RELIGIOUS BROADCAST MANAGEMENT HANDBOOK

DR. THOMAS C. DURFEY
and
JAMES A. FERRIER

Academie Books, Grand Rapids, Michigan
Zondervan Publishing House

Religious Broadcast Management Handbook
Copyright © 1986 by Thomas C. Durfey and James A. Ferrier

Academie Books is an imprint of Zondervan Publishing House, 1415 Lake Drive S.E., Grand Rapids, Michigan 49506

Library of Congress Cataloging in Publication Data
Durfey, Thomas C.
  Religious broadcast management handbook.
  Bibliography: p.
  1. Religious broadcasting—Management. I. Ferrier, James A. II. Title.
BV656.D87 1986 260 86-20548
ISBN 0-310-39741-3

All rights reserved. No part of this publication may be reproduced, stored in a retrieval system, or transmitted in any form or by any means—electronic, mechanical, photocopy, recording, or any other—except for brief quotations in printed reviews, without the prior permission of the publisher.

Printed in the United States of America

86 87 88 89 90 91 92 / 10 9 8 7 6 5 4 3 2 1

RELIGIOUS BROADCAST MANAGEMENT HANDBOOK

To our wives, who are truly partners in every sense of the word:

Ellen Nelson Durfey, whose organizing skills contributed greatly to the success of KTCR, Wagoner/Coweta, Oklahoma,

and

Connie Blackwell Ferrier, whose editing skills and long hours at the computer made this book possible.

CONTENTS

Foreword 9

Part One
Development: A Brief History of Broadcasting

Chapter 1 From the Wireless to Television 13
Chapter 2 Getting the Good News to the People 27

Part Two
Ownership Options: Making the Commitment

Chapter 3 Buying Established Stations 41
Chapter 4 Building New Stations 51

Part Three
Engineering: Making the Right Connections

Chapter 5 Positioning for FCC Grants: AM Allocations 63
Chapter 6 Waiting for the FM Window to Open 77
Chapter 7 Engineering Maintenance Programs 83

Part Four
Programming: From Music to Public Affairs

Chapter 8 Historical Development of Programming 91
Chapter 9 Format Development in a Market 97
Chapter 10 Programming for Christian Stations 109
Chapter 11 News and Public Affairs 119

Part Five
Sales and Promotions: Dollars and Sense

Chapter 12 The Importance of Promotions 135
Chapter 13 The Basics of Selling Air Time 147
Chapter 14 Other Aspects of Broadcast Sales 157
Chapter 15 Closing the Sale 171
Chapter 16 Broadcast Sales Management 181
Chapter 17 Noncommercial Operations 197

Part Six
Management: Behind the Scenes

Chapter 18	Personnel and Program Management	205
Chapter 19	Office Management	215
Chapter 20	Management From a Biblical Perspective	225

Appendices

Foreword

During my two decades as executive director of the National Religious Broadcasters, I have witnessed phenomenal expansion in Christian broadcasting. Christian radio stations are growing at the rate of one new station per week, while one Christian television station is being added every month. This growth rate far surpasses that of the secular broadcasting industry.

More than 60 million people tune in Christian television programs every month. The number of people listening to Christian radio is even higher: 73 million adults. Current statistics on the degree of duplication between television and radio audiences are not available, but it is reasonable to assume that the total in the '80s is much greater than the 1978 estimate of 128 million.

The *Religious Broadcast Management Handbook* is long overdue because the field is growing faster than people can be trained. Dr. Thomas Durfey has more than 30 years of broadcasting experience, while James Ferrier has nearly 20 years of experience as a journalist. Together they have produced a highly readable and comprehensive manual to train broadcast professionals, aid those already in the field, and inform ministries interested in expanding into radio and television.

Students will find that the complexities of broadcasting have been put into common language for easy understanding, and young broadcasters who study this book and apply it will find themselves moving up through the ranks faster.

This is a tremendous source book for established broadcasters as well, because it is full of practical material for success. Christian broadcasters actually need to know everything secular professionals in the same field know — plus a lot more!

Any ministry considering a media outreach will find a wealth of information in this book to help them get started quickly and avoid many of the pitfalls of inexperience and lack of knowledge of the field.

I believe that God wants his stations and programming to be examples of excellence and professionalism. This book should help broadcasters reach that goal.

>Ben Armstrong
> Executive Director
> National Religious Broadcasters
> Morristown, New Jersey
> November 1, 1986

Part One

Development: A Brief History of Broadcasting

Chapter 1
From the Wireless to Television

Ralph Waldo Emerson said that invention breeds invention. Certainly that has been true in the past two hundred years. The inventions of the Industrial Revolution created the need for more inventions. One of these was a tremendous need for technology that would allow rapid communication.

Until the 1800s, it was not possible to have communication without some form of transportation, from "shank's mare" to the railroad. Mail rode on the back of the Pony Express. Thus the threads of experimentation in physics and engineering that spun out of scientific theories developed after the Middle Ages led to the invention of "wireless communication" or radio.

Samuel Finley Breese Morse, a poverty-stricken painter with a fascination for electrically operated objects, worked out the theory of telegraphy in the 1830s. The first telegraph message — "What hath God wrought!" — was sent from Washington, D.C., to Baltimore and back May 24, 1844. This invention was perceived as having annihilated time. It seemed to be almost supernatural.

International communications using the Morse code began in 1866 with the completion of the transatlantic cable.

The next piece of the communications puzzle was developed by Alexander Graham Bell, a Scottish teacher of the deaf who patented his "talking telephone" in 1876 just hours before another American inventor, Elisha Gray, whose name no one now remembers. Other inventors were working on the same idea, but Bell beat everyone to the patent. After court battles with Gray were settled, the inventor formed his company, Bell Telephone. But he could raise no money to develop it, so he soon lost his patent rights as well as his company, which later became American Telephone and Telegraph (AT&T).

It is safe to assume that none of the inventors had any idea of the impact these inventions would have on the world's cultures. Many historians wrote that the "electric spark" seemed to join the natural and the spiritual worlds. Job 38:35 — "Canst thou send lightnings, that they may go, and say unto thee, Here we are?" — was often quoted by authors and orators during that period.

Practical Wireless Telegraphy

The wireless system followed the telegraph and telephone, although work was being done toward its development as early as the 1840s. Scottish physicist James Clerk-Maxwell publicized his fully developed theory on wireless waves in 1873. Some of his concepts later were proven wrong, but many of them survive. The man who demonstrated the truth of Maxwell's theory of electromagnetic action at a distance was German physicist Heinrich Hertz. His name was given to the international unit measuring the oscillations of these waves, one cycle per second. The development of radio involved many other inventions, however, and did not come to full flower until World War I.

Young Italian inventor Guglielmo Marconi experimented with equipment similar to Hertz's, and because he had the leisure and funds to experiment, he was the first to offer telegraphic services to the public, although he was more of an adaptor of existing inventions than the originator of new inventions. His mother, a member of a well-known British liquor manufacturing company, obtained an audience for him with officials in London, and he obtained the first patent in 1897 in England.

Backed by English financiers, Marconi's Wireless Telegraph Company owned most of the patents on radio operation until after World War I. Called British Marconi, it held subsidiaries around the world to supervise radio activity in each location. American Marconi controlled the radio patents in the Americas. Marconi set up International Marine Communications in 1900 to rent wireless equipment as well as furnish trained operators to military and commercial ships.

He supplied most of the world's ships with two-way radio equipment and built many ship-to-shore base stations to handle communications to and from the ships at sea. Marconi interests dominated the operation of these shore installations around the world as well. During the war, however, all allied nations shared free in the radio rights in order to advance wartime communications.

Before World War I, Marconi transmitters were spark-gap generator units producing a high voltage that arced between two metal points, one attached to an aerial, or long-wire antenna, and sometimes wired through a tuning circuit. Messages on this type of extremely noisy transmitter were pretty much confined to the use of the international Morse code that was sent out by turning the spark transmitter on and off with a telegraph key on the low-voltage side of the circuit.

A very short burst of spark energy was used for a "dot" and a longer burst of spark energy indicated a "dash." Shipboard radio operators listened to endless hours of dots and dashes throughout their watch on duty.

The encrypting system did not make for a very inviting universal broadcasting system. In fact, the coded signals were primarily meant for the safety of ships at sea and for communications related to passengers or business concerns such as shipping, cargos, and marketing. Not many people outside the shipping or naval industries listened in just for entertainment! Only a few hundred experimenters, or "hams," tried out new receiver and transmitter circuits by sending and receiving occasional messages. All who participated had to master the international Morse code. Otherwise the transmissions would have been meaningless pulses of sound.

All transmissions were sent out on a wide range of frequencies, signals that splattered from one end of a radio dial to the other. Therefore, radio messages were divided into levels of priority with disaster messages first, urgent traffic signals second, ship-to-shore messages next, and amateur testing signals last. Only one transmitter in a wide geographical area was allowed to operate at a time because every transmitter tended to interfere with every other transmitter.

General Electric Company (GE) in Schenectady, New York, born in 1892 from a merger between Thomas Edison's Electric Light Company and another manufacturer, became the owner of the patent on a less noisy transmitter, the high frequency alternator. The basic idea was that if a pure high-frequency energy of a simple constant frequency could be generated, this single-frequency signal could be transmitted simultaneously with other such signals of different frequencies. Then a receiver tuning unit could be used to separate the signals. The theory behind this system was that it might be possible to transmit up to ten or twelve signals "on the air" at the same time.

Scandinavian Ernest Alexanderson, a research engineer for GE, was in charge of building the first such alternator for Reginald Fessenden, a Canadian-born physicist, who eventually had 500 patents attributed to him. Fessenden gave GE the order to construct such an alternator to his design in 1906. But Alexanderson thought he could do better than Fessenden's design, so he proceeded to build another for the Marconi Company. The most powerful generator in the world at the time, its signals could be heard over much of the Atlantic Ocean and even in France.[1]

Alexanderson's GE research group determined that the best way to generate this high-frequency signal with enough power to radiate a decent signal was to use a large number of poles on an alternator and spin it at a very high speed. Rotating shafts abounded on board ship, so the frequency of transmission could be selected by the speed of the shaft.

Another development of this idea was to mix the constant frequency signal with the output of a telephone mouthpiece (the first microphone) and transmit the actual sounds to shipboard earphones. This permitted "radio telephony," and just as the development of Alexander

Graham Bell's telephone was destined to overtake Samuel F. B. Morse's telegraph, radio telephone was to have more value than the early wireless.

New Era Begins With the Christmas Story

The first public use of the radio telephone figuratively shook the whole world. Fessenden took the alternator constructed by Alexanderson at GE to an experimental transmission location on Christmas Eve, 1906, and sent the first voice-transmitted program from a location near Boston to ships within a five-mile radius. A broadcast on New Year's Eve reached as far as the West Indies. The Christmas program electrified radiomen and officers who had never heard anything but dots and dashes from the earphones. We cannot imagine how exciting it was for them to hear a Christmas song and a Scripture reading coming through earphones. In the midst of space travel, satellites, and computer technology, it is hard for us to understand just how great the impact of this one program was on the people of the world.

Use of ship-to-shore or shore-to-ship spark transmitters continued until World War I. During this "war to end all wars," radio technological advancements continued under the auspices of the military.

Crystal detectors had been used since about 1906 to convert the alternating current of radio frequencies into direct current to operate earphones. These simple crystal radio sets could be built by amateurs, and they continued to be in use well into the 1920s. But they were not highly efficient. The next step came when British physicist John Fleming invented a "valve," or diode, to reliably rectify the signals. His valve was an evacuated tube or case of glass surrounding two elements made of metal.

Physicist Lee de Forest, who began as a researcher with Western Electric, which was acquired by Bell in 1881 as a subsidiary, added a third element to Fleming's valve, making a "triode." The third metal element formed a grid to control the flow of electricity between the original two elements.

Called Audions, these tubes became valuable as amplifiers. This invention gave man the ability to manipulate the electron and eliminated the need for moving mechanical parts. De Forest was another inventor who, for economic reasons, had to sell many of the rights to a major invention for a mere pittance compared to its long-term value. The "beneficiary," again, was AT&T, which paid de Forest $50,000.

Major Edwin W. Armstrong, a young man in the U.S. Army Signal Corps, used the new de Forrest triodes to invent circuits for oscillators, for the regenerative (feedback) circuit, and even for the superheterodyne receiver — the circuit that forms the basis for most modern receivers. The feedback circuit was the object of one of the most bitterly contested court fights in the history of radio. Four patent-holders were involved: Armstrong for American Marconi, de Forest for AT&T, Irving Langmuir for GE, and the Telefunken Company, holder of the German Meissner patent. The courts decided in favor of de Forest, but Armstrong still claimed priority, and engineers today generally accept his claim as valid in spite of the court decision.

All the technology and inventions of those early days did not make radio broadcasting a reality for the general public. A dramatic feat by a young man from New York's East Side was the catalyst that caused the spark of public imagination to jump from the post of invention to the pole of mainstream communications. The result was the birth of broadcasting as we know it today.

David Sarnoff was operating a telegraph station in New York's Wanamaker's Department Store in 1912 when the Titanic was sinking. By spending seventy-two hours straight at his equipment and relaying messages, he became famous overnight. His feat is credited with making radio broadcasting a reality. All the technology and inventions had not accomplished what this one incident did by catching the imaginations and the hearts of the American people.[2]

From Patriotism to Profits

General Electric used its light bulb factory in Schenectady to manufacture vacuum tubes during World War I.

Afterwards these assembly lines stood idle because of the high cost of the patent rights, which were in dispute anyway. American military and political sentiment after the war was against the control of radio rights in this country by a company in Great Britain, but American Marconi had near-monopoly control. Then, in 1919, Marconi started trying to buy rights from GE for the synchronous generator invented by Alexanderson. Arrangements were made for some "horse trading." The result was the first American-owned company in the field — Radio Corporation of America (RCA) — established under GE executive Owen D. Young's leadership to hold wireless patent rights in the Americas. Meanwhile, inventions and experimentation continued.

At the University of Wisconsin, Professor Earl Terry experimented with triodes, exhausting the air from the bottles and constructing vacuum-tube transmitters. He set up an experimental station at the university to transmit weather and agricultural information for short periods of time. By 1919, according to Harold B. McCarty, first manager of WHA in Madison, Wisconsin, the experimental station maintained a regular schedule of such farm-oriented programs along with a music appreciation course and talks by various faculty members. Professor Terry's students worked practically around the clock to invent better tubes and transmission circuits while producing live programs. Historians generally agree that WHA is the oldest radio broadcast station in the world; at least, it is the oldest still on the air in the same location and with a traceable ownership.

Meanwhile, at Union College in Schenectady, German-born electrical engineering professor and inventor Charles Porteus Steinmetz led students in vacuum-tube experiments and established radiophone station 2ADD, operated solely by students from the campus. Its signals were picked up 150 miles south in New York City. Other early stations on the air were in San Diego and Detroit.

Owen D. Young, a young attorney and accountant, became a skilled diplomat in managing relationships among the early participants in the electronic field. He later was chairman of the boards of GE and RCA. He traded GE's Alexanderson generator rights to British Marconi in exchange for the radio patent rights in the Americas. RCA was established to purchase American Marconi's stock. RCA shareholders with GE in this new consortium set up by Young were: American Marconi, Westinghouse, AT&T, the United Fruit Company, Wireless Speciality Apparatus Company, and International Radio Telephone Company.

Through cross-licensing, this consortium (RCA) had access to nearly all of the patents for inventions related to wireless broadcasting (beginning to be called radio by 1920) and the use of American Marconi's shore equipment and property as well. Some of the partners to this agreement, which virtually created a monopoly, were not happy with their share of the new industry and problems arose. A lot of people in this country were not happy with the monopoly, either.

Radio Becomes a Mass Medium

During World War I, the assistant chief engineer of Westinghouse's Pittsburgh plant was Frank Conrad. Dr. Conrad constructed an experimental radiophone station at his home in East Pittsburgh and another station at the plant. After the war, Conrad played phonograph records and transmitted scores of ball games over his home apparatus on a fairly regular basis.

One evening, Westinghouse managers saw an advertisement in the evening newspaper, the *Pittsburgh Post,* to the effect that a local department store had receivers for sale that would allow customers to tune into the programs from Conrad's amateur station. For the first time, someone saw that radio broadcasting could become a mass medium and money could be made from selling receivers. The idea of radio as a public medium of communication was revolutionary. All previous efforts had been to develop the wireless as a means of communication between individuals, companies, governments, and ships to shore.

In order to sell the receivers, merchandisers saw that programming should be on the air regularly for people to tune in. So radio broadcasts essentially began as a tool of industry, that is, to sell radios, rather than as a means of entertainment or news delivery. Because Conrad's little station quickly ran out of records to play on the air, arrangements were made to get records from a music company in exchange for advertising air time — the first such transaction.

In the fall of 1920, Conrad's station at Westinghouse was relicensed as KDKA. The station's first regularly scheduled broadcast consisted of the results of the Warren G. Harding-James Cox election returns, which also were broadcast by WGR, Detroit. But KDKA continued to broadcast every evening thereafter with talks and phonograph records. By 1921, a live symphony orchestra, baseball games, and college football games had been added. KDKA holds the record for a lot of radio firsts: the first baseball game, the first football game, the first remote broadcast, the first church service, the first World Series, and many others.

In 1921, Owen Young decided to build a radio station near GE's manufacturing and research complex in Schenectady. The first manager of WGY was Kolin Hager. He recruited actors from the area for his broadcasts rather than musicians as most other stations were doing. Hager invented radio drama and began to plan a coast-to-coast radio network involving WGY, KGO in San Francisco, KOB in Denver, and WGN in Chicago. He was on his way to WGN to finalize the proposed GE network in 1926 when Young called from New York City and said he had just made a deal with David Sarnoff, now an RCA official, to form the National Broadcasting System.

Young had come to the diplomatic rescue of the industry again. The shareholder partners in RCA were quarreling because of an alleged imbalance in revenue. Westinghouse and GE were making a lot of profits selling receivers, the activity for which they had been licensed in their agreements with RCA. The Western Electric (WE) arm of AT&T was licensed to sell transmitters, but many small stations, such as college-based stations, were building their own transmitters. Western Electric persuaded the U.S. Department of Commerce to require apparatus license fees to be paid to AT&T for every transmitter that was not sold by WE. Even then, AT&T moguls believed the company was not making as much as it ought to from the RCA shareholders' deal, and they manufactured a prototype receiver to present to the White House.

This ploy infuriated GE and Westinghouse officials who complained to the government, and that resulted in a trust-busting investigation into the radio business. The Radio Act of l927 established the Federal Radio Commission (FRC) on the grounds that radio waves really are owned by the citizens of this country who have an inherent right to enjoy a share of the nation's resources. The trust-busting action resulted in two additions to FRC applications (also included in regulations of the Federal Communications Commission, which replaced the FRC in 1934): (1) "type-approved" equipment lists, that initially included mostly WE transmitters, and (2) a page of questions asking applicants whether any principal to the application had been convicted of any "restraint of trade" entanglements.

The quarrel over profits among the consortium's partners was solved by Owen Young's suggestion of a radio network, the National Broadcasting Company (NBC), which would lease long-lines from AT&T, allowing the company to operate in its area of expertise — building land-line interconnections between stations — and still make a fair share of the profits available in the new field. GE held 30 percent of NBC, RCA held 50 percent, and Westinghouse held 20 percent. AT&T sold its share of RCA in 1923, but RCA did not become an independent corporation until 1932 when an antitrust suit forced GE and Westinghouse to sell their stock in it.

An interesting development in 1985 was GE's acquisition — or perhaps we should say re-acquisition — of RCA for $6.28 billion after thirty-three years.[3]

Broadcasting Goes Commercial

Western Electric had built an AT&T toll broadcasting station, WEAF, in New York City in 1922 and sold time on the station through the new concept of a toll telephone. Everyone who wanted time on the air paid to have his message broadcast. The first such commercial broadcast was for a real estate firm advertising an apartment complex in New York's Jackson Heights district. The broadcast consisted of a talk promoting residence in this new apartment development. The toll concept of WEAF set a precedent which shaped the entire field of radio and television — selling advertising to pay for broadcast operations.

When NBC was formed, WEAF (later named WNBC) became the flagship station of the fledgling network, and WEAF's twenty-two-station network became NBC's Red Network. A network of fourteen stations, headed by RCA's station WJZ (now WABC) in New York City, became NBC's Blue Network in the 1926 merger. The famous three-note chime still used by NBC as a sound symbol was the idea of Hager and Young. The sounds are the musical notes "G," "E," and "C" for General Electric Company. Hager also fed some of his radio dramas down to New York and out over the NBC network. These were series such as "The FBI in Action" and "One Man's Family," starring Tom Lewis, a young actor fresh out of the Union College/Steinmetz experimental station 2ADD, who later married actress Loretta Young.

These dramas, comedy series such as "Amos and Andy," comedy shows with Fred Allen and Jack Benny, and musical programs such as the NBC Symphony Orchestra, offered unusual and unprecedented entertainment throughout the land. Local stations found they could increase their listening audiences with network programs. Small wonder, then, that churches and church groups sought representation on network radio.

Columbia Broadcasting System (CBS), came into existence in 1928, a replacement for Columbia Phonograph Records Network, which had replaced the United Independent Broadcasters Network. The twenty-two-affiliate network was turned into a money-making venture under its new name when a Philadelphia cigar manufacturing company heir, William S. Paley, vitalized its dying carcass with a transfusion of money. He ended up owning 50.3 percent of the stock. A third network, Mutual Broadcasting Company, evolved in the 1930s as a group of stations banding together to sell air time.

A fourth network, the America Broadcasting Company, was formed in 1940 when a Supreme Court decision caused the sale of NBC's Blue Network to Edward Noble.

From Radio to Television

From 1928 to 1931, WGY in Schenectady began experiments in broadcast television. Kolin Hager's group televised a drama, and political speeches were aired from the Capitol steps in Albany, New York. By 1936, WRGB in Schenectady was on the air as an experimental station; and, by 1939, RCA's New York City station, WNDT, was on the air. Hager's group believed they should share programs between Schenectady and New York City, so a two-hop experimental microwave was built to receive New York at Mount Beacon, across the Hudson River from Newburg, and to transmit the signal to the Catskills and from there to WRGB. Hundreds of hours of test patterns were sent out after the spectacular programming was aired from the 1939 New York World's Fair. There were, by this time, an estimated 15,000 television sets in the New York area and the Albany district.

Summary

The history of radio broadcasting dates from the 1830s and Samuel Morse's invention of the telegraph system and a code by which to communicate over it. For the next hundred years, invention built upon invention to bring mankind the telephone, radio, and television. The idea of radio as a medium for the masses was an incidental development. The main purpose of developing a radio system of networks was to sell radio sets and, later, to sell advertising. Chapter 2 is a short history of religious broadcasting.

Notes

[1] Saundra Hybells and Dana Ulloth, *Broadcasting: An Introduction to Radio and Television* (New York: D. Van Nostrand Company, 1978).

[2] Stephen Birmingham, *The Rest of Us* (New York: Little, Brown & Co., 1984), Berkeley Books, New York.

[3] "RCA May Have Short-Changed Its Stockholders in the GE Deal," *The Washington Post*, December 30, 1985, National Weekly Edition, p. 17.

Chapter 2
Getting the Good News to the People

It is extremely interesting — and perhaps significant in spiritual ways we may not fully understand — that the first voice broadcast ever made was a program celebrating the birth of Jesus Christ. The 1906 Christmas Eve shore to ship program from Brant Rock, Massachusetts, included the young Canadian experimenter Reginald Fessenden's violin rendition of Gounoud's *O Holy Night*, and a phonograph recording by a female vocalist of Handel's *Largo*. Fessenden also read the Christmas story from Luke 2.

This new invention, in the eyes of many church leaders, was to bring the worldwide victory of the kingdom of God and link mankind in unity. Apparently this was the beginning of the modern cry for universal peace, which seemed to that generation to be possible at last.

The first church worship service was aired over KDKA. The idea came from a Westinghouse engineer who was a choir member at Calvary Episcopal Church, about ten miles from the station near Pittsburgh. The Rev. James VanEtten, who was rector at that time, "considered radio a passing fad and doubted that the hookup from the sanctuary to the station would work."[1] VanEtten's curate, the Rev. Lewis B. Whittlemore, conducted the evening service for the first Sunday of the new year, 1921, becoming the first preacher to conduct a church service on the air.

The first broadcast of the church service apparently received wide acceptance by the KDKA listening audience, because it became a regular feature on the station. By 1925, there were six hundred radio stations operating in the United States, with sixty-three — or about 10 percent — of them owned by churches.[2] The revolutionary new mass communications medium at least began with the Lord having a tenth portion!

Roots of Religious Broadcasting

Early stations owned by churches or religious organizations since 1925 include WMBI, owned and operated by Moody Bible Institute in Chicago; and KFUO, operated by the Lutheran Church-Missouri Synod. The American Lutheran Church's St. Olaf College began WCAL in Northfield, Minnesota, in 1922. Several other church-owned radio stations began operations in the 1920s.

In 1924, the Greater New York Federation of Churches of the Federal Council of Churches of Christ (FCCC), the predecessor of today's National Council of Churches, began airing "National Radio Pulpit" over WEAF, still operated at that time by AT&T. (The FCCC, first established in the early 1920s, did not include the Lutheran Church's Missouri Synod and some other conservative and evangelical churches.)

The principal speaker for "National Radio Pulpit" was Dr. S. Parkes Cadman from the Greater New York Federation of Churches. The program was picked up from WEAF when it became the flagship station of the National Broadcasting System and aired across the entire new, and first, network.

NBC executives also established a relationship with the FCCC for coordinating religious programming. For a decade, six programs initiated by member churches of the council aired on free time. NBC's original policy was not to sell time to religious broadcasters, but to donate it, usually on Sunday mornings. All six of these shows had a preaching-teaching format, with the most prominent being the first program, the *National Radio Pulpit*.

In its early years, this program featured well-known speakers such as Harry Emerson Fosdick, Ralph W. Sockman, and other theologically liberal Protestant representatives, along with Dr. Cadman.[3] The Roman Catholic faith was represented in programs coordinated by the church's New York Diocesan offices, and the Jewish faith by free network time for programs arranged through the New York Rabbinical Council.

Because of NBC's agreement with the FCCC, it would not donate or sell air time to religious groups who were not members of the council. But CBS, formed in 1928, would. The result was the premiere broadcast on the first Thursday of October 1930 of "The Lutheran Hour" originating from WHK, Cleveland, Ohio. Audience response was overwhelming, with the program receiving more mail than "Amos and Andy" or all the combined programs coordinated by the council of churches.[4]

The price for a season of half-hour weekly radio broadcasts was nearly a quarter of a million dollars. Lutheran Church laymen and youth groups pledged about $100,000 to get the project off the ground, and contributions in 1931 averaged $2,000 a week, covering about half the cost of air time. CBS estimated that there were about five million listeners to this program, the inspiration of a man named Walter A. Maier.

Maier first got a taste of radio in 1922 when he addressed the members of the Walther League, the young people's organization of the Lutheran Church-Missouri Synod, over a Louisville, Kentucky, station. His talk was the convention address to the group that year. Maier served as executive secretary of the league and editor of the league's newspaper. While teaching at Concordia Seminary in St. Louis in 1924, Maier helped establish station KFUO. After preaching over this local station for four years, he envisioned a nationwide radio broadcast to teach what he felt was an authentic Christianity as opposed to the theologically liberal viewpoints then monopolizing the airwaves.

Another pioneer in the use of radio was Donald Grey Barnhouse, who began airing a weekly program — which later became "The Bible Study Hour" — in 1927 from the historic Tenth Presbyterian Church in Philadelphia.

RCA constructed a large production van on a touring-bus chassis and used it to originate TV programming from outside Radio City Music Hall studios at Rockefeller Center. This unit was kept busy with the series of inaugural telecasts from the World's Fair in 1939. The same equipment aired the

"Christmas Eve Midnight Mass" and other "National Radio Pulpit" types of religious programs during the early days of telecasting.

Radio stations gave limited amounts of air time to representative organizations of Protestantism, Catholicism, and Judaism through the 1950s, and some sold time to religious groups. A few church organizations decided they needed to operate their own stations to get enough time for the preaching and teaching they felt should be aired. All these groups discovered that access to time over the airwaves became a strategic battle to share the gospel.

Among the early radio ministries were Charles E. Fuller's "Old Fashioned Revival Hour," Theodore Epp's "Back to the Bible," M. R. De Haan's "Radio Bible Class," and Paul Myers' "Haven of Rest."

Television Expands the Electric Church

The first regularly scheduled national religious television began in 1949 when the American Broadcasting Company (ABC), formed in 1940, presented its series, "I Believe." Aired on Tuesday nights, it featured well-known theologians discussing religion in everyday life. Later in 1949, a televised puppet series was aired which dramatized parables and familiar Bible stories. By 1951, Walter Maier and his group had developed "This Is the Life," a half-hour dramatic series.

Religious television had an interesting beginning with innovative program formats, and it seemed to have a promising future. But ecclesiastical groups soon found there is no such thing as "free" television time. Production, filming, and staff costs to fill the donated network time far outweighed the combined production and air costs for radio.

Television ministries began to proliferate from the 1950s into what some call "the electronic church" but what Ben Armstrong, executive director of the National Religious Broadcasters, prefers to call "the electric church." Bishop Fulton J. Sheen, Billy Graham, Oral Roberts, Kathryn Kuhlman, and Rex Humbard launched television programs during the 50s.

With the success of spreading the gospel, however, came some controversies. The established denominations and some local churches began to fear that television was hurting church membership and finances. Also, the argument of separation of church and state began to be a public issue developed by a group of atheists and humanists and was applied to radio and television. In the 1940s, a group of militant churchmen and academicians named a committee to look into religious broadcasting. This committee of the Institute of Education by Radio came up with recommendations that put pressure on the networks not to sell time for religious programming. Conservative programs also came under fire.

Two consequences of these attacks were the formation of the National Association of Evangelicals (NAE) in 1942 and of the National Religious Broadcasters (NRB) in 1944, formed to uphold the right to spread the gospel on free and paid air time.

The first religious television station was initiated by M. G. "Pat" Robertson's Christian Broadcasting Network (CBN) in 1961 in Virginia Beach, Virginia. Another pioneer in owning and operating religious television stations is Dr. Lester Sumrall of South Bend, Indiana. In the 1970s, two more Christian networks were started: Paul Crouch's Trinity Broadcasting Network and Jim Bakker's PTL Network. In recent years, other networks and stations have been started by the Southern Baptists, Roman Catholics, and others. The latest development, of course, is the use of satellites for closed-circuit telecasts into local churches and homes by national ministries.

Dr. Armstrong says in his book, *The Electric Church:*

> The electric church has launched a revolution as dramatic as the revolution that began when Martin Luther nailed his ninety-five theses to the cathedral door at Wittenberg. Just as the Reformation brought sweeping changes in the way Christians understood their relationship to God and the way they expressed their devotion through worship, so has the electric

church. . . . Radio and television have broken through the walls of tradition we have built up around the church and have restored conditions remarkably similar to the early church.[5]

Radio and television ministries and outreaches are taken for granted in the 1980s, and more churches and groups are looking for ways to spread the gospel every day — or at least to make the public aware of the message and programs available at their meeting places. It is also possible now to get some coverage without laying out the huge sums necessary to buy air time or to prepare the stage sets, costumes, lighting, and so forth, for airing. Stations often will assist paying customers in the preparation of spot ads and/or program-length material by offering the use of a recording studio and recorded music for lead-ins and closings. Sometimes a staff announcer is available to assist in production.

Broadcast opportunities for Christians who do not have the funds or the calling to own or operate stations range from use of a limited amount of time — that really is free through public service obligations of stations — to buying program time to nonownership options for larger portions of time.

Free-Time Opportunities

As part of its operations guidelines under the FCC, every station is required to provide so much public service time. This is usually done through public service announcements, community calendars, and public affairs programs. The first two are best obtained through news releases sent by the ministry or church to local or regional stations marked as an announcement or a calendar item. The public service announcements could be at least a paragraph, while the calendar item is one or two lines beginning with the event, followed by the place, date, and time: "Chicken Supper, Faith Community Church, 200 Elm St., (town, if there are several in the audience covered by the station), Monday, May 25, at 7 p.m. Public invited. Tickets, $3.50 for adults and $1.25 for children under 12." A public service announcement might include announcement of a new pastor, in which case biographical material on him should be included as well as material about his family and when he will be taking up his new duties. Such an announcement also might involve a special meeting with a noted guest speaker, a seminar, new building plans, and so forth. These also should be as brief as possible, without a lot of adjectives or hyperbole. For use as public service, or spot, announcements in the broadcast media, the paragraph should not take longer to read aloud than 30 seconds. For use on television stations, the announcement should be accompanied by a color slide of the church. Always make the slide horizontal because no television set has a picture taller than it is wide.

Several things to keep in mind along this line include these:

• Pretend you are someone who has no knowledge of your church or organization and be sure to include everything you would want to know in such a case. That way, you will have all the facts. An announcement without "who, what, when, where, and why" will usually end up in File 13 — the wastebasket. Most new organizations are too busy to call and get the details that should have been included in the first place.

• Learn the deadlines of the various media with which you are dealing. For instance, if this is going to a newspaper (and the same news releases can be used for papers as well as radio and television), then the release should be sent to arrive at least a couple of days ahead of the deadline. Too far ahead, and your announcement may get lost. The safest thing is to contact each one by phone or through a personal visit and find out just what information is needed and when it should be sent.

• Personal contact with the person handling these announcements for the medium in which you are interested, of course, is the best way. Before visiting, however, call to find out the best time or make an appointment. Don't just drop by. A visit at the busiest time of the day only makes you an aggravation and, first impressions usually being lasting, makes it more difficult to get your releases first-class attention. Also, be careful not to overstay your welcome, and make it clear that you came by to find out how best to present your news and be a help to the person handling it and not an added burden.

• Always put your name, address, and phone number, in case the station or paper needs more information or, hopefully, decides to do a longer feature on the event.

For really important happenings, you might want to call a news conference. If you have made enough of a contact with someone in the media, find out if your event is newsworthy. If so, ask how best to go about setting up such a conference.

Another way to get your organization covered by the media without cost to you is to become acquainted with the person in charge of public affairs programming. Again, a visit by appointment will allow you to provide that person with information which could be helpful to both of you. Most persons handling such programming are looking for people with expertise or programs on various subjects of interest to your community. Talk shows, interview shows or panel programs are used regularly or intermittently by each station to fulfill its community obligations. If your group is especially involved, pro or con, in abortion, use of nuclear energy, aid for the needy or homeless, and so forth, you could be asked to appear on one of these programs. This would give you a free forum and free publicity for your organization, as well as provide information and help to the community.

Buying Time for the Gospel

The better time slots are available only for sale, and buying a fixed time allows an audience to develop. Most secular stations have a limit on the amount of time devoted to religious programming and also restrict the time slots for such programming. These stations automatically schedule weekly teaching or preaching programs on Sunday morning, and broadcasters have come to call this time period "The Sunday Morning (Religious) Ghetto."

Stringing one teaching or preaching program after another has proven to attract an audience loyal to this type of programming. Some stations play almost all of their programming in this fashion and are known as "Christian" or "religious" stations. Ministries pay the stations for the time used, and each station plays each ministry's tape in the time slot agreed upon in a contract. Then the ministry involved asks listeners for donations to pay for air time, tape, postage, production costs, and, in some instances, nonbroadcast aspects of the ministry.

This type of ministry is called "donor-based broadcasting" because of the reliance upon listener donations for operating cash flow to continue the program. Donor-based broadcasting works best on stations dedicated entirely to religious programming with Christian announcers and featuring only Christian music.

Christian music stations also include news and sports results but sell spot advertisements rather than program time. This is an "advertiser-based" broadcasting system, where the cash flow that operates the station comes from the sale of advertising. Listeners do business with advertisers, and advertisers continue to buy ads.

Leasing — a Little-Known Possibility

One method of establishing a Christian station format where none now exists is seldom done or even discussed now. This is the concept of buying bulk time wholesale or "leasing" time and then selling the time to different ministries. This concept was especially available to ministries and churches in the late 1950s and through most of the 1960s. During those years, the original bulk-buy operators were usually ethnic programmers who put Italian, Polish, Yiddish, Scandinavian, and Portuguese programming on metropolitan FM stations.

Frequency modulation (FM) stations had few listeners then and usually featured special programming with classical, easy listening, or ethnic music. In those days, few advertisers preferred FM stations for spot ads, and the revenue of these stations, often operated as sidelines of highly successful amplitude modulation (AM) stations, was minuscule. During that time, ministries could have arranged to buy large blocks of time at very low rates.

A wholesale buy might have involved 8 a.m. to 6 p.m. every day for $3000 per month. If the group that purchased the bulk time sold seven hours a day at ten dollars per half hour to various radio Bible teachers, the revenue would have covered the cost of the eight hours, an operator's salary, and postage and bookkeeping functions. The primary ministry, then, would have acquired its own hour free and still not have placed a burden on the secondary participants!

Today the tables have turned. FM stations in most markets are the preferred radio medium, and wholesale bulk sales on these stations in recent years have been rare. AM stations are now having trouble selling air time, especially daytime stations. A bulk-sales price from 8 a.m. to 4 p.m. on an AM station of $100 to $150 a day in small markets would be reasonable for both the owner and the bulk-sales operator. The cost would be much higher in larger markets. The purchaser then could reasonably charge about $20 per half-hour from national ministries for ten half-hours per day to cover his costs. Revenue from the other six half-hours would cover management and operations costs or be used by the organizer's ministry.

A bulk-sales contract must be executed with the ownership of the station and be filed at the station for public inspection. Even with deregulation, it also may be necessary for it to be filed with the FCC. The station owner retains control over programming, and his decisions override those of the bulk-buy purchaser. All of these aspects must be worked out in the contract.

A Variation on the Leased-Time Option

Leasing the station itself is a variation on the bulk-sales arrangement. The FCC treats such a lease as if it were a transfer of positive control (a majority of ownership and control) to the leasee. Therefore, a change-of-ownership FCC form must be filed with the commission and permission received before the leasee may take over the operation of a station. The concept of such a lease is that the leasee takes over all facets of total station operation for the period of the lease just as if he had actually bought the station. But he pays a fee each month instead of having to put up the capital to buy the facility outright.

When owners have an AM station that was built or purchased a few decades ago and co-own an FM station that has become a big income producer, they might consider leasing the old AM station for a reasonable fee, less than the amortization rate on high-cost borrowed money necessary to build a new facility at today's prices.

Another option is available: buying or building a station outright. Those interested in this option should understand, however, that *ownership means total commitment*. The owner must operate the station all the time, every day, including holidays, for 365 days a year. Ownership not only requires most of the owner's time, it requires a major financial investment. Buying a pre-existing station allows the new owner to change the format, if necessary, and establish a Christian facility. Building a new station for the purpose of showcasing a Christian format involves filing with the FCC and gaining its approval. These possibilities will be discussed in Part Two.

Summary

From its roots in the eighteenth century, the rapid growth of broadcast technology has opened bold new opportunities for ministries to reach the masses with their messages. Many Christians would like to have a Christian station in their communities. As we have seen, there are several options, depending on the intensity of responsibility and commitment, on the broadcast opportunities in the community, and on the financial resources available.

The degree of responsibility felt, and the degree of commitment toward, spreading the gospel depend on the individual group or ministry. The broadcast opportunities range from seeking free time through news releases, community calendars, public service announcements, or public service programs, to buying spot ads or program time on a daily or weekly basis to establishing a Christian-format station in the community through purchasing bulk time or through a leasing agreement. Station operation opportunities include buying an established station or building a new one. The choices must be based on a calling from the Lord as to which is best for your ministry, on availability of funds, and on finding someone with the right expertise to help you. Christians should try harder for excellence than non-believers do.

Notes

[1] Ben Armstrong, *The Electric Church*, (Nashville: Thomas Nelson, 1979), p. 20.

[2] Ralph M. Jennings, *Policies and Practices of Selected National Religious Bodies as Related to Broadcasting in the Public Interest* (Ann Arbor, Michigan: University Microfilms, Inc., 1969), p. 14.

[3] Interview with Kolin Hager for a videotape lesson, *The Birth of Broadcasting — Radio* (Tulsa, Oklahoma: Oral Roberts University, 1981).

[4] Armstrong, p. 38.

[5] Ibid., pp. 9,10.

Part Two

Ownership Options: Making the Commitment

Chapter 3
Buying Established Stations

"Above all else, brethren," broadcasting is a business. Stations have employees to pay, equipment to buy and maintain, utilities and rent to pay, music to obtain, use fees, and other expenses to pay each month. An owner has to raise the funds to meet these obligations. Most broadcast station owners raise the money by selling air time.

The Value of a Station

There are many methods of estimating the industry-accepted value of a broadcast station. Figuring the value of the equipment is not one of these methods, because the equipment is only a fraction of the considered value of a successful station. On the other hand, the value of the equipment at a loser station may be more than the market value of the station itself. The value of the station is more closely related to the total annual billing, or the total accounts receivable for the year.

Billing is the worth of the advertising aired on a station during a given time. The worth of a station ranges from one and one-half to two and one-half times the annual billing. For example, suppose an AM daytime station has advertisers spending about $12,000 a month. The annual billing would be about $144,000 a year, and the value of the station would be about $216,000, or one and one-half times the billing. If the station is at 1000 watts and can easily apply for a power increase to 5000 watts, that would double the population covered. With the improved coverage, the station would be valued at about $300,000 — or twice the amount of the annual billings.

An FM station in the same market with the same billing, and with a 3-kilowatt assignment, so that the population covered is approximately the same as the 1000-watt AM station, would have a fair market value of $350,000 to

$375,000. This higher worth is not because of coverage expandability, because FM stations are assigned by channel to maximum power capability and usually are fulfilling their entire coverage potential when first built. The higher value is because of the popularity of stations in the FM band and the potential of increasing the billing.

In smaller markets, the projected possible billing can be forecast from a couple of directions. Divide the total population covered by the station by the number of signals popular in its coverage area. If there are five popular signals in the area and about 500,000 people, then the achievable billing figure is about $100,000 per year, or about $1 per person who, given an equal chance, might be a loyal listener in the coverage area.

Another method for calculating potential revenue is to take 2 percent of the total annual retail sales in the city-grade signal area and divide by the number of advertising media selling in the area. Let us say the marketing area has total retail sales of $42 million a year and that two newspapers, a shopper's guide, two radio stations (including the one in question), an independent UHF station, and an outdoor advertising (billboards, etc.) agency are actively selling advertising in the market area. This would make seven active sales media in the area. Two percent of $42 million is $840,000. When we divide by seven media, we find that the potential billing for the station in question is $120,000.

In a small market, a radio station may get more than its "fair share" of business by aggressive sales techniques and excellent or exciting local programming. In larger markets, the rates for ads are related to rating points, and a growing audience will mean an increase in billings. The formulas for these calculations will be included among the details of ratings systems and methods discussed in chapters 12 and 14.

The following formulas and the ones given above are based on co-author Durfey's extensive experience in the field.

How to Estimate Total Billings

The cost per thousand listeners will partially determine the rates charged at a station. For radio, two to five dollars per thousand listeners is an acceptable local rate. With six thousand listeners at a given hour, each 30-second ad would be worth $12 to $30.

Another way to estimate the total potential billing is to find how much each major business in the community spends on radio per average month. A list of these businesses can be compiled from business category listings in the telephone company's Yellow Pages directory. Also, directories published by the Radio Advertising Bureau (RAB) document advertising budgets and profiles of various businesses.[1]

The maximum billing of any station is 80 percent of the total number of ad slots per month times the maximum rate the market will pay. Obviously, most stations for sale will seldom be near the top of the billing limit. When looking for a station to buy, hunt for one that has very little billing so the station can be paid for from increased billing. If operating costs at a particular station need to be expanded quite a bit to achieve the increased billing, then it may not be a wise purchase.

"Cash flow" essentially means net monthly collections less the total of bills paid. If money is borrowed to facilitate the purchase, the cash flow must be sufficient to cover the debt retirement costs.

One other method for determining market value of a radio property is to multiply cash flow by a factor of 5 to 10. A station with $3,000 to $4,000 cash flow per month would be worth from $200,000 to $300,000, depending on expandability and potential.

Normally the price of a property and the predicted increase in billing should be such that the *increased cash flow* will be maintained at 2 percent of the purchase price per month. When considering a particular station, if you are not certain that programming and sales improvements will yield this increase in cash flow, do not buy this property.

Table 3.1 shows expenses and income of a 1000-watt small suburban-country market station for November 1985.

Table 3.1
Typical Small Station Monthly Balance Sheet

MONTHLY EXPENSES PAYROLL	
November 1	$2,150
November 15	2,220
Federal Depository	785
Commissions	664
	$5,819
OPERATING EXPENSES	
Electric	$257
Heating Oil	159
Rent	125
Plumber	25
Photocopies	40
Hardware	58
Printer	150
Sports Talent Fee	80
Telephones	536
Insurance	100
Church Telephone Line	37
Media General Transcription	80
	$1,647
MUSIC COPYRIGHT FEES	
ASCAP	$88
BMI	96
SESAC	36
	$220
OTHER EXPENSES	
Debt Retirement	$1,789
Non-Competition Agreement*	250
Travel	225
Miscellaneous	195
	$2,459
TOTAL MONTHLY EXPENSES	$10,145
MONTHLY INCOME	
National Ministries	$4,250
Local Ministries	1,000
OU Football (in season)	1,400
Local Sports Sponsers	1,500
Local News/Interview Shows	820
Gospel Music Countdown Show	880
Promotion/Contest	1,200
Miscellaneous	600
	$11,650
TOTAL MONTHLY INCOME	$11,650
TYPICAL NET MONTHLY INCOME	$1,505

Buying Established Stations

   * The Non-Competition Agreement expense represents a monthly payout to the previous owner as partial payment for the purchase of the station. The former owner agrees not to buy or build a competing station in the same market.

Table 3.1 shows operating expenses between $9,000 and $12,000 per month for a 1-kilowatt (kw) daytime station with a modest staff. If the rent had been a normal amount instead of the incredible bargain the station enjoys for being on a dirt road at the transmitter site, the payroll (less commission) would have represented about half the monthly expenses, which is a more typical situation. A 3kw FM station would have about one and one-half times the above expenses because ordinarily it is on the air eighteen hours a day instead of twelve. The format of the station also somewhat determines the expenses. An automated Easy-Listening operation or a religious station with taped teaching programs represents the least expensive operation. Contemporary music disc jockeys (deejays) and intensive local-regional news coverage represent high-cost station operations.

As shown in Table 3.1, the same station took in $11,650 during a typical month. The cash flow varies at this typical 1kw AM station from about $1,000 to $4,000 per month, depending on which expenses are included and how many ads or programs are sold and collected. The cash flow for the month shown in Table 3.1 is $1,500.

This station was purchased as a 500-watt station licensed to one city with a leveraged buyout: low down payment of $20,000 and assumption of a fairly large note of $150,000. The new owners knew several options existed to boost the station's growth. They knew that it could be moved toward another city, that the FCC would allow double the power rating to 1000 watts output, and that operations could be consolidated at the transmitter, thus cutting overhead expenses.

Sellers usually want to sell stock and take any and all profits on the sale of a station as "capital gains," which are taxed at half or less than half the rate of ordinary income.

Most of the time, buyers want to purchase assets because they can be "valued up" for a tax advantage where the stock represents capital investment only. Hardware can be valued at the maximum possible price and then depreciated, while stock is capital and cannot be depreciated. A good certified public accountant (CPA) can make all the difference between a reasonable profit and a high cash flow contaminated with high taxes. The tax laws allow a business to plan the conduct of its operations to minimize taxes. The expenses of a good CPA and a good attorney to help plan accounting procedures and methods of operations that will minimize taxes are well-justified by the resulting savings.

Copyright Fees

Copyright fees to the American Society of Composers, Authors and Publishers (ASCAP), Broadcast Music, Inc. (BMI), and the Society of European Stage Authors and Composers (SESAC) represent a form of "taxes."

ASCAP was the first group of music writers to organize into a guild or union to protect songwriters and is still the largest. Names of composers such as Irving Berlin, Sammy Kahn, Richard Rodgers and Oscar Hammerstein make up the early roster of ASCAP. These organizations collect a small fee from every piece of "their" sheet music sold, every piece of "their" music played in a public performance, and a percentage of income taken in at every broadcast station. This fee has a sliding scale for broadcast stations, from 2 to 7 percent, depending on the income of the individual station.

At one time, these fees might have been much larger. In 1938, the legal leadership of ASCAP announced that the intended fee for radio stations would be more than double that of previous years — 10 percent or more of gross revenues. Radio stations reacted in 1939 by establishing BMI to license copyrighted music for air play. Almost every radio station on the air in 1939 became a "shareholder" of BMI and agreed to play no ASCAP music.

In place of already copyrighted music, the stations played public domain music. This music is old enough not to come under copyright laws and includes folk songs by Stephen Foster and other classical music, hymns or older church songs, and spirituals. In 1939, many original local songs, mostly country music selections, also were played by the stations in revolt against the system. They were then copyrighted by BMI and licensed back to the stations that created them.

ASCAP could not withstand the boycott for long and capitulated with a less demanding contract for radio-play rights. Today, ASCAP and BMI fees are about equal, and the fees of SESAC are lower.

SESAC licenses mostly patriotic songs and hymns along with songs of civic clubs. For example, if a station broadcasts a parade or a Rotary Club meeting, music fees involved may be SESAC's.

An interesting anecdote involving SESAC and music licenses concerns WGY in Schenectady, New York. The station had an "After Hours" program advertised as "Music from midnight until a new day's dawn over your General Electric Station, WGY, Schenectady," according to the program liner. The program consisted of 45 rotation-per-minute (rpm) records selected carefully by the music library staff in groups of ten or twelve, or just enough records to fit comfortably on one of the six-by-nine-inch plastic RCA record players being sold in the consumer electronics ads for the new 45-rpm records RCA was pushing at the time against the more popular 78-rpm records, or the 33⅓-rpm long-playing albums. This 45-rpm player, if not shut off, would repeat the last record to fall on the turntable *ad infinitum.*

Fully licensed broadcast engineers were required by FCC rules to be on duty at 50kw transmitters during all broadcast times in those days. So WGY apparently thought it could avoid a SESAC contract by carefully monitoring all music being played from the station. Record librarians were told to cull out all SESAC-licensed records from the transmitter packets as well. But someone goofed. SESAC investigators had moved into a nearby motel room to tape WGY twenty-four hours a day. You guessed it! One of the records in one of the night's turntable packages was SESAC music and, according to broadcast legend, it ended up as the last record of the package.

The engineer on duty picked that time to take a little snooze, and the contraband record played twelve or fourteen times in a row. As the government-authorized fine for each "unauthorized performance" was five hundred dollars, the resulting fine was more than the proposed SESAC blanket license. The station, according to the story, proceeded to do the smart thing — settle out of court. Consequently, even if a station plays very little music, a blanket license is the usual practice regardless of format. It may be more economical in the long run, even though it seems unfair in the case of Christian stations that only feature teaching ministries and little or no music.

Debt Retirement

Another item in the expense column is referred to as "debt retirement." This refers to the monthly payment on a bank loan. In a leveraged buyout, very little cash is brought into the purchase by the principals, who hope to increase the cash flow enough to cover payments on loans. Such loans usually generate interest of two to four points above the current prime interest rate, the rate most banks charge their preferred customers. In the mid 1980s, this rate had hovered between 9 and 14 percent per annum.

Most local banks believe broadcasting represents a substantial risk because, in the better stations, equipment value is such a small fraction of the total station worth. Banks typically desire "hard" assets to mortgage for such buyout loans. But certain sophisticated lending institutions in larger cities have eyed the substantial cash flows typical of successful stations and developed a desire to fund this kind of transaction.

The sales price of almost any station increases over a period of time. Even losers set a price escalation because poor operators think they should get their accumulated operating losses back from the sale of the station. Sometimes these continuing losses are rolled up into a credit-line loan at the local bank, and any buyer must pay enough to cover the accumulated debt of the station. In many purchase transactions, the major portion of the debt is arranged through a lending institution with a willing seller taking a second mortgage for a large part of the remainder of the purchase price. This reduces the down payment (for buyers with a proven sales track record) to as low as $10,000 to $20,000. Then the proof of how the cash flow gets increased to meet expenses and debt reduction rests directly on the new owner.

The onus of debt reduction is diminished when the entrepreneur files for and successfully receives an uncontested grant for a new facility. Building a new station is discussed in chapter 4.

Summary

Christian or secular, broadcasting costs money and should be operated responsibly as a business. In fact, Christian businesses should be *more ethical* in practices and *prompter* in paying bills, which means using sound fiscal policies. These policies should begin with the purchase of the station or stations. With so many ways of calculating the market value of a station, prospective buyers should figure several of these formulas when evaluating an existing station. Careful analysis *before* a purchase will help ensure that the bottom line will be in the black *after* the purchase.

Notes

[1] Radio Advertising Bureau, Inc., 485 Lexington Ave., New York, N.Y. 10017.

Chapter 4
Building New Stations

The cost of a new radio station varies with the tower height, cost of land, and power of the station, but the total cost is closely related to the cost of the equipment plus the first three months operating expenses. The FCC has opened several hundred FM channels in various communities throughout the United States in its "Docket 80-90." FM stations are assigned to communities by computer; and, in general, citizens may file only for the frequencies designated and only for the communities designated in the published list as well.

The exact location of an FM tower is constrained by "short-spacing" to existing and-or designated frequencies within fixed mileages from the desired location. The FCC publishes a chart designating the permissable separation by power or class of station. Class B, or 50,000-watt, stations are the most powerful FM facilities authorized in the Northeast. Class C, or 100,000-watt, stations are the most powerful stations authorized in most of the rest of the country. The FCC has divided the country into two high-power zones. But Class A stations are granted on the basis of 3,000 watts effective radiated power at 300 feet above average terrain throughout the country. These are the smaller community FM allocations. The majority of the Docket 80-90 new assignments are for Class A stations.

The FCC has announced these frequencies to be considered for filing on a randomly chosen "window" basis. Early in 1985, the commission divided all the new FM allocations by frequencies and put the channel numbers on separate pieces of paper in a large drum. Officials then pulled out the channel numbers at random, noting that the first drawn was Channel _____, the second was Channel _____, etc., until all frequencies were drawn. This placed an index on ordering (randomly selected) new channels.

Each channel was then detailed with the newly designated communities of application. The facilities for any given community would come due for filing in a thirty-day window, and the windows would open one or two frequency groupings per month as announced by the FCC.

Some of the windows have been opened, and citizens have filed for new facilities at most of the locations. If more than one applicant files for the same facility, the FCC holds a hearing to determine the best party to own the new station.

Contact the FCC for a list of the 80-90 windows. The FCC has been opening about two windows per month. If someone is interested in an allocation for a certain community, a good idea of when the appropriate window will be opened can be gained by estimating from the first window, opened in September 1985. To file for the desired window, a prospective owner would need to get organized beforehand because an application cannot be prepared properly within the thirty-day time limit provided for in the window itself.

Preparation for an FCC Application

Several areas of information need to be organized to prepare for filing an application with the FCC. The commission wants to know who the new owners will be, whether the ownership will be an individual or a corporation, whether the finances of the owner are in order, and whether a proper site for the tower has been located. This information, along with an engineering report will need to be pulled together before the application can be filed.

How to set up a corporation: It usually takes more than thirty days to organize a corporation. The prospective name must be researched at the Secretary of State's office at the state capital to be sure it has not already been used. The franchise tax must be filed with the appropriate papers, and a certificate of incorporation must be returned. Bylaws must be written, and the complete minutes of the corporation filed. This implies setting aside some money to be used as capital by the new corporation. All this takes at least thirty days. There are many other details to take care of close to the filing date, so a new corporation needs to be in place before the actual filing for a new station is done.

Finances: Is the cash available to buy the station and operate it for at least three months? Will loans or letters of credit need to be arranged? In the past, the FCC required applicants to prove the availability of financing, but now there is just a box on the application to check indicating that you have the funds available. Do not try to stretch the truth with a "statement of faith." This has to be a statement of "materialized" fact! There must be money in the bank or a written promise from an investor or a loan institution that the funds will be available.

Christians particularly need to be careful in this aspect. The FCC does not understand "faith financing" and crisis funding. A lot of lip service is given to building new Christian stations, but not much cash is available. Believers may have good intentions but may not part with the actual money. According to an old adage, the road to you-know-where is paved with good intentions!

Everyone has been to a circus or a carnival where a fellow in a booth has three shells. He asks, "Which shell has the pea under it?" Hands move the shells around, and after the guesses are all in, the guy lifts first one, then another shell. "Here it is!" And the game goes on. There's another shell game in Christian broadcasting: "Which shell has the Christian capital under it to build a new station?" If the prospective owner waits until the last thirty days to start moving the shells around, he will be sadly disappointed nearly every time.

The money must be available before the applicant files! One possibility is to persuade a businessman to buy the land, tower, antenna, and transmitting equipment, and lease it to you over a ten-year period. He is assured of getting his money back and can get a tax break on the equipment write-off. A further fail-safe is the worth of the station. But even Christian businessmen must be convinced that this is a good business venture. Let us look at an approach that will usually convince a prospective financier. Start with a listing of construction costs:

Table 4.1
Typical Construction Costs for a Small Station

	NEW	USED
Land for site	$5,000	$5,000
Tower	15,000	5,000
Transmission Line & Antenna	5,000	5,000
Transmitter	16,000	6,000
Monitor	5,000	3,000
Studio Equipment	25,000	5,000
Consoles, Turntables		
Tape and Cassette Recorders		
Cart Machines		
Production/New Studio	10,000	4,000
Building vs. Mobile Home	30,000	5,000
TOTALS	$111,000	$38,000

Suppose the prospective buyer has accumulated all the studio stereo equipment. He can get this into the "lease" for cash to operate with, and here is how. Let us assume that a businessman puts up $50,000 to buy all the land and equipment needed. If the payments are $500 per month for 120 months, the investor will get back about twice his investment. Now, suppose you give him 20 percent of the stock of the station. In a viable market, the station will be worth about $200,000 the day it is built, with almost no billing accounts. If it were to be sold, the investor would get his money back in a payout from the buyer and get $40,000 for his share of the sale price. In addition, the investor-leasor will have received the tax investment credit and equipment depreciation allowance against the lease payments.

About five years down the road, with excellent billings, the station would be worth about $350,000. At this point, the investor would have all his investment dollars returned, enjoyed a substantial tax break, and also have received $70,000 from the sale price. Such an investor will want to know what the buyer is going to supply — which is the knowledge and skill to wire all the equipment into an operating system, the ability to program the facility properly, and, above all, the ability, drive, and competence to sell air time so that billings will cover the lease payments plus operating expenses. These financial arrangements usually cannot be completed in thirty days.

Site selection: The details of site selection for FM applications will be covered in Part Three, the engineering chapters, but it is necessary here to note that this process is of utmost importance. For an FM station, the location of the antenna at a point of commanding elevation above the city of license and area covered is the keystone to proper coverage of the market. FM works essentially by line of sight, so if the station owner were to climb to the proposed site with a pair of binoculars, what he would see is what he would get in coverage. Another fact to remember is that not every hilltop owner wants a tower on his land. Many people do not want the bother.

Other considerations involve government agencies other than the FCC. If the tower is to be more than 199 feet tall, an environmental impact report must be filed with the Environmental Protection Agency. Some of the questions the agency wants answered are:

- Is the new tower to be near any bird sanctuaries or in the flyway of flocks of birds?
- Is the tower going to stand out against a national seashore landscape or near a national monument?
- If the tower is going to cause problems to the natural habitat or mar the landscape, can a careful study justify its construction?

The Federal Aviation Administration (FAA) gets involved if the tower is near an airport. A special form must be obtained from the FAA, filled out, and filed with them. A tower should be at least six miles from any airport.

Also, almost every area of this country large enough to support a broadcast station has enacted zoning regulations. The prospective owner needs to be reasonably assured of getting a building permit for the new tower by the time of filing an application with the FCC. The assurance can be in the form of a firm lease or an option to purchase. Once a tentative site is located, it would be advisable to check the location against co-channel and first, second, and third adjacent frequencies to determine the separation of the antenna sites. Computer analysis services such as Dataworld[1] and Compucon[2] have spherical geometry programs that give a printout of distances to problem stations or allocations based on the geographic coordinates provided by the client.

Information on Starting an AM Station

A proposed rule being considered by the FCC would open up the high, or top, end of the AM band for new stations on frequencies above 1600khz. These stations would use power up to 5000 watts, primarily nondirectional, day and night operations, that would depend on expanded-dial AM receivers coming to the marketplace so the new stations could be tuned in. AM allocations differ from FM assignments in that, in establishing a new AM station, the entrepreneur is welcome to ask for any frequency and power that fits. The FCC rule has established protected-field strength contours, and any signal that is greater than a regulated ratio must be minimized toward the established station.

This may give rise to directional antennas (DA) so that the planned signal may be minimized in given directions. In AM, the entire tower radiates, and directional antennas consist of more than one tower. DA's cost more than non-directional antennas. The engineering aspects of AM applications get complicated very rapidly and usually are handled by consulting engineers. But it is possible to get an idea of available AM channels in an area by listening to every frequency on the AM dial. Frequencies with little or no activity may be candidates for application.

The FCC has designated certain frequencies as Class I operations with 50,000-watt power output that dominate whole segments of the country. On some of these frequencies, the FCC permits daytime-only Class II operations. These stations are not authorized for significant nighttime operations because of the nighttime skywave phenomena. Some of the electric wave that is radiated from the tower goes up into the ionosphere, a portion of the atmosphere that is almost a vacuum, where electrons and ions float around in that rarefied atmosphere. The electric wave that gets up into this area of the ionosphere is bent back down to earth in the nighttime hours. This reflected wave comes back down to the earth about 800 to 1,200 miles from the transmitter and causes interference to any station on the same frequency. This skywave phenomena precludes Class II stations from operations that would interfere with Class I operations on the same frequency. The Class I operations were the first established on those frequencies and have priority on channels that send signals for hundreds and hundreds of miles to their protected contours.

The FCC has provided a group of frequencies to cover an intermediate-sized area. These are called regional, or Class III, stations. Many of these stations are full-time operations. Most of them use directional antennas at night, but some use directional antennas day and night with one pattern in the daytime and another at night. These directional antennas allow a regional station to protect other Class III stations on the same and/or nearby frequencies and still cover its market.

In addition, the FCC had set aside a group of frequencies for "local" stations to cover a smaller city or town. These Class IV stations are on 1230khz, 1240khz, 1340khz, 1400khz, and 1490khz and were permitted 250 watts day and night. Then the FCC allowed them 1000 watts during daylight hours and 250 watts at night. As of 1985, many Class IV stations have been permitted to raise their power to 1000 watts day *and* night.

In filing for an AM station, the applicant must choose a frequency that permits operation in the chosen market while causing no interference to other stations. The details of such interference and of filing the engineering procedures will be discussed more fully in Part Three. The financial, ownership, and programming aspects of an AM application are the same as for commercial FM applications.

The programming aspects of an FCC application have evolved since 1975 from the height of a special-ascertainment-of-community-needs era to a slightly less regulated regimen, but the prospective broadcaster still must operate "in the public interest." This concept goes back to the original basis for governmental regulation of radio waves: that they are owned by the public because they are a natural resource. All citizens have an inherent right to enjoy these resources, and when the resource is limited (there are only so many radio waves available), the government has a right to intervene with business affairs to regulate the use of the resource on behalf of its citizens. There has to be a balance between the public affairs programming considered ideal by the staff members of the FCC and the marketing niche that a station's rigorous format maintains. The history of radio programming is a fascinating profile of the marketing growth of the medium. (See chapter 8.)

FCC Television Applications

Television stations are assigned by channel to communities on a computer list by the FCC in a similar fashion to the FM assignment lists. The televison channels are divided into Very High Frequency (VHF) channels from 2-13 and Ultra High Frequency (UHF) channels from 14-84. The VHF stations are cheaper to build, as well as to operate, and cover more area for a given transmitter power than UHF stations. Unfortunately, most VHF channels already have been assigned and are in operation. Some major population areas still have UHF allocations available, although most are at least in the construction stage. The main new regulation of the 1980s is the authorization of an entirely new class of broadcast stations: Low-Power TV (LPTV).

These LPTV stations were made available on the basis of the "TV Translator Station" rules and, in effect, permit UHF stations of powers up to 1000 watts to transmit output power on channels that fit certain mileage separation standards. The new rules permit the TV equivalent of AM Class IV or FM Class A stations, especially for smaller communities. The problem with applying for these low-power TV stations is that the cost is approximately five to ten times the cost of a radio station of comparable coverage. The programming also is much more expensive, harder to broadcast, and less versatile than radio; nevertheless, Christian TV stations are going on line at the rate of about one a month.

The ownership forms, financial statements, and programming forms used in filing for a new television station are similar to those used for a new radio station. The amount of capital needed is much larger, of course, and the programming aspects are a little more complex than for radio applications. Many LPTV channels have already been filed for, and quite a few have been granted by the FCC and not yet built. Some of the channels in this category are becoming available for new filings on a first come-first served basis. Many of the LPTV stations that were built in the last few years are in, at, or near bankruptcy proceedings. Financial institutions involved would welcome new entrepreneurial investors.

These operators have learned that everything seems to cost more for television than radio. Studio facilities, news gathering activities, and programming cost about the same for LPTV stations as for full-power stations, except that the cost of power to the transmitter is less. Also, LPTV stations are optional for the area cable systems to carry, and most choose not to carry the LPTV stations. Many ministries, then, choose to produce programming for use directly on cable access channels. The cost of such programming per viewer seems reasonable in the larger markets, but the viability of this activity in smaller markets is questionable.

The concepts, development, and costs of radio and television programming will be explored in Part Four.

Summary

The main steps in getting an application together for an 80-90 FM construction permit, which are similar for AM and for television, are these:

1. Unless the owner is a single individual, form a legal entity to file for the station, such as a corporation or a partnership.

2. Get the finances together. Either deposit the cash in a savings account or make firm financial arrangements in writing with a person or agency which will finance the project.

3. Find an appropriate tower site on high ground (for FM or TV), with a firm lease agreement or option. It must be far enough from airports, birds, flora, or fauna, etc., a site that has been checked to make sure it is not short-spaced to existing or already allocated channels.

4. Prepare the engineering part of the application (See Part Three), and file when the appropriate window is open for 80-90 FM applications or when TV channels become available to the community of interest.

Notes

[1] Dataworld, Inc., 1302 18th St., N.W., Washington, D.C. 20036.

[2] Compucon, Inc., P.O. Box 809006, Dallas, Texas 75380-9006.

Part Three

Engineering: Making the Right Connections

Chapter 5
Positioning for FCC Grants: AM Allocations

The FCC allocation rules have changed drastically, especially for the AM band. Formerly, only proposed new AM stations for communities not served by any radio signals were available for filing. At this time, any AM signal that does not interfere with an existing or proposed station and covers a community with the appropriate signal level is available.

Before filing an application, the legal, financial and programming boxes must be checked and the exhibits produced, and the applicable engineering section completed. Most applications are accepted for filing with a built-in time period during which opposing applications are sought by the FCC for the same facilities. When competing applications are filed for the same facilities, the FCC will either hold a comparative hearing or use a lottery system to determine which applicant will be issued a construction permit to build the station. Regardless of the method of issuing the construction permit, the FCC has certain criteria for which it looks in selecting preferred applicants.

In the case of a lottery, the commission has decided to enhance the chances of minority owners being drawn by doubling the number of slips in the hat for applications with minority members in the dominant ownership positions. Blacks, Hispanics, Asian-Americans, American Indians, and women constitute the minority groups the FCC believes are under-represented among broadcast owners.

In order to weight the drawing or hearing, minority group members must hold the controlling interest in the applicant organization and be active participants in the management of the station. Points are awarded also for "integration of local ownership and management," an FCC phrase for broadcast owners who live in the same community as the broadcast station and manage the facility. Extra points are awarded when the owners already are residents of the community before the application is filed, but some points are available when the owners testify that they intend to move to the area, live there, and operate the station. Minority group ownership is most valuable when it results also in integration of local ownership and management.

Other Issues Important to the FCC

In addition to minority group members holding a controlling interest and integration of local control and management, the FCC looks for "307(b) issues." Section 307(b) of the Communications Act of 1934, as amended, concerns the FCC's "equitable distribution of stations" among the communities of our nation. As the population of many communities has grown from a few hundred in the 1950s to a few thousand by the 1970s to more than fifty thousand by the mid 1980s, the FCC would rather see an application for a community of fifty thousand that has no locally identifiable broadcast service than to see an application for essentially the same facilities for a big city thirty miles away that already has several broadcast outlets.

The other concern under that section is the size of the population in the appropriate coverage area. The wiser an applicant can be in locating the transmitting site and in controlling output, antenna-gain, and various other engineering parameters to maximize the total population covered, the better the applicant's chances in the hearing. This is especially true for "white areas," or groups of people outside the service area of any station. At a 1960s FM hearing, such a "white area" was the determining factor causing application approval for a station covering about 2,000 people. The FCC hearing examiner decided those people, recognized in the statistical population counts of all the applicants' service areas, should be served by the one applicant whose transmitter site was best located to cover the "underserved" area.

Diversification in programming could enhance an application designated for hearing. Adding a Top 40 station to an area with three or four pop music stations does not add to the diversity of programming for an area. FCC hearing officers do not necessarily prefer religious format stations. Actually, they may be prejudiced against such programming. A careful analysis of the programming in an area and a selected diversification in the proposed format could enhance the position of the new applicant. For example, let us say an area has four FM and three AM stations. The FM formats are Adult Contemporary, Album-Oriented Rock, Contemporary Country, and Beautiful Music. The AMs are News/Talk, Oldies, and Country. Just as a new FM frequency opens up, let us say that the Beautiful Music station changes to Top 40. The FCC would much rather see an application specifying Beautiful Music for that market than a proposed Top 40 format. (The various programming formats are discussed in chapter 9.)

FCC hearing examiners, or administrative law judges as they are now known, apparently like first-time ownership proposals from applicants with broadcast experience. Applications from people who have already owned stations are somewhat discounted in favor of giving new owner-operators their first chance at broadcast ownership, but the judges do seem to give preference to people who have worked in the field as announcers or technicians. Certainly applicants who approach a hearing should know the operations and ownership/FCC vocabulary well enough to answer questions intelligently. Obviously having a bankruptcy in one's past or having been involved with labor disputes could be harmful to an applicant's chances. Having been convicted of any "restraint of trade" activity could remove the application from consideration at all. Any principal of the application must have less than twelve applications "in the works" at the time of the hearing. Any given owner is allowed an interest in twelve AM, twelve FM, and twelve TV stations at any one time. That includes applications in progress and already operating stations.

There Is Still an AM Radio Band

Yes, Virginia, there is still an AM radio band! What was all of broadcasting thirty years ago has fewer listeners than FM now but is still a viable medium, especially for Christian broadcasters. A slogan of the 1950s and early 1960s — "Find a market, find a frequency" — applies once again, because the FCC has removed its "first service to a community" rule. The engineering operation of that maxim depends on finding a market. That is getting harder and harder to do. Most markets are over "radioed," but some good-sized markets have no Christian broadcasting. Perhaps the cheapest way to get the gospel out to these markets is to build a new AM station.

Once a market is selected that can support the new AM station, a frequency that will work for that market must be selected. One obvious way to get started on the search for an AM frequency is to get a good, sensitive AM radio and listen to all the frequencies that come into the area during the daytime. Listen for holes in the AM band that might permit a new station.

AM stations are protected to their predicted contours on the FCC's M-3 ground conductivity map, unless actual field meter readings prove these estimated contours are incorrect. A new station would cause interference to an existing station if the 0.025mv/m "nuisance" contour reaches the 0.5mv/m contour of the existing station. The 0.025mv/m contour of the new station is predicted by using the FCC M-3 map of ground conductivities and the Field Strength Versus Distance Ground Conductivity Log-Log graphs located near the M-3 map in the rules. (See the examples of graphs and maps in Appendix 1.) The higher the power and the greater the ground conductivity, the farther the 0.025mv/m signal goes. At 1530khz and 1kw from a quarter-wave antenna, the 0.025 predicted contour goes 160 miles towards an existing station in 15 ground conductivity. If the ground conductivity was less, say an 8, then the signal would go 125 miles to the 0.025mv/m contour. Five hundred watts on 1270khz would go about as far as the 1kw on

1530khz, and 500 watts on 950khz is about equivalent to 5kw on 1390khz. Therefore, as the several curves in Part 73, Section 184, Paragraph 19 of the FCC rules indicate, the signal strength at a distance of given ground conductivity for a given power varies with the frequency and is increased as the frequency is decreased. (See FCC rules for a complete set of curves.)

After finding a quiet spot on the dial, the adjacent frequencies must be studied also. At 10khz on either side of the chosen frequencies, the 0.5mv/m contour of existing and proposed stations must not cross. For example, the 1530khz Wagoner, Oklahoma, 0.5mv/m contour must not cross the 1520khz Oklahoma City 0.5mv/m contour. At 20khz from the proposed station, on either side, the 2mv/m contour of one must not cross the 25mv/m of the other. Thus the 2mv/m Wagoner contour cannot cross the 25mv/m contour of KKOJ's 1550khz signal in Sapulpa, Oklahoma. At 30khz separation, the 25mv/m contour must not cross. With 40khz separation, the two stations may be licensed to the same town, however. Keep in mind that these interference ratios are reciprocal, that the proposed station may neither accept nor cause interference with any existing station or other proposal. A field strength meter helps by allowing a determination of signal strength for existing stations near the proposal frequency to determine the power level allowable for the new station. This power level must be great enough to allow the signal to cover all of the city of license with a 5mv/m signal in order to be licensed to that city.

The frequencies that are often the easiest to work with are the local AM frequencies. The frequencies of 1490, 1450, 1400, 1340, 1240 and 1230khz are designated by the FCC as "local frequencies" and are assigned 1kw day and night, usually from a 150-foot tower. The first step for the proposal is to see if the frequency would fit in the community with 250 watts causing no interference. Once that is established, the 1kw facilities are authorized almost automatically. That is because of the history of these frequencies. They were licensed originally for 250 watt stations day and night with given interference ratios, but in the 1970s were allowed to go to 1kw days as well as maintain the 250 watt nighttime. And in the mid 1980s, they have been allowed 1kw day and night, regardless of the mutual interference caused and received. Therefore, the FCC is a little more lenient on these frequencies, especially in cities or towns that have no radio service.

Directional Stations

Another area where the relaxing of rules benefits those who would like to start an AM station is on the Class I frequencies for either daytime Class II operations or deeply directional Class II day and night stations. Whenever there are two or more towers in a station's antenna array, the station is directional. Directional antennas serve two primary purposes with probably the most important being to direct the signal away from areas that might otherwise cause interference.

Let us say that without a directional antenna, the station could radiate 850 watts toward a particular Class I station. With one additional tower, the applicant could design an antenna coverage pattern to suppress the signal toward the dominant station while pouring more than 5000 watts in other directions, being licensed as a 5kw station. The other reason for a directional array is to put the power over the people. If the station in the example above was so strategically located that there was a partially populated area in the 850-watt direction (called "null") from this site toward the dominant station and that the high power directions (called "lobes" or "main beam") covered the main cities of interest, an efficient system could be created.

The power rating of a station refers to the average non-directional power effect. For example, whenever a 5kw station is directionalized to limit radiation in one or more directions, then there must be lobes or concentrations of power in one or more directions that are more power-effective than the 5000 watts. The effective power in these main beams, or lobes, is often nearly twice the rated output of the station. Of course, directional antennas are more expensive to build and maintain than nondirectional single-tower antennas. DAs require two or more antenna towers with special sampling coils attached to expensive antenna monitors as well as a separate tower-feed transmission line to each tower and a separate tower tuning unit at the base of each tower. All DAs require a special phase network to send the power to each tower in the desired fashion.

A turnkey two-tower DA would cost approximately $150,000 in 1986 dollars. The station would have to bill at least $2000 more a month than a nondirectional installation to be worth the effort of a DA. But DAs are especially helpful in suppressing skywave interference to preexisting dominant stations in Class I frequencies. If a pattern can be chosen so that the signal is suppressed toward dominant 50kw stations and also toward any stations on channel (10, 20, or 30khz away from main channel), while still putting the main beams in the desired heavy-population directions, the population served may well double or triple.

Class II operations where the smaller station is six hundred to eight hundred miles from the dominant station usually will fit, barring any groundwave interference in adjacent channels. There are special curves to determine the daytime power allowed toward the dominant station, but a dead giveaway is discovering another operation closer to the dominant station with a reasonable sunrise to sunset power. If your proposed daytime contours would not interfere with that station, chances are that the proposed operation would fit with the dominant station with regard to the skyway interference tables and graphs.

When the listening survey of a chosen market turns up daytime silence on a list of frequencies, it is fortunate if a local channel also shows up on the list. More probable, however, is that a Class II frequency will turn up. These include 670, 720, 770, 780, 880, 890, 1020, 1030, 1100, 1120, 1180, 1210 khz and allow smaller stations than 50kw to co-exist on the channel. Some frequencies are foreign clear-channel frequencies such as 680, 710, 810, 850, 940, 1000, 1060, 1070, 1080, 1090, 1110, 1130, 1140, 1170, 1190, 1500, 1510, 1520, 1530,

1540, 1550, and 1560, and must protect Canada, Mexico, or the Bahamas. Canada and Mexico may receive little or no radiation on their border with the United States, rather than at any station's protected contours.

Plot a "Spaghetti" Map

Once a frequency or frequencies that seem quiet are determined, for a modest fee firms such as Dataworld (see Notes, chapter 4 for address) will list all the stations on each submitted frequency and 30khz on each side of that frequency so the proposed operation's feasibility may be further examined. Once all the potential stations that might cause or accept interference to your proposed frequency use are listed, the next chore is to plot the protected coverage areas of these stations on a big map, commonly called a spaghetti map because all the signal contours look like spilled spaghetti. Start with stations 30khz above and below the filing frequency, and within twenty miles of the proposed site, by plotting their 25mv/m coverage contours, which is easy if they are nondirectional. Because every station has been required to file this contour with the FCC, these figures may be found in the station's file in the FCC reference room or in the station's public file.

Plot the 2mv/m and the 25mv/m contours of any stations within 50 miles of the proposed site which operate 20khz on either side of the proposed frequency. Next, plot the 0.5mv/m signal contours of all stations within 100 miles of the proposed site for stations 10khz either side of the proposed frequency. Then plot on the map all stations on the proposed frequency within 300 miles of the proposed site and show their 0.025 contours. It must be shown that the proposed 25mv/m contour does not cross the 25mv/m contour of stations 30khz away from the proposed frequency, or the 2mv/m contour of any stations 20khz away, or that the 2mv/m contour will not cross the 25mv/m contour of stations 20khz away. The proposed 0.5mv/m contour must not cross any 0.5mv/m signal from stations 10khz away. Then the 0.025mv/m "nuisance" contour must not cross the 0.5mv/m signal contour of stations in the same frequency and their 0.025mv/m contour must not cross the 0.5 contour from the proposed station.

Every contour should be labeled for reference. If the contours fit without crossing any other station's protected contour, then the application may be filed for the daytime use of the frequency. Class IV stations practically get the nighttime service free of extra work, but all other frequencies guard the nighttime service with very complicated rules.

Signals from AM stations go up into the ionosphere and at night are bent down, or reflected, to great distances from the antenna. Try tuning around the radio dial at night and hear the distant signals that come in loud and clear. This implies deep directional protection from minor stations on the same frequency if nighttime service is to be established. A discussion of the procedures for establishing such coverage is beyond the scope of this handbook. The reader should contact a consulting engineer for planning.

If the frequency search turns up a Class III or regional channel, the applicant may file for 500 to 5000 watts. On Class I channels, any daytime power from 250 watts up to 50,000 watts that fits may be licensed.

Class III Channels

The Class III channels include 550, 560, 570, 580, 590, 600, 610, 620, 630, 790, 910, 920, 930, 950, 960, 970, 980, 1150, 1250, 1260, 1270, 1280, 1290, 1300, 1310, 1320, 1330, 1350, 1360, 1370, 1380, 1390, 1410, 1420, 1430, 1440, 1460, 1470, 1480, 1590, and 1600 khz. The groundwave criteria are the same for these frequencies, but the nighttime restrictions are more relaxed than for the clear channels. There is some talk around regulatory circles that there might be more relaxation of nighttime restrictions on the Class III channels, moving toward the concept of the Class IV rules, although not quite as simple. The move, if any, seems to be aimed toward protection of Class III nighttime signals to their nighttime city grade interference-free coverage contours, rather than to other coverage contour levels. Some Class III stations have accepted interference to their 5mv/m or even 10mv/m nighttime signal level, as long as their entire city is covered with a useful signal, then other stations are thought to be licensable on the same channel.

The more stations there are on the same frequency at night, the more general the interference effect. Just one competing station may send an intelligible signal into the nighttime area of a dominant station. It is possible that more than one station added to this interference will yield less interference than just the one other station. It is true that several nearly equal class stations' nighttime signals mixed onto another station's city signal gives an unintelligible hash to interfere with the desired signal, and they mix nonarithmetically so that the addition of another nighttime signal may add very little extra interference to the already interference-laden desired signal.

Class III stations already have received generous postsunset operating powers. In 1983, daytime AM stations were issued power levels at which they could operate between sunset and 6 p.m. local time during the shorter days of the winter months. The computer-designated FCC-authorized power levels varied from 2 or 3 watts to 500 watts, and the higher power levels usually were allocated to the Class III daytimers.

As of 1986, the FCC is accepting applications for all AM frequencies, regardless of whether the proposed community of license is served by aural signals at the time of filing or not. Applications for Class I frequencies were opened up in the late 1970s. Class III and Class IV frequencies have remained available, now with maximum power specified that will work interference-free, as long as it is at or above the minimum of 250 watts on Class II and Class IV channels and 500w on Class III channels. Before 1985, Class III channels were only authorized power levels of 500w, 1kw, 2.5kw, and 5kw. Now applications will be considered for any power more than 500w up to 5kw that fits and covers the city limits.

To file for an AM frequency, first listen around the radio dial, then prepare a spaghetti map, using the maximum power level above the minimum for the class of station that permits interference-free operation. Sometimes it is helpful to use a field meter to measure signal levels of existing stations, especially in hilly or mountainous terrain. The FCC M-3 map is not absolutely accurate, and detailed ground conductivity studies have created many an application's feasibility. All stations with DAs have field meters. A person who wants to file for a station can learn to operate a field meter, and probably borrow one occasionally, by volunteering to help out with a DA adjustment. Get to know the chief engineer of a DA station nearby and help him or her in exchange for instruction in operating the meter and in interpreting the readings. This is a good way to obtain free field radiation and ground conductivity information.

Field meter readings are analyzed by plotting the mv/m reading at a distance from the antenna on log-log paper. Many readings made within a range of 0.2 miles to 1 mile from the antenna, at least every tenth of a mile in carefully measured-off distances in a given direction, should be plotted with the measurements at longer distances. Once plotted, the graph with these points is placed over the FCC standard log-log plot for the frequency involved. The graph with the points is slid vertically up and down with the one-mile vertical lines held together until the curvature defined by the points matches up with a ground conductivity curve on the standard FCC graph. Then the ground conductivity curve(s) that are matched up are traced through on the plot of points and labeled, and the slanted straight-line is traced out as well. Where the slanted straight-line crosses the one-mile mark on the plotted graph, the value of the unattenuated radiation at one mile is read from the Field Strength axis numbers. This gives the unattenuated radiation in the direction of the measurements from the station measured.

One kilowatt stations should have 175 to 240mv/m unattenuated radiation, depending on tower height, with an average being about 190mv/m. This is a check on the results for ground conductivity. That is, when the curve is fitted to the correct horizontal radiation in the direction of the measurements, a station's signal path should travel through the ground conductivities shown on the traced-through plot.

Measuring existing stations shows only the ground conductivity toward the proposed site, not the other way around. These measurements also show the actual signal strength of a station toward the proposed site. AM allocations are sometimes achievable only through such field measurement techniques. A spaghetti map drawn with actual field meter-determined coverage contours usually will determine a slightly greater space for the proposed signal.

How to Carry Out an On-Site Test

Occasionally it is productive to determine the ground conductivity *from* a proposed site. Unless there is a transmitter operating in the broadcast band from the proposed site, a little tower, ground system, and a test-site transmitter will need to be set up. Determine the quietest spot on the dial for daytime operation at the site and apply to the FCC for a test-site authorization with the frequencies and power desired. The authorization will list the days and hours to which the test site transmitter is limited. The field measurements made on this test site transmitter will enable the points to be plotted and curve fit. It will determine ground conductivity toward problem areas and also will determine the distance to various contours of the proposed operation should the ground conductivities be less than those of the M-3 map.

In some cases it is possible to file for a lower power, build the station, and then make the measurements when the lower-wattage signal is in place. This may well determine if the power of the little station may be raised by application for a power increase. Field measurements seldom show an increase of ground conductivity over that predicted by the FCC M-3 map and usually show the ground conductivity as less. Green leaves on the trees during a dry spell will decrease the ground conductivity in seasonal reductions not recognized by the commission staff. They believe that the ground conductivity is more stable than field engineers have found it to be.

New Receivers on the Way

In densely populated areas, new AM station frequencies may be a little harder to find in the main AM dial range (540 to 1600khz). But the FCC is strongly considering opening up 1600 through 1800 on the top end of the AM dial for 5kw non-directional full-time operation. The only problem is that it will take awhile for new receivers to become active in the field. Author, FCC attorney, and registered FCC consulting engineer Larry Perry told a 1984 meeting of the Gospel Music Broadcasters in Nashville that special digital transmissions are destined to replace regular modulation techniques on the AM band, that these new digital broadcasts will sound better in stereo than Stereo FM now does, and that a 1mv/m signal strength with digital transmission will sound just as clear as the 25mv/m analog signal does now. These digital AM systems at 1kw will have the coverage of 50kw stations — but not until there are enough of those new receivers out there!

Summary

All the criteria suggest that an applicant who anticipates a hearing (or lottery) should construct the application with a minority owner-partner; with all parties having previously worked in broadcasting without ownership interests; with all parties, if not filing for their hometown, then willing to move to the town of the application and help manage the station they have built in the best location to cover the most people in an area without similar service; with a program format that increases the diversity of signals heard in the community, which, of course, features plenty of public affairs programming of community interest!

But the first step is to find a location, market, and frequency to propose, then plot out all the necessary contours using detailed maps. The AM engineering section of the FCC Form 301 demands detailed maps, one of the proposed tower site and one that indicates the proposed 25mv/m, 5mv/m, 2mv/m and 0.5mv/m coverage contours with the proposed area and population covered. Aerial photographs of the proposed site also are required as well as the spaghetti map discussed above with a narrative describing how the map(s) were prepared. A vertical sketch plan of the proposed tower also must be filed.

Other decisions that must be made are whether to go to a directional station, and which class station is possible and desirable.

But the bottom line in the decision to go this route could be that building a new AM station is the cheapest way to get out the gospel in that area.

Chapter 6
Waiting for the FM Window to Open

There are many tasks that can be accomplished while waiting to file for that 80-90 frequency. The first task is to find a site for the transmitter. Look for a 300- to 500-foot tower, preferably atop a hill or mountain overlooking the community. Investigate a side mount tower-use lease allowing the FM antenna to be placed part-way up the tower. The usual charge for this is $1 per foot of tower height per month. If the antenna is mounted three hundred feet up a tower, the usual fee would be $300 per month to park the antenna there with the transmitter at the foot of the tower. This corresponds to the rent on land and amortization of the tower itself. Arrangements like this also reduce the capital necessary for starting a new station.

If this type of tower attachment arrangement can be found, get the geographic coordinates of the tower and spend $60 to $70 at Dataworld to check out the spacing between the proposed transmissions on the channel being assigned and other stations on that frequency and adjacent channels. If the printout shows no short-spacing, sign a contract with the tower operator. Otherwise, it may be necessary to get the use of land to erect a tower. In that case, get an "option to lease or purchase" from the landowner and determine the geographic coordinates for the spot where the tower is to be erected. Give these coordinates to Dataworld to check out short-spacing on the proposed channel.

After the site has been chosen, a corporation or other legal entity of ownership needs to be established to build, own, and operate the station. It might be helpful to find a minority partner to give the application some priority with the FCC. Once the ownership entity is organized and the transmitter site nailed down, buy the seven-and-one-half-inch Coast and Geodetic Survey Quadrangle Maps that cover ten to twelve miles in each direction from the site. At the tower site, draw a north-south line, and an east-west line, and the 45-degree bisectors at NE/SW and NW/SE directions. If not intersected by one of the above, draw a radial over the city of license. Extend each of these radials in their directions onto adjacent maps. Draw a circle with a two-mile radius, using the site as the center. From this two-mile distance, draw one-tenth-of-a-mile markers out each radial until the ten-mile mark is reached on each radial. At each place where a 0.1 mile hatch mark crosses each radial, read the elevation above sea level and record it in a tabulation by radial. For each radial, add all the elevation readings and divide by the number of readings in the list. This number yields the average elevation of the radial above sea level. This must be done for each of the eight radials and the radial over the town as well (if needed).

Determine the tower height or the spot on an existing tower to attach your antenna by calculating the height above the average terrain. Subtract the elevation at the base of the tower from the average elevation of each radial. Add these "elevation of site above average elevation of radial" numbers and divide by eight (omit separate ninth radial drawn to cover community from this calculation). Add enough tower height to reach 328 feet above the average elevation of the radials. If the elevation at the base of the tower is more than 300 feet above the average elevation of the radials, then add about 100 to 150 feet above this by tower height to get the antenna above the tops of any trees and determine how high the center of the antenna (the middle radiator of a three-bay antenna, for instance) will be above the average elevation of the radials. This is the Height Above Average Terrain (HAAT).

Now consult the FCC application Form 301, Section V-B, "FM Broadcast Engineering Data," on page 3 of Section V-B (or FCC 301, p. 13). Calculate the height of the antenna radiation center above average elevation of each radial direction by subtracting the average elevation for the radial from the height of antenna radiation center above sea level. (This is the height up the tower to the center of the array added to the height above sea level of the tower base.) Convert each difference, if they are in feet, to meters by multiplying by 0.3048. Use both feet and meters in the application unless new FCC Form 301 instructions say otherwise. If the HAAT is more than 328 feet, reduce power according to the "Height of Antenna Radiation Center vs. Equivalent Coverage Powers" graph in the FCC rules to determine the appropriate power for increased antenna heights.

The 3.16mv/m contour is the 70-DBU contour in FCC figure 73.333, figure 1 in the FCC rules. Use the sliding scale cut from the following page. Select the power in kilowatts of radiation and line up the power on the sliding scale with the horizontal line at 40 on the vertical scale of the figure 1 graph. Slide the cutout (usually to the right) until the right hand side of the slide lines up with the height of antenna radiation center above average elevation of the northeast radial, and make a mark on the main graph to the immediate right of the slider at the 70 mark (using the numbers "F in DBU above 1mv/m" in the center of the sliding scale, that is, just to the right of the 70-mark on the slider), and put a mark on the figure 1 graph.

The slanting curved lines extended to the right of the figure 1 graph indicate the miles from the antenna for this coverage contour. Between five and ten miles are imaginary curved lines indicated by hatch marks in the graph. Each hatch mark represents another mile. It will probably be necessary to estimate the distance by guessing how far between the five to ten mile curve the particular mark for the proposed site occurs. The usual distance for 3kw at 100 meters or 320 feet is about seven miles from the antenna. Higher antenna heights above a radial will go farther. Lesser heights will not go as far, of course.

The 1mv/m contour is the 60-DBU number on the slides. Calculate from the figure 1 graph how far the 1mv/m contour will go in a like fashion using the 60 level on the slider. This is about twelve to eighteen miles with an average of fifteen or sixteen miles from the antenna to the 1mv/m contour. The distance in miles and km to the 70-DBU and the 60-DBU contours for each direction from north, to the east through south and west back to northwest is tabulated on Form 301. Get an air sectional map of the proposed coverage area and outline the city limits on the map. Note the transmitter site and draw the eight radials on the map out to about the twenty-mile distance, then plot the distance out to the 60-DBU and the 70-DBU contours. Connect all the 70-DBU contour points with a smooth interconnecting line to indicate the predicted coverage area. Does the 70-DBU contour cover the entire community of license? If so, check the "Yes" box on Form 301. Now plot the 60-DBU contour on a similar basis as the 70-DBU above.

Cut the scale of miles from the edge of the map and attach it with rubber cement to the portion of the map being used. Cut an eight-and-one-half-inch by 11-inch portion of interest from the huge air sectional map. The sum of distance to contour for all eight 60-DBU distances divided by eight and then squared and multiplied by 3.14 gives the area within the 60-DBU contour in square miles. Use kilometer distances to get km2 area. (A better method involves the use of a solar planimeter.)

Using U.S. Census Department data, determine the population covered by the 60-DBU contour or have Dataworld calculate it for you. Type area(s) and population figures on the air sectional map using adhesive labels. Draw a vertical section plan of the proposed tower with heights asked for on the last page of the engineering forms. Measure heights in both meters and in feet. An environmental impact statement concerning the effect on the surrounding terrain of the proposed structure is required. It will include zoning, flyway for birds, any state or national parks, any wildlife sanctuaries, etc. Fill out Form V-G and submit with the rest of Form 301.

Use the check sheet in Appendix 2 to review the entire application before submitting. Write a letter of transmittal and have the clerk at the FCC secretary's office stamp your copy of the letter of transmittal and keep it on file. Publish the required public notice in the daily paper twice in the week following the filing date and twice the next week. Use the form attached in Appendix 2.

Then wait to be designated for a hearing. It is best to check the local paper of the area in question to see how many different applications have been filed for the same facilities. A hearing with one other contender will cost more than $10,000 in legal fees, and five or six other contenders might cost as much as $100,000 in legal fees. Each contending application must be analyzed for strong and weak points and a schedule of hearing items agreed upon among attorneys and the FCC. Interrogatories are submitted among applicants to establish facts preliminary to the hearing. Replies to these questionnaires are submitted and motions made. At any time during the attempts to "determine the issues," some parties may be posturing to be bought out or offer to buy out other parties. Some parties may propose a merger. All in all, this period usually results in fewer total applications actually reaching a hearing.

Some applicants may drop out, and mergers can drop the number of applications in contention to two or three from seven or eight. It is probably not possible to make it through this stage without an attorney. With 80-90 FM applications, all initial filing procedures must be completed accurately or the application will not be accepted for filing. If the applicant takes the time and trouble to carefully check his application against the check list, it will probably be accepted for filing. At least one in ten is not accepted. This procedure also may reduce the field a little at the beginning.

The geographical fit, heights above terrain for each radial, distances to contours along each radial, and area and population contained within the 60-DBU contour, are all obtainable from Dataworld (for about $200). This service may be well worth the price as a double check.

Watch for the window to open, and best wishes!

Summary

In filing for an 80-90 FM station, check and double-check all the calculations because the FCC will throw out any

Religious Broadcast Management Handbook

application with faulty engineering figures. When in doubt, it pays to bring in an experienced engineering service. It also pays to have a lawyer to deal with any competition for the same frequency.

Chapter 7
Engineering Maintenance Programs

After the station has been built, the main engineering chore involves maintenance. The Communications Act of 1934, as amended, requires the FCC to insist that a licensed operator be on duty at every transmitter whenever it is operating. In the 1930s and 1940s all licensed operators were required to pass an FCC examination for a First Class radio telephone license. This test is said to have been equivalent to the finals at a two-year electronics college. At each station, one of these engineers was designated as "chief" and assigned the responsibility for all the technical aspects of the broadcast station.

Now all operators have to do to get a license is fill out a form and send it to the FCC. The resulting Third Class Permit must be posted near the transmitter operating point. There must be a Third Class operator on duty at the transmitter or the transmitter operating point at all times in order to fulfill the operating requirements. It is usually up to the program director to see that every announcer also serving as an operator has the appropriate license or permit and that the permits are posted properly. The chief operator no longer is required to have a First Class license. Now, anyone who is technically qualified to be chief engineer may perform those duties regardless of the class of license held.

Sometimes the studios are not located at the transmitter site. At these studios, the transmitter must be remote controlled from the studio operating point — usually over a phone line or as part of the studio-transmitter-link (STL) equipment — and licenses are posted at the operating point.

Maintenance of Radio Station Equipment

Typical radio station equipment consists of studio input equipment such as microphones, turntables, reel-to-reel tape recorders, cartridge recorders, playback and cassette recorders, compact disk players, short wave receivers, and telephone lines. All of these are arranged around a mixing console that is used to switch sequence or fade between audio sources. The output of the console is sent to the transmitter by audio wiring, telephone lines, or microwave circuits. At the transmitter location, which is sometimes the same as the studio, the audio processing equipment takes the audio from the studio and keeps it loud. Many of the signal processing units separate the audio by octaves and process each narrow range of audio frequencies individually then recombine them for transmitting. The audio is then sent to the AM transmitter or to the FM exciter. The output of the FM exciter is amplified by the transmitter and sent up a transmission line to the antenna which is mounted on a tower.

Matching Impedance

In AM output, the entire tower radiates. The output of the AM transmitter is sent down a transmission line to an antenna tuning unit at the base of the tower that matches the transmission-line impedance to the impedance of the tower. Impedance is the opposition or resistance of an electrical circuit to the flow of an alternating current (AC) of an individual frequency.

Measured in ohms, it is a combination of resistance and reactance. Although there is a maximum transfer of energy in an inpedance-matched circuit, other acceptable ways of transferring audio exist than the use of impedance matching. For example, "bridging" circuits put low impedance circuit energy into high impedance inputs.

Many new equipment purchases are made because a chief engineer tells an owner or a manager, "You need this new gadget to match the impedance." That should be a cue for the manager to investigate further, because this is a favorite excuse of some chief engineers to allow them to purchase a new "toy." The right question for the engineer who comes up with this suggestion is: "How will this help us to make more money?"

Preventive Maintenance

Chief engineers should establish a preventive maintenance program. Dirt is the prime enemy of electronic and mechanical equipment. It causes noise and misoperation of contacts in electronics and wears out mechanical parts. A chief engineer should have a file card on each piece of equipment stating when it was bought, the model and serial numbers, and maintenance notes. Such information may be filed on a microcomputer, as well. The engineer then can arrange the cards in such a way as to assure that each piece of equipment is checked for maintenance at least once every three months.

For tape recorders, cassettes, and cart machines, the maintenance operation consists of thorough cleaning of all parts and of the lubrication of all moving parts according to the shop manuals. Transmitters need cleaning, and parts may need to be tightened because the cooling fan causes vibrations. At least all the mounted parts should be checked for proper tightness. This kind of preventive maintenance takes at least one day a week in a relatively simple operating radio station. Larger operations with high power, AM directional antennas, and AM-FM combinations take two to four days a week for preventive maintenance. Managers should make certain that their engineers are on a preventive maintenance program, because this reduces the opportunity for crises that might lead to being off the air for a period of time.

Consider using older equipment as standby or redundant equipment. That way, if a new piece of equipment should fail, it would at least be possible to be on the air with the standby. The oldest equipment usually is relegated to the station's newsroom, the rationale being that broadcasting news involves only voice frequencies which do not require the same fine tuning or fidelity of operation as music.

The older equipment gets, the harder (and the more expensive) it is to obtain parts. In some cases, parts are simply not available any longer. When the cost of maintenance becomes greater than the cost of payments for new equipment, the old pieces should be retired. Many operations retire equipment or give it to schools or universities when the amortization, or write-off, is completed. In most cases, this is from three to five years. With all the rapid electronic advances in broadcast equipment, some stations seek to remain competitive in their markets by replacing equipment every three years. Other stations operate at half-price or less by purchasing this used equipment from the more progressive stations.

Television stations need to add cameras, film chains, satellite feeds, and video tape machines to the audio sources that radio stations use and mix through switchers, which sequence, fade, and effect together the video sources and send them (usually by microwave) to the transmitter. Preventive maintenance principles are the same for television and radio stations.

Automation Adds to Maintenance Chores

A new factor in broadcast operations is automation. Television stations often use a computer sequencer to insert advertisements between network programming or syndicated taped programming. Radio automation exists to sequence program elements without a deejay having to be present. Radio automation often includes satellite-fed disc-jockeyed musical programming and automatically sequenced local inserts and ads. The cost of such automated systems and the quality provided must be weighed against the quality that can be achieved with a more traditional manual system. The cost/benefit analysis will give different outcomes in different markets. But wherever automated systems are used, more engineering maintenance is required.

The three most important aspects of a TV or FM site are height, height, and height of the antenna. For AM, however, the location should be in the best ground conductivity area, which probably will be in a swamp or near a river or lake. Under each AM radiating tower is a ground system with 120 equally spaced quarter-wavelength-long #8 or #10 soft-drawn bare copper wires bonded to a copper ground screen at the base of the tower. If a tower were to fall, the results should be obvious. When a ground system is buried three to six inches below the surface, acids in the soil will cause equally obvious results, but in this case the cause is invisible. The signal strength is greatly reduced when the ground system deteriorates, therefore the importance of its maintenance cannot be overstressed. The ground system probably should be replaced every ten years.

FCC-Required Records

Each year the FCC requires that a "Proof of Performance" test be made on the system. This is a series of measurements taken to determine the fidelity and distortion of a broadcast system. The engineer must make this series of measurements yearly and keep the written report of them on file pending any FCC inspection. The system must measure up to an official set of criteria, otherwise circuits must be repaired or modified until the system does pass proof of performance.

Operating log regulations have been greatly relaxed in the 1980s so that only the tower lighting observations need to be recorded daily as well as the times for power changes (in AM) or changes in directional antenna pattern. Weekly recorded data now includes the Emergency Broadcast System (EBS) tests, received and transmitted. These transmissions consist of a precise dual audio tone and a message about emergencies that must be broadcast each week. The tones open special receivers in the community (mostly at other broadcast stations) where the received test must be noted. Records of this type must be maintained at the station from two to five years or until license renewal is completed, then the retention cycle begins again.

In addition, a public file must be maintained at the station. This includes a community-problems list, usually prepared by management and filed monthly or quarterly. The FCC requires stations to research their communities to determine controversial issues and problems and to keep a list of these. The most important ten problems on file are to be reviewed at least quarterly. Other papers required to be kept in the public file include every document and letter written to the FCC — license renewal forms, applications for any changes such as an upgrade of facilities, etc. — and all notices and letters from the FCC. The station's copy of *The Public and Broadcasting: A Procedure Manual* and a copy of the station's ownership statement are to be kept in the public file. The file should have a transcript of the renewal notice and the times when it was aired as well as information on how legally qualified candidates for public office may use the station. Last, but not least, the public file should be home for all the letters received from listeners during the last three years.

Summary

A good engineering maintenance program includes keeping all equipment clean and in operating order, keeping good records on the equipment and on the maintenance procedures, and keeping the public file up to date in order to meet FCC standards. Management's role is to obtain a good chief engineer and periodically investigate to make sure job duties are being fulfilled in a way that will enhance and protect the operation of the station and its integrity before the FCC.

Part Four

Programming: From Music to Public Affairs

Chapter 8
Historical Development of Programming

During the Great Depression of the 1930s, the still-new concept of radio programming for public entertainment helped to lighten the hard times for millions of people. The networks featured drama, comedy, music, quiz shows, and religious programming. Radio receivers were reasonably priced, and the entertainment was free. When "Amos 'n' Andy" was on the air in those early days, the streets were deserted. In movie theaters, films would be interrupted at 7 p.m. so fans of the radio show could hear it.[1]

National sponsors paid the networks handsome sums to have their products brought to the attention of those millions of listeners. The stations also made a dollar or two from each advertisement. Local sponsors yearned to be aired next to the popular shows at the rate of $10 to $20 for each 20-second advertisement.

Station operators aired on-going daytime shows about everyday life in certain families living in fictional towns. Sponsored by soap product companies, these became known as "soap operas." A variety of entertainment was aired in the evenings, most of it fed to the stations from a national network. One or two local newscasts a day were joined to their corresponding network feeds of national news and commentary. Mid-mornings brought the "Man on the Street" program or the "Breakfast Club." Religious programs were placed where the broadcasters of the day thought they belonged: on Sundays, usually in the morning. There were only one or two stations in each market, and they made a lot of money, usually by carrying the excellent network programs.

This romance between the local stations and the networks continued through World War II, when all the emerging experimental television stations (except WRGB, Schenectady, New York) were shut down because of the war effort. The technology that would have gone into television receivers was channeled instead into the development of radar equipment, which was top-secret. But the war helped radio grow and flourish. In fact, radio news came of age through carrying reports of the battles. Edward R. Murrow's broadcasts of Nazi air raids on London were a classic example of radio's ability to present news coverage as events unfolded. Radio rallied all three shifts of defense workers to their war production jobs in factories all over the United States.

Although FM had been invented in 1933, the receiver technology was needed for tank-to-base two-way radio use. Most FM stations, which usually were duplicating AM programs and being received by very few receivers, were shut down during the war, leaving the door wide open for the AM band. Few transmitters were available to build new stations, so owners of existing AM stations did very well during the war.

For about a year after World War II, technology was changing from war materiel to television receivers. People yearned to see the radio stars in action, so television cameras were moved into radio studios. Famous comedians were on radio and television simultaneously, along with such shows as "Arthur Godfrey and Friends" and "The Firestone Hour" music program.

TV sets sold as fast as they could be manufactured. By 1949, most American neighborhoods had at least one TV set, and neighbors often visited those lucky or rich enough to own one to catch a glimpse of the new medium, especially when "Uncle Milty" was on. A plastic-faced natural for television, Milton Berle mugged it up weekly and, like "Amos 'n' Andy" in the previous decade, traffic all but stopped during the "Milton Berle Show," Sid Caesar's "Show of Shows" and the "Ed Sullivan Show."

Radio was caught short by this television boom. Listeners to the traditional radio network fare wanted pictures as well. Typical radio operations then kept a transmitter engineer, an engineer to spin records at the studio, and an announcer on duty at all times. Some innovative new operators — mostly recent war veterans — cut costs by setting up shop in the transmitter building and hiring announcers licensed as transmitter engineers. This new breed of announcers played phonograph records and talked directly to the local audience. A few independent (nonnetwork) stations had perfected this deejay style of broadcasting in the mid 1930s, notably Martin Block of WNEW's "Make-Believe Ballroom" in New York City. As smaller stations — sometimes the new daytime-only stations — picked up this format and sold time locally, radio began to get back on its feet financially.

Format Concept Streamlines Radio Programming

The biggest breakthrough for local independents came with new concepts in the management of music programming. Until 1954, most disc jockeys played the records of their choice, but modern "Top 40" radio was born in Omaha, Nebraska, one night in 1954. Legendary program director Bill Stewart told author Claude Hall that he was sitting in a bar across from the KOWH studios one night with Todd Storz and the jukebox kept playing the same song. After several hours, the bar closed and everyone left but Stewart and Storz who lingered on a few minutes. Stewart said that while the waitress was waiting for them to leave, she put her own money in the jukebox and played the same rock 'n' roll song three times that customers had been playing all evening! This incident gave them the idea of a "closed music list" which was instituted at KOWH for the first time. The station, which had been moving down in the ratings, was turned around.[2]

What Top 40 pioneer Todd Storz and program director Bill Stewart realized that night was not only the tolerance for, but the preference for, repetition in popular music. The key to music management in modern-format stations is the closed music list. That is, music selections controlled by management rather than by the whims of the announcers.

The other aspect of the system involves the high rotation of key records within the closed list. As few as four and as many as twelve to seventeen records are kept in high rotation, or repetition cycles, depending on the station and the type of format.

So Top 40 or popular-music radio became the first format to sweep America. Historic Top 40 formatted stations in four- to eight-station markets captured 75 to 80 percent of the radio audiences. Listeners wanted recognizable music, the kind they put quarters into jukeboxes to hear. Other formats soon followed.

Radio format pioneer Gordon McLendon set up KABL, Oakland, California, as a Beautiful Music station by recording smooth old and new favorites played softly by stringed-instrument orchestras onto tape in thirteen-minute segments. Announcers played the taped segment and did two minutes of talk, which was mostly commercials and image announcements. KABL used the bell and clanging sounds of the San Francisco cable cars in association with its call letters. WPAT in Patterson, New Jersey, copied this "13-2" format and developed a tremendous New York City audience.

McLendon credited Bill Stewart also with putting polish on the programming at his KLIF, Dallas, station with news shows. This station became one of the most notable popular music stations in the world in the late 1950s. McLenden saw very quickly the power of radio in covering local news. As early as 1957, he told the Georgia Association of Broadcasters that his station localized as many news stories as possible. He explained how to keep a list of the most newsworthy (or likely to be) civic, religious, and business leaders in the community. The list was categorized according to specifics such as oil, banking, society, etc. When a story broke concerning one of these fields, the station called the local leader for his comments.

In those days television news was pretty well locked into the studio, but even the smallest radio station could use the telephone! McLendon then developed an all-news format which he used at Station XETRA, in Tiajuana, Mexico, and beamed across the border from San Diego to Los Angeles.

The basic concept in format radio programming was to control the elements of disc jockey-news programming and tailor these elements to a specific portion of the population — the "target" demographics. If an audience of fifteen- to twenty-five-year-old listeners is desired, the biggest element of programming — popular music — is tailored to this age group's tastes. If the target demographic group is eighteen- to thirty-five-year-olds, then adult contemporary music is featured. If the target is affluent thirty-five to fifty-four-year-olds, then beautiful music or, in larger markets, all-news operations would get their attention.

The proper music-news mix has been researched for each demographic group. Each target audience has its preference for contests, promotions, approaches to advertisements, etc. Each element of programming, to be successful, has to fit the specific tastes of the audience desired.

The 1960s brought even more AM stations to the air in growth areas of the United States, and during the 1970s the FM band began to achieve popularity. This multiplied by two or four the number of viable stations in most markets. The more stations covering a given market, the more sharply each station must focus its format. The available music product really determines the formats. Progressive rock stations were not possible before that kind of music was available on records. Urban contemporary formats were born when FM stereo transmissions hit the ghetto-blasters with ethnic music. Christian music format stations with contemporary Christian music would not have been possible in the early 1970s, because there were not enough recordings available for a realistic music rotation until very late in the 1970s to early 1980s. Country music stations emerged in the late 1950s and early 1960s when enough of that kind of music provided the means for such a format.

Also, the technology to mount the format in question needed to be in place. The development of the quarter-inch reel-to-reel magnetic tape recorder in standardized speeds and tape-editing procedures gave the local independent station program director the chance to get it perfect before broadcasting. RCA developed 45-rpm records in the early 1950s, and they seemed to popularize the recorded music business. More records began to sell than had the older, more awkward 78-rpm discs. Automatic tape playing devices for playing short messages with an automatic cueing system enabled disc jockeys to air one custom-made sound after another in rapid succession and revolutionized radio production techniques.

In television, videotape recording multiplied the number of shows available, and portable videotape recording techniques revolutionized news reporting. Stereo FM broadcasts, developed at WGFM in Schenectady by General Electric, went a long way toward popularizing the FM band. The appropriate application of new technology to the lifestyle needs of the population in a given area is one way a new medium becomes commercially viable. Chapter 9 discusses format development in a market.

Summary

The advent of television and rapidly changing technology forced radio to make radical changes after the glory days of the 1930s. Network radio gave way to emerging independent stations with specialized formats targeted at specific segments of the local community. Format radio developed as the music industry diversified and more records were available in a variety of styles. Today's successful program director is constantly monitoring the tastes of the community and adapting the station's format to gain maximum listenership.

Notes

[1] Stanley W. Head and Christopher H. Sterling, *Broadcasting in America* (Boston: Houghton Mifflin Company, 1982), p. 160.

[2] Claude Hall and Barbara Hall, *This Business of Radio Programming* (New York: Billboard Publications, 1977), p. 162-174.

Chapter 9
Format Development in a Market

From the late 1950s to the late 1960s, teenagers controlled the radios in homes. The Top 40 formats were targeted to teenagers who turned on the radios in cars and in kitchens before and after school to hear their favorite deejays. Then small portable radios and Sony Walkmen made listening more personal. No longer was it necessary to force adult ears to listen to "that outrageous music" because teens could be told, "Use your own radio and earphones." This trimmed the number of adults tuned in to Top 40 operations, so the formats became more sophisticated and competitive, with some stations focusing more on the young demographic groups and others toward older groups.

Teen Top 40 formats became Contemporary Hits Radio (CHR), and the stations targeting the older generation became Adult Contemporary (AC) operations. The difference was not only in the music and the size of the play list, but the entire orientation of the station. If it was snowy and cold out before school, the CHR morning deejay would say, "Dress warm and put on your boots. It's a tough one out there today." But an AC announcer would say, "If you're dressing the kids for school this morning, better put on their boots, and get out hats and mittens for 'em, 'cause the wind chill factor today is minus 10 degrees!"

A market of 250,000 to 500,000 population typically has a roster of the following formats:

FORMAT TYPE	KNOWN AS	TARGET DEMOGRAPHIC AGE
Contemporary Hits Radio	CHR	12-25
Adult Contemporary	AC	25-34
Album-Oriented Rock	AOR	18-34
Country	C	18-64
Contemporary Country	CC	18-34
All News	N	25-64
All Talk	T	25-64

News/Talk	NT	25-64
Beautiful Music	B or EZ	35-64
Classical	Classic	35-64
Religious	Rel	35-64
Ethnic	E	25-64
Urban Contemporary	UC	15-34
Music of Your Life	MOYL	35-64
Oldies	O	35-64

The change in orientation for ads also is apparent: Concerts advertised on CHR tend to be for the teenage idols, while the AC ads are for Barry Manilow or John Denver. AC stations tend to sell "yuppie" cars such as Porches and BMWs, while CHR's sell Chevies and K cars. CHR stations feature ads for drive-ins or fast-food chains, while AC station ads tout family restaurants, clubs, or resorts. CHR contests involve calling in by phone, while AC contests might involve writing something down. CHR personalities tend to talk less during each break and be more slogan oriented, while AC disc jockeys chat a little more and do community-oriented bits. CHR stations often do little or no news. When news is featured, it is in very short casts, while AC stations seem to have professional five-minute newscasts every hour with comments from the principals in the stories. They make a strong effort to be comprehensive.

A Contemporary Country format is distinguished from old-line, or authentic, country by shorter talk breaks and more up-to-date Nashville commercial music. It plays fewer oldies or Bluegrass and has a very polished AC sound but with up-to-the-minute Nashville releases.

Urban Contemporary plays commercial black music (the Motown sound) and, in some markets, mixes in the top of the Latin music charts.

AOR is an amalgamation of progressive rock station features with album cuts of the best rock artists, sometimes without the song having been listed on any pop chart, because adult rock connoisseurs know and love certain artists. An AOR format nearly always is used by an FM stereo station.

Format Development in a Market

The distinction between All-News, All-Talk, and News-Talk formats should be obvious. Talk radio became popular when good telephone hybrid circuits became available, giving a talk show host the technical ability to talk into a microphone on the air and simultaneously over the telephone, while airing the highest quality incoming telephone comments as well. All News cycles an hour of news with updates throughout the day. Combination News-Talk stations feature all news in the morning and afternoon drive periods of 6 to 9 a.m. and 3 to 6 p.m. but feature talk programs between the intensive news blocks.

Beautiful Music or EZ formats usually are automated and use syndicated music for twelve or thirteen minute sweeps, then ads for two or three minutes, and news or weather or community calender events, followed by another music segment. Syndicated music is records put onto reel-to-reel tape with 25hz tones at the end of each selection. The automatic circuits listen and switch to another program element when the tone arrives.

Ethnic stations often feature music and announcers in a language other than English.

Oldies stations usually feature the rock of the 1950s-1970s.

MYOL is a Big-Band based format featuring oldies from fifty years ago up to the mid 1960s with a Benny Goodman-Glenn Miller flavor. Pioneered by Al Hamm first in Connecticut in the late 1970s, MYOL has revitalized several older AM operations.

Programming for religious stations will be discussed in chapter 10.

Music Management and Audience Research

Once the ownership has chosen the demographic target or best competitive format niche in the market, the program director has the job of implementing the format. Most formats are plotted out on a clock to graphically tell the announcer or deejay on duty the type of music to play and the succession of these music types throughout the show.

All music is picked by the management of the station, and no personal records may be brought into the station. The records are selected in various categories, and some categories are featured more prominently than others. Let us say we are programming an Adult Contemporary station. The categories of music rotation might be as follows:

Fast rising hits	HH
(New releases by top artists that probably will be hits)	
Charted songs	H
(Songs listed in Billboard and other hit lists)	
Recurrent	R
(Songs on the way down but still on the charts)	
Oldies	O1
(Big hits from six months to two years ago)	
Classic oldies	O2
(Top 10 hits from five to twenty years earlier)	

The more exciting the station's sound, the more emphasis will be given to the H and HH categories. A typical music clock would look like this:

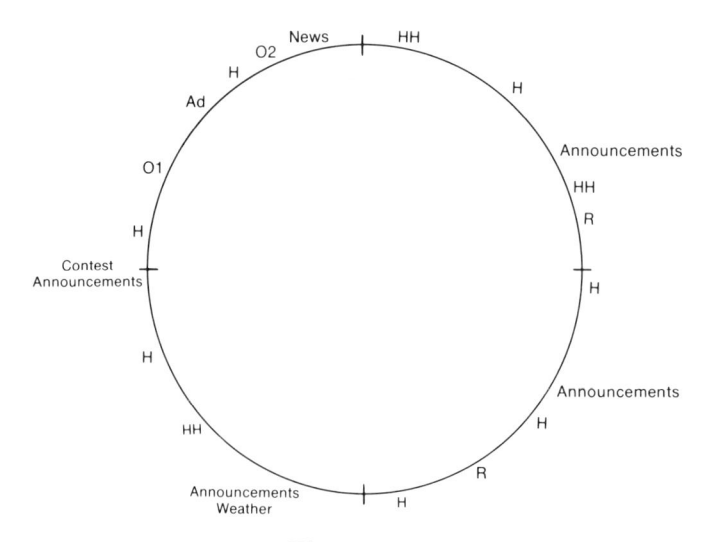

Figure 9.1

The exact placement of music types on the clock would be determined to a large extent by the market involved. If five records were in the HH category, the sound of those records would repeat every hour and a half. If forty records were in the H category, the nonduplicated period would be about six hours. If two dozen records were in each of the R, H, O1, and O2 categories, these categories would repeat every other day. Although this may seem extremely tight to the reader with little format radio experience, the numbers given here are extremely generous. Many tighter play lists can be found among currently operating stations. Naturally, with a tight play list, the exact record played is of utmost importance, so that is where the program director or, in some very large stations, a music director, must excel in professionalism.

Great Top 40 program directors of old knew what the audience would love, even though they may not personally have liked the record at all. In the late-1950s, nearly everything Elvis Presley recorded became an instant hit. In the mid 1960s, almost every Beatles cut had the same effect. HH selections depend a lot on the artist and the timeliness and sound of the release. Tip sheets such as the "Gavin Report," "Monday Morning Quarterback," and "Hitmakers" give the play list changes by America's top program directors at the top-rated stations in the country. If top directors are adding a certain record to their HH list, then the release at least bears some attention. *All the music that comes in must be auditioned.* Many great program directors have an ear for what their audience will want. Others need the charts. All of them have to do research.

Call-out research in music involves recording the "hook" of the song. The "hook" is the brief musical passage most readily identifiable from a given song, the part that, if you heard it, you would know exactly what song it was and how intensely you enjoyed the tune when you heard it for the first time. In call-out research, a group of listeners who typify the target demographic of the station is recruited to participate in the study. This group, including up to one hundred persons, is called about once a month, played the hooks of half a dozen songs, and asked to rank the songs in order according to their preference.

If call-out research ranks a couple of releases on the top two or three slots with great consistency and the song is getting tip-sheet "adds" at other research-oriented stations that the program director respects, then adding it to the HH category is probably merited. In call-out research, program directors also get a feeling for the general sound of music preferred by the research sample.

A variation on the call-out is to have 100 to 200 people come into an auditorium to rate songs. The room may be rigged with a test answering system, where each test seating position is equipped with four or five buttons connected to circuits that will show the percentage of audience making each choice. Otherwise, computer cards can be used, on which participants pencil in numerical answers in columns. The program director welcomes the group, tells something about a station promotion, hands out concert tickets, and plays several hooks to the group. Groups involved in preference-order ratings give several trends and specific hit choices every time they meet.

Another form of overall station programming feedback comes from a research method called "focus groups." These are groups of seven to fifteen people who represent every aspect of listeners in a neighborhood. Ideally, focus groups should be formed in every neighborhood of a market. These groups meet informally with the station management, frequently in the community room of the branch bank or in one of the group member's homes over coffee and pastries. Members of the group are asked questions about their lifestyles and how radio fits into their lives. It takes a very perceptive researcher to cull programming maneuvers out of focus group meetings, but trends can be identified and broad needs met from this kind of research.

Once the HH rotation is set, the weekly changes in HH force changes all the way down the play list. If there are five records in HH and three are moved out, those three will be moved to the H category which means that it also must be reshuffled. Three records will be peeled off the bottom of that list. Maybe a couple more can be added to the H list that particular week that have not been hot enough to be on the HH list at all but are worthy of going into the H rotation. Then you have a total of five records to remove from the H rotation that week. Most of those five go into the Recurrent rotation, and that means five other records come off the R list and go onto the shelf. Oldies are changed weekly with another package of oldies equivalent in sound.

Records arrive free from record distributors. The program director calls the agents of the record companies periodically to ask about the acceptance of new products and to get fresh artist information. He sends the weekly Top Hit list from the station to each label and adds a personal note when HH additions are made. He also sends additions, deletions, and play lists to the tip sheets, although these are not solicited. Any mention in the tip sheets about the station puts it in the big league category in the minds of the program director's peers, and record distributors will continue to give good service if they believe the station is a trend setter.

Ads Run Second to Music

The music element of most station formats is the largest single ingredient in a format hour. Other large influential elements of programming during the hour include ads and news. In a successful commercial station, the ads are second only to the music element of the clock hour. Ads must be well-produced, recorded in advance, and perfect. The program director supervises the production of ads to assure a balance of different voices and different styles of production. Styles of the produced ads might include multiple voices, dramatic skits, humorous cuts, sound-effect usage, music behind the ads, and dry cuts. Good copy is the basis for clever, selling ads. A good variety of styles and excellent voices and production will get listeners just for the ads! A good program director makes his ads a tune-in factor, not a tune-out irritant.

Music "beds" for ads provide a mood setting for the message and should end with a definite musical ending (up and out) right after the last word. One way to create one of these beds is to record the beginning ten or fifteen seconds of a song onto tape and splice the definite ending of that song (or any other in the same key) for fifteen or twenty seconds onto the end so that the total tape time is thirty seconds. Then run the music behind the narration of the script mixed onto a second tape machine. When choosing the music, never select vocal renditions that would blur the voice reading the script. A broadcast adage to remember is, *"Never talk over a vocal."* Use only instrumental beds.

The use of music under announcements not only enhances the mood but gives musical continuity to the total station sound. For local television ads, develop a good radio ad with a music bed and then illustrate the ad with portable camera shots made at the store location. The script should be written with the illustration video in mind. Music beds for such radio and TV production have been produced with professional musicians playing original music written and performed especially for music beds. These are available on disc for a fee, either a purchase price or, more usually, for lease payments. One set of basic beds is available from the L.A. Air Force on a buyout basis at a reasonable cost.[1]

Media General of Memphis, Tennessee, offers a complete transcription service. Transcriptions are the discs that contain the music beds and jingles. The Media General people usually combine the transcription service with custom-made vocal station-break jingles for a fee that ranges from $80 to $250 or more a month, depending on the market size and specific package leased. Several sets of transcriptions are available with different target demographics in mind, such as "Thunder Country" for country stations, or "Trendsetter" for CHR and AC stations, according to Bob Blowe, who has been sales manager for Media General for years.

Competitive transcription services such as TM of Dallas offer similar services. Smart management shops around for the best sound at the best deal. Many of these transcription lease deals have a half-cash/half-trade arrangement whereby the company gets fifty ads a month to sell on the station in addition to the cash payment. But beware of the wording on this kind of contract that permits the company to let the time build up over the term of the contract and extend for long periods after the termination date. Negotiate with the transcription service to have its allotment of ads cancel monthly or quarterly and expire completely at the end of the contract. Otherwise, the sales from the transcription service could overload the spot inventory and choke off revenue at some future date.

Another problem with the trade portion of the transcription service deal is that the company may have the same client nationally that an individual station is trying to sell advertising to through the local agent. WHVW (Hyde Park/Poughkeepsie, New York) had this trouble in the late 1960s when the station sold ads to a nationally known company through its local office manager, and one of the transcription services wanted to place the company's ads on the station as part of a trade arrangement. Of course, this would have meant no revenue for the station! A word to the wise is sufficient: Examine these contracts thoroughly before agreeing to any transcription deal.

The program director needs to schedule each announcer to do production in such a fashion as to rotate voices on the ads. If the station has a small staff, sometimes the sound of the station is greatly enhanced by utilizing good weekend voices or even hiring some free-lance talent to do production a few hours a week. By having excellent-sounding ads on the air, a station has a quality sound throughout the week, regardless of staff size.

It is assumed that all 30-second ads will be 29 to 31 seconds in length. Maintaining this standard is important because of being fair to every advertiser, but especially important for stations affiliated with a network. If ads played locally are to cover public service announcements on the network, both need to end at the same time.

Production personnel need to know how to dub the reel-to-reel tape announcement to cart. Cart, short for cartridge, is an endless loop of tape with a recording mechanism that records a special tone at the beginning of the message on a hidden magnetic track. When the carts are played back, the playback unit listens for the "stop" tone on the special track, and when the tone is detected, the cart stops, ready to play the beginning of the announcement again. If two different pieces of copy for the same merchant are recorded onto the same cart, the announcements will alternate because they are on the same endless loop of tape. Variations on a theme of copy to bring three ads to a cart for an advertiser that has seven announcements per day will put up different copy at any given fixed time of the day. When the number of ads scheduled for a day is not evenly divisable by the number of ads recorded, then the ads will cycle through the day in a fashion different from the cycle of the following day and will give a maximum variety of ads each day throughout the week.

The cart labels should give enough information at a glance, for the announcer on duty to tell if the right cart is ready to go, and phonograph record stickers should give information helpful to the deejay. When the program director or the music director puts records into the play list rotations, he also affixes a sticker to the record that looks like this:

```
:35 F
8/85 HH
Cold
```

The record sticker shows that this 45-rpm single was added to an HH rotation in August of 1985, that it has a fast tempo, uses a 35-second intro until the vocal hits, and ends cold. That is, there is singing on the last note of the record. The deejay uses the intro timing or the tail timing to plan short bits using the instrumental portion of the record under his voice. The tempo information helps the deejay plan the tempo mix, and the HH shows the category of the song.

Format Development in a Market

Cartridge labels are actually file-folder labels that look like this:

> Security National Bank
> 3—30 sec.: TCD
> End Q: . . . "on the Coweta curve."

At a glance, the operator finds the client, Security National Bank, alphabetically under S and knows there are three cuts of their ad on the cart and that all three have the End Q (cue) indicated on the last line of the label. The initials are for the announcer on the production so the deejay can alternate voices on playback. Other End Qs might include: "music up and out" or "address and phone number."

News Placement

The next largest element in programming is news. At some stations, the news director is in charge of news. At other stations, the program director is in charge of the news director. At any rate, the program director usually decides how many minutes of news per hour or per day belong in the format and the clock hour placement of that news. The Frank Magid/Gallup nationwide poll shows most American radio listeners prefer their news at the top of the hour. Could this be because most stations already place their news at the top of the hour?

There are other placements for news if a station wants to defend against the programming clock of other stations. One of the obvious ploys is to place the five-minute cast at half past the hour. Another is to place the news just before the top of the hour, as WTRY, Troy, New York, did in 1956. Their slogan was: "News of the hour before the hour!" The station's prime competitor was prestigious WGY, Schenectady. The fifty-five-minute placement allowed the wire copy to clear the "World in Brief" that usually started printing at about thirty minutes past the hour. WHVW (Hudson Valley, New York) had "News alive at 45 on Channel 95," and some

FM stations of the 1970s ran "20-20" news watch, with weather at twenty minutes after the hour and news at twenty minutes before.

Content and delivery style, as broad concepts, are somewhat determined by the program director. The higher the age group in the target demographics, the slower and more dignified the delivery and the pace, with business news and adult-oriented stories emphasized. AC stations use a more staccato style of delivery and stories that appeal to "30-year-old junior executives with one little kid." Some progressive-rock AOR stations use a very left-wing progressive story orientation and a "laid-back" delivery. Details of newsroom operation and promotions in programming will be handled in subsequent chapters.

Summary

Radio formats have developed into an exacting "science." Owners and program directors decide on a target audience and then design a format to appeal to the selected demographics. The most successful program directors are the ones who can anticipate what will appeal to the targeted audience. Research into the audience's likes and dislikes, however, always is necessary. Several methods of market research are possible, including call-out research and focus group meetings. The most important element in most station formats is the music, with advertisements running a close second, followed by news. The delivery style of the news and its content are broadly determined by the program director.

Notes

[1] The L.A. Air Force, Terry Moss Productions, P. O. Box 944, Long Beach, CA 90801.

Chapter 10
Programming for Christian Stations

Religious programming stations and Christian programming stations are not the same thing. The latter broadcasts only programs or music that are Bible-based and generally accepted as Christian, while Religious Programming stations may carry programs from any world religion. Moslem, Buddhist, Bahai, or Jewish programs may be interspersed with Christian programs. (See Appendix 3 for a statement of Christian television principles drawn up by the National Religious Broadcasters.)

The biggest difference in Christian station formats is the amount of music featured. This concept is found reflected today in a spectrum ranging from all talk or teaching to all music and no Bible-teaching programs. The history of the Christian station is the heritage of the taped teaching programs, while the all-music Christian station is a development of the late 1970s and early 1980s.

With the Charismatic Renewal and the restoration of the office of teacher in the Church came a rise in the number of taped ministries buying time on Christian stations and a growing audience to listen to them. Program directors of stations that broadcast ministry taped programming usually group the Charismatic Movement speakers in time slots near each other. Ministers have found that the audience for one taped program stays for the next and that the audience for a group of such programs is greater than the audience garnered if only one such taped program is played.

In like fashion, Evangelical or Fundamentalist Bible teachers are grouped together for broadcast. Again, the listenership for such programs tends to build when they are placed near each other. Many stations group the traditional teaching in the morning, with the Charismatics grouped in the afternoon. If a second Christian station is established in an area where the preceding scheduling is being used, it would do well to reverse the groupings so that Charismatic ministries are in the morning and traditionalists in the afternoon. This gives a second opportunity for some of the followers of established programs to listen to their favorite speaker and gives the new station an immediate listening audience.

Some of the Charismatic speakers who have taped programs are Kenneth Hagin, R. W. Shambach, Fred Price, Charles Capps, Kenneth Copeland, Marilyn Hickey, Robert Tilton, Terry Law, and Lewis Caplan of "Jewish Voice." Traditional ministry programs include the H.M.S. Richards program, Dr. James Dobson, Charles Stanley, J. Vernon McGee, and Theodore Epp. More recently, some program directors are classifying the Chuck Smith, John McArthur and Charles Swindoll tapes as "buffer" programs, because they tend to address modern themes from a Bible base without condemning or extolling topics favored by Charismatic speakers. For this reason, these buffer ministries seem to be popular with Charismatic and non-Charismatic audiences alike.

KTCR, Wagoner/Coweta, Oklahoma, serves the southeast suburbs of Tulsa. Mark Fitzgerald, general manager, and Kendall Durfey, program director, have laid out the following schedule for the station:

6-7 a.m. — Charismatics (Fred Price, Kenneth Hagin, R. W. Shambach, "World Missionary Evangelism")

7-8:15 a.m. — Local, ABC, and sports news; Paul Harvey; state news, and community interview (public affairs)

8:15 a.m. — H. M. S. Richards

8:30 a.m. — Dr. James Dobson's "Focus on the Family"

9 a.m. — "In Touch" with Dr. Charles Stanley

9:30 — "Through the Bible" with Dr. J. Vernon McGee

10 a.m. — "Word for Today" with Chuck Smith

10:30 — "Grace to You" with John MacArthur

11 a.m. — "Insight for Living" with Charles Swindoll

11:30 a.m. — "Faith Seminar of the Air" with Kenneth Hagin

11:45 a.m. — "Ever Increasing Faith" with Fred Price

Noon — ABC news, Paul Harvey, local news, sports

12:30 p.m. — "Success-N-Life" with Robert Tilton.

Charismatic ministry tapes eventually will be placed in the 1 to 3 p.m. slot; local ministries are aired from 3 to 5 p.m.; and ABC news, community interviews, Paul Harvey, state news and sports are run from 5 to 6 p.m. At this stage in its development, the station is playing some music in the 1 to 2:30 p.m. and 3 to 5 p.m. slots. The mix of music leans toward Southern gospel because this type of music is not featured very much on any other station in the Tulsa area. Also, listeners thirty years of age and older tend to listen to program lengths of fifteen and thirty minutes, and music that attracts that age group is the obvious choice to feature on a station formatted to appeal to adults.

Contemporary Christian Music Stations

Newer Christian stations, primarily FM stereo stations, have been developed around music, especially the newer Christian contemporary music. KCFO (FM) Tulsa is a leader in such formats. Awarded the prestigious "Station of the Year" award for 1984, KCFO has been the leader in Christian music programming in the 1980s. The FM Stereo Class C (100,000 watt) station stopped featuring taped ministries programs in 1979 and began featuring all music Christian programming. The music was programmed on a Hot Clock, just as a secular station would be, with generous music rotations, ads, news, and promotions, except that all the elements were Christian in content. Listenership developed into the thousands, and KCFO reached a ratings stance of about number ten in a twenty-station market. It rated as high as second, third, or fourth place in its target demographic — eighteen- to thirty-five-year-olds. In 1986, KCFO brought some teaching ministries back in the evening hours.

The assistant station manager and the program director who polished up this format have moved on to other stations, the former to KLTY, Dallas, and the latter to KRDS in Phoenix. KLTY switched to Christian adult contemporary music in August of 1985 and by the end of the year was rated by the Birch rating service in the top 20 percent of the radio listenership in the Dallas-Fort Worth metroplex. KLTY is consulted by Burkhart/Abrams of Atlanta and uses both call-out and focus-group research to target a female audience between eighteen and thirty-four years of age.

Donor-Based Stations

The major distinction between the program format station and the Christian music station is more financial than programming in nature. Stations that feature taped ministry programming total up the expense for operating the station, divide by the number of minutes to sell, and charge each ministry enough to operate the station, pay employees, and cover any other costs. Many radio speakers have an offer, a book, a cassette, or lessons that they sell or use as "a gift for a suggested donation of $5 or more." Others urge listeners to write and send a donation if they "feel led to," but mainly they urge listeners just to write. Then the mail department of the ministry will correspond with those who respond, sending more appeals and offers than are available on the broadcasts. Directly from the air appeals or through the mail, the radio teachers and speakers must make more than enough money from the listeners to pay for their mailing costs, air time, tapes, tape duplication, and other ministry activities.

The radio stations involved are listener supported and part of a donor-based system. The ministries that buy time on the station must take in one and one-half to two times the air time cost each month from each station in order to sustain their efforts. Therefore, the listeners to a given station must be present in sufficient numbers with sufficient commitment for the ministries' broadcasting activities to survive. Stations that cannot generate enough mail are canceled and new markets tried. In the industrial northeast, Bible-teaching stations typically have less than 1 percent of the available audience; therefore, only powerful stations that cover millions in population have a large enough audience size to operate a successful donor-based station.

In the Bible Belt, smaller market stations have significant ratings for such programming and seem to do very well in donor-base formats. When such stations do play music, the music *must* have an adult appeal. As we reviewed in the chapter on the history of radio, the network radio program of the 1930s and 1940s was fifteen or thirty minutes long. People who remember radio when programming consisted of individual programs are thirty-five at the youngest and probably forty to fifty years old. These are the people who tend to remain loyal to the AM band and listen to religious programs on donor-based stations. Therefore, newer kinds of music have little appeal to this group, although the songs have Christian lyrics.

A few stations in the United States have adopted a format almost identical to an Adult Contemporary station, except all the music has Christian lyrics. Songs by such artists as the Imperials, Sandi Patti, Amy Grant, Russ Taff, Michael Card, Dallas Holm, Carman, Steve Green, Steve Camp, and White Heart make up the heart of the play list. Benson and Word and their derivative companies, along with Sparrow, are the three largest Christian music companies and supply most of the records. *Music Line, Contemporary Christian Magazine, Singing News,* and the Christian charts that periodically occur in *Billboard* magazine provide the essence of all the industry tip sheets. *Music Line* concentrates on contemporary sounds while *Singing News* emphasizes Southern gospel music.

All charts change a little every month, and according to one Tulsa area program director, the charts are also sixty to ninety days behind the play-list rotations. He said that the maximum "adds" and "take-offs" from all play-list rotations would be six or seven songs with the superhit list rotating ten records, the H category about fifteen or sixteen, and the recurrent list twenty-four, with the gold by request from the entire Adult Contemporary library. The program director's ear must be the chief factor in most "add" choices. Tip sheets tend to be too far behind because magazines must be "put to bed" four to six weeks before they hit the streets.

Response to area Christian bookstore sales of music and records and music call-out research becomes an extremely important aspect of music management. Contemporary Christian station programmers have complained that the major record sources are stingy. They say better service is available from secular record companies such as CBS or Music Corporation of America (MCA). This seems short-sighted on the part of the Christian companies, because the free exposure given their products creates a potentially greater market.

Advertising-Based Stations

Establishing a Christian music station involves an advertising-based operation. Unlike donor-based stations where listeners give to the ministries' broadcasts, who in turn pay for station air time, the advertising-based station must sell 20-sec., 30-sec., and/or 60-sec. ads to local, regional, and sometimes national advertisers. Each ad costs from $2 to $50 depending upon market size and listenership. At $20,000 billing a month and $5 for each ad, that is 4,000 ads per month that must be sold, written, produced, broadcast and billed — 135 ads a day or about 10 an hour. The problem is not in billing, broadcasting, or even writing and producing these ads, but in *selling them*! Smaller stations in smaller markets have had a hard time attracting and retaining competent sales personnel. Before anyone decides to establish a Christian music station, he or she must love selling air time and/or have one or more dedicated partners or friends who love selling air time.

Promotions on Christian music stations also must be taken into consideration. Bible-teaching tape stations promote to some extent, but music operations promote almost exactly as secular stations do. Chapter 12 discusses broadcast station promotions.

Christian Television Programming

Christians have been complaining about the fare on television and have filed for, and obtained, licenses for independent TV stations in dozens of communities around the United States. The programming on these stations has varied from all-Christian content to "family television." The all-Christian formatted stations are somewhat like the Bible teacher formatted radio stations, but with pictures. Many of the stalwart radio speakers have added greenery to a set and televised the radio talk, featuring a son, wife, or daughter who sings.

A newer format for Christian television programming is the Christian "Johnny Carson Show" and features an evangelist talk-show host chatting with Christian authors and musicians. The best of these, in our opinion, is the "700 Club" from the Christian Broadcasting Network (CBN) of Virginia Beach. Hosts Pat Robertson, Ben Kinchlow, and Danuta Soderman interview such guests as Pat Boone, Phyllis Schafly, and Rosey Grier, as well as educational and political figures. They also run many short features of how ordinary people meet and solve common financial, social, emotional, or spiritual problems. The show often features investigative news magazine pieces and has great appeal to a general audience as well as the Christian audience.

Another version of the Christian talk show is Trinity Broadcasting Network's "Praise the Lord" program originating from Santa Ana, California, featuring hosts Paul and Jan Crouch. It also uses a talk-show format but without the investigative news magazine pieces. A third version is "PTL Club," hosted by Jim and Tammy Bakker and originating in Charlotte, North Carolina. Usually the same guests are featured on all of these shows at one time or another. All three of these programs are fed by satellite transponder to TV stations and cable headends in the continental United States.

Evangelist Richard Roberts has a one-hour morning show fed live via satellite from Tulsa that features gospel and contemporary music as well as interviews. Evangelist

Jimmy Swaggart has a daily show from Baton Rouge that features his own music, back-up singers, band, and sermons. All of the above buy time on TV stations, and ask for donations.

A Christian television station tries to air all the programs that will buy time in its area. Many of them run repeat performances of the same program in the same day. Regional churches sponsor the-camera-goes-to-church programs purchased and produced locally. With this arrangement, a Christian station can program about twelve hours a day. Many add another four to six hours of local Christian talk programming, mostly to solicit local donations.

Blending Secular and Christian Programming

Family television is a concept that places the best of Christian programming on the air with the best secular programming in a competitive independent station programming stance. Prime time programs might include a Christian children's story; news from Cable News Network (CNN); local news, sports, and weather; the CBN half-hour continuing drama "Another Life"; "Little House on the Prairie"; the "Merv Griffin Show"; a feature movie; national news; and then the "700 Club," running opposite Johnny Carson. The two dramatic series, movies, Merv Griffin and national news must have locally produced ads that have been sold by local sales people. And it is not always possible to recruit sales or production personnel who are able to sell and to write, shoot, narrate, and produce adequate local advertising for these spots.

To operate a local TV station with a break-even budget of about $25,000 to $35,000 a month, more than 1,500 commercials a month at $20 each must be sold, produced, and run. That is seventy-five spots a day, and at schedules of about three a day per client, the station would need twenty-five clients whose spots would have to be updated monthly. It would keep a commercial production crew of two or three people busy just updating those commercials and another crew to keep up with each pair of salespersons.

So television spot sales imply five or six extra staff members more than radio in order to visualize the ads and to stay even with the station's creditors — one of which is the local electric utility, because a full-power UHF transmitter draws about $10,000 a month in electricity!

Another problem with advertising sales on a family TV formatted station is the assumption that the shareholders are primarily Christians. The Christians in the community will be under the impression that the station will be a "Christian" station. When the family station format signs on, many Christians in the audience will be disappointed. Their image of "Christian" television usually does not include any secular content. This disappointment may be reflected in the sales. Some Christian stations "sneak" on the air almost undetected and struggle along with no promotional money so that very few people seem to know the facility is broadcasting. Sales and promotions are discussed in Part Five.

Summary

Donor-based radio stations usually offer a variety of ministry programs grouped for maximum audience appeal. Charismatic shows are separated from Evangelical and Fundamentalist programs by "buffer" ministries that appeal to both audiences.

Christian music stations rely on advertising revenues and select their music in ways similar to secular stations; however, up-to-date research data for Christian music is more difficult to obtain.

Christian and family television is similar in programming to Christian radio, but the operating and production costs are substantially greater.

Chapter 11
News and Public Affairs

The predominant musical taste of a station's marketing area is extremely important. Audience preference for a certain kind of music plays the largest role in determining the type of programming format selected for the station; however, local news can make the biggest difference in listenership for stations located in smaller market areas, especially those in competition with big city signals. The music program and the ads/spots/production elements of the big city signals naturally will have highly paid creative development as opposed to the lower budget operations of the smaller market station. The revenue potential for the bigger stations from the smaller market area, however, does not warrant detailed coverage of its events by the bigger stations.

The smaller station, therefore, is able to cover local stories in much greater depth and detail than the larger station with many such areas to cover. People usually tune into their local station in order to learn about local happenings, so local news should be a source of ad revenue because of its high audience draw.

The cost and efficiency of newsroom operation determines the profit that can be made in local news. The person with responsibility for news at a station usually has the title of news director. In some operations, he answers to the program director, in others, to the station manager. Either way, the news director should organize the newsroom in a way to get more stories faster. There are two organizational techniques that maximize efficiency.

Techniques of Organizing News Sources

The first technique is the establishment of a "who's who" file, a listing of all possible news sources cross-indexed by office or responsibility. This file should contain the names, addresses, office and home phone numbers of the mayor, councilmen, judges, key law enforcement officials, fire and school officials, and key businessmen. The news director should become personally acquainted with all of the major figures on the local news scene, so he can determine whether the party can be called at home and up to what hour of the night or how early in the morning. This information should be recorded on the card catalog of the file.

The news director should post the meeting dates of all area legislative bodies or boards. If a reporter is not sent to each meeting according to this schedule, a call to one of the participants in the meeting can garner information for newscasts. Occasionally, the meeting agenda is available through a phone call to the recording secretary of the group. This information is often of value the morning before an evening meeting for use in a story telling the high points planned for that meeting. A station *always* should have the results from meetings that have been previewed in this manner. Otherwise, listeners are "left hanging" and will find some other source for their news. The obvious meetings to be covered are county and city government, school boards, and regulatory commissions such as public works or airport authorities.

A prime source for news is the local newspaper. The newscaster should read the paper thoroughly and keep an eye out for notices of future meetings or criminal trials.

The story of a drunk driving accident may say that the person charged with vehicular homicide has a trial date set for March 19, almost a month away. Notice that the person has been charged "with" vehicular homicide, not "for" vehicular homicide. Saying "for" convicts the accused person without a trial and could interfere with the proper judicial process. Police and court stories require careful handling. The key is to attribute the facts to the source of information — "according to police reports," "a police spokesman said," "court records show," or similar attributions. Above all, make sure the facts and quotations are correct.

Stories about trial dates being set, petition dates and deadlines, political party caucus schedules, and other upcoming events appear in local papers. Newspapers usually have larger news staffs than radio and TV news operations, so broadcasters regularly take advantage of print coverage to save time and legwork. News directors do need to check whether a particular story has been copyrighted. Copyrighted stories must be credited to the newspaper. In any event, information drawn from print sources should be rewritten for hearing rather than reading. Broadcast news uses shorter, simpler sentences that can be easily understood by the audience.

The second organizational technique is to create a "future file," a collection of file folders dated 1 to 31 for the current month and monthly files for future months. The clipping about the trial would go in the file for the 19th. Then, on each date, look at the folder for that day and the next several days to be reminded of upcoming events that may be worthy of coverage.

Remove those stories for the day and follow up on them. Call the clerk of court a couple of days ahead to see if the trial has been postponed, then announce that fact or the fact that the trial is to be held as scheduled. Always briefly recapitulate the facts in the case for the benefit of listeners who did not hear the original story. Never assume that your audience knows everything you know about a given story.

If a caucus is coming up for one of the political parties on the following night (another story from the folders), call the party chairperson and do a story on what will be discussed at the upcoming meeting. Arrange with that person to get the results of the meeting right after adjournment. The secret for the success of a "futures file" is consistency — feed the file daily and use the file daily.

In smaller markets, there will be some folders with next to nothing or nothing at all in them every month. But other days will make up for the slim ones. In every size market, the system works and is an aid to news directing every time it is used properly.

Local News Coverage

Print reporters have a regular "beat," a particular schedule of meetings, events, or offices that they are responsible for covering. They attend court hearings and trials, talk to clerks of court and attorneys, and, in general, hang around the sources of information. The radio reporter or the news director, however, usually is confined to the newsroom and must use the telephone to cover these beats. A news director, therefore, must establish a regular calling list: calls that are made more than once a day, daily calls, every-other-day calls, and weekly calls.

The standard news call list at a typical small market station might look like this:

State Police

County Sheriff's Office.

City Police and Fire Dispatcher(s).

Outlying Police and Fire Dispatcher(s).

By calling regularly, the news director keeps in contact with the news sources and renews acquaintanceships on a regular basis. Phone contact is not as good as a print reporter's visits in person, but it works. The important thing is to build a rapport with your sources. If they know you and know they can trust you to deal fairly with them, they will soon begin to call you when anything important is happening. That makes the job a lot easier.

Most news directors work a 5 a.m.-to-noon shift, because morning drive times are the most important news times. A good practice is for the news director to take an occasional afternoon, perhaps once a month, to visit two, three, or four of the contacts he calls regularly on the telephone. The next visiting afternoon, he could take several more and continue until he has seen in person everyone on the list.

The presence of a station representative is required at some community meetings and press conferences. Although most county or city board meetings are routine, the news director or station reporter should attend almost every meeting. Otherwise, the station is perceived as not caring about the city or county at all. The best way to cover such meetings is to take notes on the highlights of resolutions, passed or not passed, noting opposition to any item. If a major controversy develops, try to get a statement from the leadership of each faction on audio cassette. Edit these down to twenty to forty seconds and lift onto cart. Include both comments in the ensuing news stories, and listeners will know the station was represented live at the meeting.

News releases will be sent to the station by many groups and organizations. Usually these will need to be rewritten in the station's style, and many times the facts will need to be verified. They can be a good source of information about upcoming special events or activities that will need to be covered live. The item, when read on the air, should be one brief paragraph taking thirty seconds or less to read. TV station news directors should build up a file of color slides of area churches, government buildings, museums, libraries, etc. to use with stories involving these locations, if live shots are not available. The slides should be made horizontally.

If not worthy of inclusion in the regular news slots, some of the releases that come in may be useful for a community calendar. Also, at times, a station may have some spots free that are normally allotted to commercials that can be used for public service announcements (PSAs). Prior to the 1980s deregulation, in order to achieve license renewal, broadcast stations were required to promise how many PSAs would be aired each week. This promise, and check up on performance of the promises by the FCC, has been discontinued as a requirement for license renewal. Stations are left to be judged in this area by the marketplace instead of the government.

Another area of the news that can build community trust and help develop an audience for the station is public affairs. News directors should be on the lookout for articulate spokespersons on topics of concern to the local community. Holidays are good times for special community programming, especially programs that can be pretaped allowing station personnel to spend more time with their own families. Church programs and holiday concerts are ideal for pretaping.

Public Affairs Programming

Most issues of vital community importance are broadcast on public affairs programs. The news is expected to be factual and free from bias and opinion (which also is a matter of opinion) and any "opinion" is to be labeled as such. But in public affairs programming, advocates of various viewpoints are offered a stage on which to present their opinions. Various spokespersons for the different views are invited to appear. The station usually presents the program on a regular basis — daily or weekly — and invites the protagonists in as guests on a rotating basis.

One format for public affairs took the nations' stations by storm in the 1960s. This was the telephone talk show, where guests representing a certain viewpoint on a community issue could field questions and comments from listening citizens. WHVW in Hyde Park/Poughkeepsie, New York, pioneered the first telephone talk show between New York City and Albany. The station at first avoided the customary delay device because the five seconds delay gave a confusing echo to the listeners. The delay seldom gives broadcasters the chance to remove maligning comments, which are too subtle to be judged as offensive in five seconds. The station did install such a device, however, after profanity from one caller went out on the air.

Not only must the broadcaster defend against violations of the Fairness Doctrine, but indecent, immoral, and profane comments must be kept off the airwaves. The greatest listenership for the station is believed to have been during especially controversial "open line" broadcasts.

Many stations bury their so-called public affairs programming at 5 a.m. on Sundays. Others feature such programs and sell participating sponsors on them. Banks, hospitals, and other institutions of similar nature are likely candidates for this kind of sponsorship. Stations with primarily religious programming can find several topics to discuss: abortion, public versus church schools, and taxation issues, to name a few. Monthly reports from mayors, school superintendents, sheriffs, and police chiefs in the listening area are other suggestions. State and national legislators from the area usually are happy to take part in such programming, which can take the form of a telephone talk show, an interview, or a panel forum. It is the program director's job to make sure that a balance of viewpoints is maintained in public affairs programming.

Too often religious broadcasting stations ignore local news and public affairs programming, but these programs are key factors in building a strong, loyal audience. Potential listeners who would normally bypass a Christian station can be attracted by sound news coverage and public affairs programming.

The Fairness Doctrine

Regardless of the sources of news stories, the news operation must strive to be fair, to offer as often as possible all sides of any issue. If the Democrats speak on something, Republican leaders should be called for a comment. The station should not crusade for any particular issue or any particular candidate, but strive to achieve balance. Editorials, short spots that present the station management's viewpoint or stand on an issue may be aired, but these should be separate and not confused with objective news stories. This concept of "balance" was developed regulatorily over the years by the FCC.

In the late 1930s, radio station WAAB, Boston, had been using its facilities to air the owner's partisan ideas on community issues to the exclusion of any other viewpoints. When the station filed for license renewal in 1940, the Mayflower Company filed for the same facilities. In the renewal hearing, the FCC discovered that WAAB's policy had been to broadcast editorials urging the election of selected candidates for political office and supporting one side in a public controversy without corresponding objective coverage of other candidates and other positions on an issue.

"It is clear," the commission found, "that the purpose of these editorials was to win public support for some person or view favored by those in control of the station."[1] Although the station's license was renewed, the FCC issued a dictum that prohibited editorializing:

> A truly free radio cannot be used to advocate the causes of the licensee. It cannot be used to support the candidacies of his friends. It cannot be devoted to the support of principles he happens to regard most favorably. In brief, the broadcaster cannot be an advocate.[2]

World War II rallied most Americans to a common cause, but the commission's ruling in the Mayflower-WAAB hearing was criticized by groups and individuals who felt the prohibition against editorials was an unconstitutional restraint of a licensee's freedom of speech. By 1948, the FCC had held public hearings on the decision and in 1949 issued a new opinion allowing licensees to editorialize provided they maintain overall fairness. The FCC stated that "the identified expression of the licensee's personal viewpoint as part of the more general presentation of views or comments on the various issues" may be aired, but they also said:

> But the opportunity of licensees to present such views as they may have on matters of controversy may not be utilized to achieve a partisan or one-sided presentation of issues. Licensee editorialization is but one aspect of freedom of expression by means of radio. Only insofar as it is exercised in conformity with the paramount right of the public to hear a reasonably balanced presentation of all reasonable viewpoints on particular issues can such editorialization be considered to be consistent with the licensee's duty to operate in the public interest. For the licensee is a trustee impressed with the duty of preserving for the public generally radio as a medium of free expression and fair presentation.[3]

This FCC stance became known as the Fairness Doctrine. This ruling was tested in the early 1960s at a religious broadcasting station in a town just outside York, Pennsylvania. WGCB is a 1000-watt AM station licensed to Red Lion, Pennsylvania, and operated in the 1960s by the

Rev. Murray Norris. One of the programs carried regularly by the station was that of the Rev. Billy James Hargis of Tulsa, who had a patriotic, anticommunist ministry. Hargis discussed a book on one of his programs that was critical of then FBI Director J. Edgar Hoover and Republican Senator Barry Goldwater of Arizona. In his comments, Hargis suggested that the author, Fred J. Cook, had been associated with known communists and homosexuals.

Cook considered the comments unfair. He obtained Hargis' broadcast station list and wrote his objections to everyone on the list that had carried that particular program. Several of the stations offered him free time to rebut the allegations, but Norris would not offer free time. He did offer Cook air time at the same rate that Hargis had paid. The author refused the offer and took his complaint to the FCC, which ordered the station to *give* him reply time. The Radio-Television News Directors Association saw this case as a chance to overthrow the Fairness Doctrine as a violation of freedom of speech and joined WGCB against the FCC in a U.S. District Court appeal. In June 1969, the U.S. Supreme Court unanimously upheld the FCC's application of the Fairness Doctrine:

> Although broadcasting is clearly a medium affected by a First Amendment interest . . . differences in the characteristics of news media justify differences in the First Amendment standards applied to them . . . the right of free speech of a broadcaster . . . does not embrace a right to snuff out the free speech of others . . . When there are substantially more individuals who want to broadcast than there are frequencies to allocate, it is idle to posit an unbridgeable First Amendment right to broadcast comparable to the right of every individual to speak, write, or publish.[4]

The bottom line for broadcasters is that the FCC expects them to seek out issues of significant importance in their coverage areas and to broadcast divergent viewpoints concerning each of these issues. If any individual or group is maligned or anyone's character impugned in any broadcast, this individual or group must be informed of the broadcast, supplied with a tape or a transcript of the program, and offered free reply time. This is not necessarily "equal time," but merely enough time for an adequate reply to be made. If the purported maligning or impugnment of character is made in a pretaped program, the licensee is obligated to notify the party in question prior to the broadcast of the tape.

It is possible for an otherwise conscientious broadcaster to miss such alleged offensive programs and receive reply requests from potentially aggrieved parties. In that case, it is wise to comply with the request for free reply time, regardless of the nature of the reply.

In the early 1980s, a pastor with conservative views aired a church service over Channel 39 in Dallas which included a sermon condemning homosexual lifestyles. The gay community felt maligned and asked the owners for reply time. The ownership of the station then was the Christian Broadcasting Network, headed by author-evangelist Dr. Pat Robertson, who is also a graduate of Yale Law School. The spokesperson for the gays got the free time.

Program Director's Report

The best way for management to keep track of the varied aspects and responsibilities of programming is by using the program director's report form.

The program director's report form is divided into several sections: music, news, public affairs, personnel, and technical sections.

The technical section of the form provides a system for informing the chief engineer and the manager about equipment malfunctions. What better monitoring of equipment performance than to have deejays and newspeople note when machines misfire or string tapes fail to play or records skip or sound bad? These are written up on a "discrepancy sheet" which the PD scans several times a day. Many of the problems involve a minor adjustment or cleaning and are easily rectified by the PD.

News and Public Affairs

The news and public affairs section of the PD report addresses the management's criteria of news and the FCC's concern for public affairs programming. In news, management wants to know how many "firsts" the station had — how many stories it aired first as opposed to "scoops" by the competition, and the news topics that dominated the newscasts throughout the week. From the topics listed, the manager becomes aware of current news topics and, in talking with businessmen, can include phrases such as, "I believe our news department broke that story first," etc. Owners and managers deserve to get a quick briefing on the background of what's going on in town.

The public affairs programming report is a holdover from the days when stations needed to report in a narrative to the FCC all the outstanding public affairs programming carried during the license period. Although the FCC no longer requires such explicit reporting in this area, it does hold the licensee responsible for serving the community or communities of license in the public interest. A program director who has the pulse of the community accurately reflects the needs of the area in the topics discussed on the public affairs programs. Each quarter (a three-month period), the management must update the station's local public affairs file with a list of what the station perceives as the top 10 problems of the area and what programs or programming, if any, the station proposes to air in addressing these problems. The PD's public affairs report provides input to management in these important areas of concern to the FCC.

Unfortunately, many religious stations do not broadcast much, if any, public affairs or community programming. A simple local telephone interview show or a live or taped interview program discussing problems of local importance is not that hard to do and would fulfill the FCC concept of service to the coverage area. It would also head off any competition at license renewal time. In addition, the station can sell ads in and around the public affairs program.

The music reporting form keeps the station music selection system honest and free from any form of "payola."

Because of the history of record-company bribes to disc jockeys, the FCC wants to be assured that each station manages its music rotation with integrity. Back in the late 1950s, when Top 40 stations were rising to the top of the ratings in each market, some record promoters took advantage of the tentative and developing music management techniques to pay deejay's bribes directly in order to ensure air play for their records. Some of America's top deejay's were caught up in this scandal.

Music management began to clean up its act in the early 60s until "drugola" replaced "payola." Some hard rock albums arrived at stations with glassine envelopes in them, and some 45rpm records were shipped with a 35mm can full of a tobacco-like, but illegal, substance. The FCC then began to admonish music managers to get the drug lyrics off the air. The results of these shenanigans included the requiring of "payola/drugola" statements to be signed by deejays to the effect that each person hired to host music programs has not and will not accept any remuneration, gift, or benefit from playing or promising to play any program element other than in the rotation established by the management. These signed forms also should be placed in each individual employee folder.

When the PD has a continuing record of the music removed from play lists and added to rotations, with the reasons for this action, the station has established a pattern of music management that maintains the integrity of the station management.

A copy of the various portions of the Program Director's Report Form appears in Appendix 4.

Summary

Broadcasters should not let limited staffing keep them from covering the local news scene and carrying public affairs programming. Careful organization with "who's who" and futures files can save news directors a lot of time, and most news beats can be covered by telephone and with the use of the local newspaper.

Balanced, fair news and public affairs programming will build listenership and avoid problems with the FCC's Fairness Doctrine.

Notes

[1] "In the Matter of the Mayflower Broadcasting Corporation and the Yankee Network," WAAB 8 FCC 333, 338, January 1941.

[2] Ibid.

[3] "Report in the Matter of Editorializing by Broadcast Licensees," FCC Docket No. 8516, June 1, 1949.

[4] "Red Lion Broadcasting Co. vs. FCC," (395 US 367, 386-388, 1969)

Part Five

Sales and Promotions — Dollars and Sense

Chapter 12
The Importance of Promotions

Four basic elements are necessary for the success of a radio or television station: the music format, news and advertising, which vary as second in importance, and promotions. Promotions can make the difference in whether a station is near the top or the bottom of the ratings.

Great radio stations have a contest or other type of promotion in operation all the time. Designing the contests is an ongoing chore for the program director, chairman of the fun and games department.

Some contests are centered around specific holidays, others are merely seasonal, but all must be constructed to be saleable — that is, they should be tailored so that sponsors' ads fit into them. Some stations run a promotion at the same time as a contest. Promotions can tie into holidays, community events, or trends. Good program directors keep a promotions calendar to remind themselves about successful promotions or contests that will bear repeating. Even small contests are good programming when they are just plain fun. A calendar of typical contests and promotions might include the following ideas.

CALENDAR OF CONTESTS, PROMOTIONS
JANUARY
Ski Weekend Giveaway. Set up a free ski weekend with a ski lodge including transportation, ski equipment rental, dining, and so on. The slogan could be, "Register for a ski weekend giveaway at participating merchants (advertisers)."

March of Dimes Month. WHVW is licensed to Hyde Park, New York, home of Franklin D. Roosevelt, who founded the March of Dimes. In the 1960s, the station began placing dimes, ten per foot, end to end until a "mile of dimes" was laid out on the driveway at the FDR National

Historic Site in Hyde Park. The event, broadcast live via shortwave to the station, featured area youth choirs, bands, talks with area public officials, and coverage of the thousands of loyal listeners who drove through to donate their dimes. The proceeds went to the March of Dimes and the advertising revenue to the station. This live all-day remote broadcast was first held on FDR's birthday, then moved to the Sunday that falls closest to his birthday.

FEBRUARY
(Cartridge) Cart-Stop Contest. Put the numbers 1, 2, 3, 4, and 5 each on a separate piece of paper, shake them up in a hat, and have someone draw them out one at a time to get a sequence, such as 3, 1, 5, 2, 4. Then record a series of chopping sounds like this: three chops, stop the cart; one chop, stop the cart; five chops, stop the cart, and so on, until the entire random sequence is recorded. The contest slogan might be "Win a cherry pie from XYZ Bakery." Have listeners call in their guesses as to how many chops it will take George to cut down the cherry tree during a certain hour. Air the callers giving their guesses. Press the random cart button, and if a guess matches the number of chops that is aired, the caller wins the cherry pie from the sponsor. This is a fun contest.

Heart Contest. Tie a heart contest to Valentine's Day and sell ads to candy stores, bakeries, jewelry stores, and florists. KTCR played a montage of songs by a variety of artists whose initials spelled out H-E-A-R-T. The first caller guessing the artists won a prize from one of the advertising sponsors.

MARCH
Spring Into Spring Contest. This contest is operated as a variation of the cart-stop described above. How many pulls will it take — from one to five — to start a lawn-mower? The caller with the correct guess gets a lawnmower blade sharpened. The grand prize could be a new lawnmower.

Predict the Temperature. Have listeners send in a postcard with a prediction as to which day the temperature will first reach a certain reading (e.g., eighty degrees). Entries with the correct date win garden supplies, seeds, plants, etc., provided by the advertising sponsor.

APRIL
Easter Egg Hunt. Hide candy eggs on the courthouse lawn. Use service organizations to help with the kids. Jaycees, Optimists, or Lions Clubs are good choices for help with youth. Work in local talent for entertainment and invite all area kids through eight years of age to hunt for eggs. Broadcast live from this community event featuring interviews with the children and their parents, as well as with representatives of participating civic groups.

MAY
Salute the Graduate. Tape mini-interviews with high school seniors with their name, scholastic major, extracurricular activities, college or employment plans. Sell advertising to community-minded merchants as a "Class of '??" promotion.

Indianapolis 500 Race Month. Tie in all auto sponsors. Put numbers 1 to 33 in a hat, draw at random and assign race car numbers to each sponsor. If his car comes in first, the $200 May ad package is free! This is an example of a sponsor promotion, as opposed to the earlier examples of community or listener promotions.

JUNE
Bridal Fair. Hold a bridal fashion and wedding gift show using sponsors to promote it.

Fishing Show. Give fishing and water reports and recreation forecasts. Boat dealers, fishing docks, recreational equipment stores, etc. are ideal sponsors for this kind of promotion.

Theme Park Ticket Giveaway. Listeners register at summer sponsors to win free tickets to Six Flags or a similar park.

Bumper Stickers. Distribute bumper stickers with the station's call letters and frequency through advertisers — especially convenience stores. Then have a spotter drive around the area and announce the license tag numbers of cars displaying a bumper sticker. The owners of the cars with the announced tag numbers have to call the station within a specified time in order to claim their prizes.

JULY

Fourth of July Events. Broadcast live from area parades, picnics, or other events. Feature area talent and on-the-spot interviews. Food companies or area restaurants who plan to have booths at the event are likely sponsors.

AUGUST

Back-to-School Safety Promotions. "John Doe Motors reminds all area drivers to watch out for children boarding buses or crossing the streets now that schools are in session again."

Meet the Football Players. Record high school stars giving their names, positions, grades, and majors with statements such as "We're going to have a great year!" Add a tag, "Brought to you by such-and-such sponsors."

SEPTEMBER

Community Day Ceremonies for Labor Day. KRMG (AM) in Tulsa hosts a "Great Raft Race" down the Arkansas River. Participating groups and individuals try to get down the river to a finish line first in their class of craft. In the listeners' "Pokie Okie" class there is no time competition; they only have to complete the course!

OCTOBER

Pumpkin Patch Contest. Give away pumpkins to kids for Halloween.

NOVEMBER

Shoot-the-Turkey Contest. This contest is a cart-stop game. The object is to see how many shots from one to five it will take to shoot the turkey. A deejay plays the random cart with the recorded shots and listeners who guess correctly win a turkey.

DECEMBER

Christmas Promotions. Any number of variations can be made on this theme. Feature once or twice an hour letters to Santa, Christmas customs, community Christmas cards, or area choirs recorded singing Christmas music early in the Fall. The station can gain listeners by having all the churches listening for their choir. Ads can be sold to local sponsors for these features.

Christmas Greetings. Sell "Merry Christmas" messages to area professionals and politicians who do not normally buy time.

Year's News in Review. Summarize the top stories of the year and review the top musical hits of the year between Christmas and New Year's. Sell ads to sponsors for these highlights.

All Christmas Music. Play holiday music between Thanksgiving and Christmas. Promote the "Christmas spirit" at your station.

When Is a Contest a Lottery?

Each contest or promotion must be fully developed for the air personnel. "Fully developed" means the program director must type out explicit instructions detailing where each cart is located, what to say, when to play which cart, what to say when a listener calls, when to put the caller on, exactly how to determine a winner, and so on. All such instructions should make it clear that station employees or their families are ineligible, so that everyone knows the contest is not rigged. The FCC puts broadcast licenses in jeopardy for *fraudulent contests*. Thus the program director and, ultimately, the station manager must have details of every contest on file to explain any listener complaints.

The major concern for compliance with FCC rules is in the area of whether a contest is a promotion or a lottery. The FCC defines a lottery as *a contest offering something of value as a prize, with the prize, for which there is a consideration, to be awarded by chance* (drawing, etc.).

Any prize that a station would offer would be something of value, and since giving away too many things of value would cost the station too much, the "something of value" is usually given away by chance. Any random selection process constitutes chance, such as drawing for a name from slips of paper with individual names (sign-up slips) or guessing how many shots it will take to kill the turkey. (Shots are recorded in random order on cart.) Most station contests contain two of the FCC's three elements of a lottery, but to be judged a lottery, all three elements must be present. The third element is the most troublesome for broadcasters.

"Consideration" is defined as the condition where the chance to win is paid for by the participants. In the 1940s, pupils from one parochial school used to go door to door with a punch board and ask, "Would you buy a chance on a new car to benefit our school?" A quarter would give the donor the right to punch out a number from the board to see if that number matched the winners' chart on the back. The quarter was the consideration.

Most broadcasters give out prizes by chance but they must make sure there is no consideration in the game or contest. Calling the station on the telephone is not considered consideration, nor is going into a store to register as long as no purchase is required.

An example of a seemingly innocuous contest that actually involved all three elements occurred at the Hyde Park station, WHVW. The Hyde Park Chamber of Commerce wanted to run a Sales Day promotion with a TV set giveaway program. All that shoppers needed to do was write their name and phone number on the back of a cash register receipt at any participating store and deposit it in the box next to the register. The station told the merchants' association that the promotional announcements could not be aired because the TV set contest was a lottery. All three elements were present: prize, chance, and consideration. The register receipts constituted consideration because a purchase was required to participate in the drawing.

Beware of Potential Hazards in Promotions

Be careful not to tell listeners to do something that might cause a public nuisance, encourage them to trespass on private property, or result in disruption of traffic. In 1950, Dick Mills, a morning radio personality at WEOK, Poughkeepsie, told his listeners, "This is a dead town — no St. Patrick's Day parade planned or anything! Tell you what. Let's do something about it! Meet me at noon down at the corner of Main and Market (the main traffic intersection downtown) and we'll start our own parade." Then he forgot about his parade plans.

The Poughkeepsie police called the station about 1 p.m. on St. Patrick's Day and said, "There are about 4000 people holding up traffic at the main intersection in the city, and they are all asking for Dick Mills."

Well, they had their parade, and everyone talked about it. But the station was fortunate. Nowadays such a prank promotion would undoubtedly precipitate a lawsuit and a hefty fine from the city as well. Treasure hunt contests, for example, could block traffic or encourage people to trespass on other people's property. This type of promotion must be very carefully planned.

Out-of-Media and Christian Promotions

Christian stations often find their best promotions are in connection with churches — an out-of-media promotion. For example, KTCR Radio, Wagoner/Coweta, Oklahoma, has good quality Bible bookmarks and telephone message pads printed up, each with the station's call letters and frequency. The manager visits every pastor in town, explains the station's ministry, and gives the pastor some phone message pads for his office and bookmarks to hand out to the congregation. The manager invites the pastors to become involved with the station and to put information about it into the church's Sunday bulletins.

Out-of-media promotions, or those that operate in ways other than over the station's own airwaves, are very effective. Some of the best of this type involve billboards, because most cars have radios, and drivers see local radio or TV news billboards before reaching home. Many broadcast stations use newspaper ads as well. Bumper-sticker or window-sticker campaigns use listener's bumpers as mobile billboards. No matter what the plan, out-of-media promotions are designed to draw nonlisteners or nonviewers to the station.

Other Christian station promotion ideas include a skate night when station deejays spin Christian music to which youth groups can skate, and a Christian Station fun park night when listeners may be admitted to area fun or theme parks free or at a discounted rate. One station held a gospel sing and picnic in a public park and invited listeners. Concert ticket promotions are fun for station listeners. Some visiting artists will introduce station personalities or use the deejays as concert emcees.

Promotions and Ratings Systems

On-air promotions build audience numbers by keeping occasional or short-term listeners tuned in for longer periods of time. This concept is called "quarter-hour maintenance." The most efficient such contest is a promotion that relates to the method of a rating service canvassing technique. In the 1950s, C. E. Hooper prepared the data for his "Hooper Ratings," using the telephone coincidence technique. He dialed random numbers and asked anyone answering the phone: "Are you listening to the radio?" and "What station is it tuned to?"

The promotion found best suited to this survey technique was a cash-call contest. The listener stayed tuned to determine the cash amount in the jackpot. When called by the station, the listener had to answer the phone with the words, "My favorite station is _____," to be eligible to play. The deejay asked the listener if he or she knew how much was in the jackpot during this hour. If the question was answered correctly, the listener won. If not, the jackpot was augmented for the next hour. This method was effective because it trained listeners to identify incoming phone calls with a contest motive, so that when a Hooper enumerator called, the response would be conditional.

Some Top 40 stations promoting cash-call contests achieved more than 80 percent of the available audience in six- to eight-station markets.

The mid 1960s brought the Pulse rating system. The sampling method involved typical neighborhoods, and interviewers canvassed all the homes in the designated area with "recall" interviews in the home or roster recall interviews. Residents' memories were prodded by the roster that the enumerators carried, which listed stations by call letter, frequency, deejays' names, logo, and featured newscasters' names. Most people did not remember their listening patterns from eight to twelve hours before the interview in very much detail. What they tended to remember was the station whose call letters they heard the most frequently, even from a short encounter with the station. Thus a station that repeated its call letters between songs and had deejays with memorable names may have received a better rating than it deserved.

Recallability of deejay names was a facet of Pulse rating techniques that was taken very seriously by that great radio programming consultant Bill Drake of Drake-Chennault, Inc. Drake actually conducted research on how well members of his target demographic area remembered the names used by air personalities at his stations. A list of names was read to participants, then a few days later another list was read to the participants who were asked to identify any names that had been on the first list. The winners were the names given to Drake station jocks, such as Johnny Donovan, Keven Kennedy, and others. WHVW, Hyde Park, used to have quite a large turnover for the weekend deejay position. Then station management began telling part-time deejays that they must use a certain name, such as "Kevin Kennedy," which had already become familiar to listeners as their on-the-air nom de plume.

Prospective employees who balked at not using their own names were asked, "Well, how would you like to play the lead in a very successful Broadway play?" When they agreed that this would be "making it" in the acting profession, they were told to consider success in the disk jockey field as playing the part of deejay Kevin Kennedy every weekend on the station. Employees usually bought the idea when it was presented in this manner. WHVW must have had a dozen "Kevin Kennedys" over the course of a five- or six-year period. Usually, "Kevin" was rated the number one deejay on weekends!

The Pulse contest during that period was a prize wagon promotion using a station wagon or van loaded with gorgeous prizes cruising through suburban areas from about 10 a.m. to 8 p.m. If a listener spotted the van and stopped it, he would get certain prizes; or, if the van driver came to the door, whoever answered the door and mentioned WHVW would get prizes. Notice the conditioning of response to someone ringing the doorbell!

The third, and presently viable, ratings service is ARBITRON, the ratings system of American Research Bureau (ARB). This system uses diaries sent to the homes of selected sample groups and asks survey participants to keep records of their listening or viewing habits.

The best contest defense for this system is a form of music bingo. Cards are printed up with the names of artists in bingo card squares. The station plays songs by these artists in a given hour in such a pattern that some cards have the artists' names in sequence up or down or across. These numbered cards are distributed through convenience stores and service stations to generate sponsor traffic. The first person to call in with a winning card which verifies the artist sequence for the preceding hour wins big prizes. This contest is difficult to coordinate, but it is an effective weapon in the ARB ratings battle because listeners are conditioned to keep track of a listening element of a certain station. A variation of this is to have the listener write down the exact songs played from 7:05 a.m. through 7:30 a.m., then send in the list for station judges to verify. To avoid too many winners, the prize is awarded to the one chosen at random from among all the correct entries or the one with the earliest postmark. This conditions participants not only to listen to a 25-minute period of the morning drive time, but to keep a self-written diary of their listening and to mail it in to the station. Typical prizes are TV sets, stereos, cars, and condominiums, usually contributed by advertising sponsors.

Another version of high dollar prize volume is the prize catalog contest. A large four-color brochure with special numbering is sent to each resident in an area by zip code mailing. The main message is: "You may already be a winner! Just check the number on your prize packet and stay tuned for your number to be read over the air!" Prizes include TV sets, VCRs, sports cars, fishing boats, yachts, and trips around the country or the world. A Dallas station estimated that $8 million to $12 million in prizes was given away during this ten- to thirteen-week promotion.

Can Audiences Be Bought?

These types of contests give rise to the question, "Can the audience be bought?" The answer is a qualified "Yes." But there is a pretty big qualification: The station with the big-bucks giveaways already must be excellent on the air. It must have the best researched music, air personalities, news and public affairs programming, and the most entertaining commercials within a large market. Another station with a similar format is always nipping at its heels. Such a station will assure its position with a big-bucks giveaway or lose it to the other station using the big-bucks giveaway. In other words, the station's reputation essentially is built on quality, but the deciding factor between two stations of equal quality can be these giveaways. Also, less superior stations can gain ratings points with giveaways, but probably cannot "buy" the number one or two ratings position.

TV ratings/contests are much more subtle because network stations have little to do with most of their programming content, as the networks themselves maintain program control. To build viewership, independent stations can offer such special viewing as the best movies from network packages, and news departments can run such features as strips of five- to ten-minute mini-documentaries on each newscast for a week. But TV stations seldom have high-dollar contests to augment ratings.

Summary

Promotions and contests are effective devices to generate larger audiences and more enthusiasm with advertisers. Imaginative and careful planning throughout the year — particularly during the rating season — can have a profound impact on a station's success.

Watching the operations of the contests and promotions at the station for conformity to FCC rules and regulations is just one of the duties of the program director.

Chapter 13
The Basics of Selling Air Time

Broadcasting is commonly divided into three parts: engineering, programming, and sales. Engineering gets the channel or frequency and puts the signal on the air. Programming selects the shows, format, and image, and builds an audience. Sales delivers this audience to paying clients. So we have these three — engineering, programming, and sales — and the most important of these is sales!

More than 90 percent of American broadcast stations are commercial stations, as opposed to public or educational noncommercial stations. Commercial stations must make money to stay on the air, and the only way to make money is to sell air time. Depending on the structure of the format and operations of the station or stations, either program time or spot advertising is offered for sale. Unless this air time is sold, the station will not be able to pay its bills.

Spending money on a budgetary basis is a management function involving priorities and trade-offs. In a broadcast operation, spending is guided by industrywide criteria, FCC criteria, and commonsense. Selling, however, is an art combined with a science. While the science aspects may be written down, the art of selling develops with experience. That is why not everyone who attempts sales activities succeeds at the profession.

If a station has revenue, it can spend money, which is why most station managers are selected according to their proven ability to generate income from sales. Most general managers or station managers began as sales managers or sales personnel. They have proven their revenue production capability before taking over the reins of the station. The most promising route to management is through the skills of a salesperson, so the aspiring manager must learn to excel in the sales arts and learn to manage other sales people.

How do you get started in sales? Opportunities vary. In 1963, when author Durfey was in his mid-twenties, he found himself the majority stockholder and president of a radio station. Three months after the station signed-on, the volume of business being broadcast was minimal. The station began selling the Christmas ads a little late. Before those seasonal sales were started, President John F. Kennedy was shot. The nation went into a state of mourning. Area stations canceled commercials and either carried news live from the networks or played subdued classical pieces. After the funeral, the stations put their commercials back on the air, but Durfey's station lost a substantial percentage of income. In addition, most of the Christmas business had been placed a couple of weeks before on the other stations in town.

Durfey's back was against the wall. He picked up a rate card and a coverage map and hit the sidewalk selling. Special Christmas packages at $50 and $75, multiplied by two or three closes an afternoon for a month, got a respectable Christmas sponsorship for the fledgling station after all. Necessity changed a young engineer and programmer into a salesman. He had to sell successfully or face bankruptcy. Other stations may not have this drastic a need; however, the motivation should be as great.

Some people are more self-motivated than others. One way to become more highly motivated is to listen to cassette tapes of the great motivational teachers and to lively motivational music every morning, according to author Zig Ziglar in *Secrets of Closing the Sale*.[1] Ziglar emphasizes also that to become more effective at sales, a salesperson should exercise regularly to maintain physical stamina, study constantly to fill the mind with useful knowledge and skills, and maintain spiritual and emotional growth. He adds that the salesperson is no better than the individual himself.

Another point Ziglar makes is that salespersons should take time to train their voices. That training already is partially accomplished if the broadcast sales aspirant has served as an announcer. A good course in announcing, acting, or oral interpretation of literature also would fill the bill on voice training. Several professional announcers have received further voice training by singing or by taking vocal lessons from professional solo-singing coaches.

The Anatomy of a Sale

Once a person is prepared physically, mentally, emotionally, and spiritually, he or she must acquire the skills for sales. The best way to begin is with a description of the components of this dynamic process called "a sale."

A sale can be represented in six or seven phases: prospecting, qualifying, preparing, presenting, meeting or answering objections, closing, and servicing the accounts.

Prospecting, or finding a need and filling it, begins the process of selling. There are many ways to find new clients for a broadcast station. Among them are "cold calls" and referrals. Although most client contact will be initiated by telephoning for an appointment, there are times when a new salesman should spend time walking around a business area and introducing himself to the store managers and determining the name of the person in charge of advertising. Leave a card (perhaps two or three) and ask the people you meet to pass them along to their business friends. Ziglar points out that each person has fifty to seventy-five friends in his or her sphere of influence, so business cards have a way of getting around — which is what the salesperson wants!

While in a particular store, it is a good idea to look around and take notes. What kind of people make up the store's clientele? Note the brand names featured. What is unusual about the store? How do the prices compare with other stores? Note the location and describe the decor. On a note card, record the name and phone number(s) of the person(s) who make advertising decisions.

Qualifying the business as a potential client, or acting on the information acquired in the initial call is the second step. There are a number of questions to be answered: What could the broadcast station do to help this business? Is the business big enough to support the cost of a substantial advertising schedule? What has been gleaned from other stations or other media, such as newspapers, outdoor advertising, or business friends concerning this potential client's advertising budget? If possible, contact a media credit checking organization to find out about the potential client's credit. Does he pay his bills on time? The answers to the qualifying questions are used in the preparation of a presentation for the client, once it has been determined that the station might help the business and that the potential client can afford the station's rates. (Prospecting and qualifying will be discussed in greater depth in the next chapter.)

Preparation basically includes a rate card and a coverage map with a written summary of the station's programming. A written summary of the proposed schedule must also be prepared. Presenting two or three suggested plans is the best idea: one with excellent coverage and a high price tag, one an economy package, and one in the middle of the price range. This information should be showcased in a presentation folder or a clear plastic binder. At smaller stations, the salesperson should invent copy for an advertising spot script to possibly run on the station. Such an ad, written — and usually produced — before a client actually places an order is called a "spec-spot," because it is prepared on speculation.

After the presentation is prepared, make an appointment with the client's decision maker. Dress up when calling on accounts, because first impressions count! Dress conservatively, which means a business suit and tie for men and a suit with a skirt or a business-style dress for women. Get your shoes shined. Carry a briefcase or attache case with your written materials in it. Remember the client's name: it is music to his ears. When within visual range of the client, smile! Let that first impression be of a friendly professional.

Then greet the client or his representative, "Mr. Client, we have been thinking about you for a couple of weeks and believe that we have come up with something to help you make more money. Do you have a place where we can sit down and talk about it?"

The Basics of Selling Air Time

Did anyone ever buy insurance standing up? If the salesperson and Mr. Client are going to have a serious discussion, it will not be over the counter while he waits on customers and the salesperson paces back and forth tracking him. Mr. Client's ideal response would be, "Come into my office," and, as he closes the door, telling his assistant or secretary, "Hold my calls, please."

The atmosphere between these two extremes of paying scant attention or paying total attention to the presentation will reveal how interested Mr. Client is in what the station has to offer.

After sitting down, exchange pleasantries and hand the prospect his copy of the proposal. Be sure to keep a reference copy. Depending on his style of personality, go over the pages one by one as the client turns them, summarizing briefly (not reading) the content and meaning of a page. The meaning of that page is solely what benefits the client about it. If answering the questions in the above phase gave any clues as to what city or area of the city most of this client's customers come from, point out that the station covers that area or city. The last page of the written proposal should contain a list of the three different packages with the schedule and prices for each. It is usually a good idea to take a tape of the sample commercial(s) along. Once the points are made, stop talking benefits and play the tape. Don't talk long enough to wear out the client.

Objections can be handled several ways. One of the better ways is to turn them into questions — and then answer them. Throughout the proposal stage, answer any questions raised by the prospective client. If he says, "The price is too high," that is an objection.

A typical exchange of objections and answers might evolve as follows:

"The price is too high."

"What do you feel bothers you — the cost per ad or the cost per thousand?"

"The cost per ad. I spent less than half that per spot on WXXX."

"Well, Mr. Client, which would you rather have, half a page in the *Valley Weekly* or half a page in the *Valley Shopper?*"

"The Shopper, of course."

"Why?"

"Because it has twice the readership!"

"If you had to pay a little more for the *Shopper*, would it be worth it?"

"Sure. That's why I do it every week."

"Well, that's how we feel at WAAA, also. The survey shows that we have about twice the listeners in the eighteen-to-thirty-four age group, and that is the group you really want to reach, isn't it?"

"Well, yes."

"Then spending a little more for a lot more listeners targeted for your message is worth something. Now, just like your wise decision to use the *Shopper*, don't you feel that we are an efficient buy?"

The answer, hopefully, will be "Yes."

Finally, *close the deal, or ask for the buy.* Play the commercials, if they have not been played already. Ask which one the client particularly liked — "the straight one or the funny one?" If he picks one, ask, "Would you rather start Monday or Friday?" When he gives you a date, write it on the contract (which was prepared and brought along with the presentation package). Ask questions about desired frequency of ads, depending on which plan — A, B, or C — that he has selected from the written proposal's last page. Write out the schedule on that portion of the contract.

When the contract is completely filled out, put the pen on the contract pad and hand it to the client.

"If you will just okay the schedule, we will get you started."

He signs. The client bought the package because he is convinced that the ads will bring him some new customers. Thank him and leave the office with a smile. After all, you got an order, and an order is worth a smile. As a matter of fact, a salesperson should never lose his smile, even when he does not get an order. There may be a next time. Back at the station, make arrangements to get the ads run, produced, and in the correct form for airing. Make certain that traffic personnel schedule the ads. If this is not done immediately, perhaps because other calls intervene, make certain enough time is allowed to complete the order before the business day ends and the support people — those in copy, traffic, and production — leave.

Service means taking care of the client back at the station. The attitude of service should continue to be the hallmark of a salesperson-client relationship. Call a couple of times each month with fresh copy or copy ideas. Talk briefly about upcoming sales or special seasonal needs of the client. Offer station sports or other special events packages as an add-on to his current schedule. Let the client know he has a station that cares about his business.

You need to make three or four quality calls like this each day five days a week. Also, three or four service calls a day should be made. During the morning hours of 8 to 9:30 a.m., you will need to use the telephone to make appointments. Some service work can be done on the telephone, but every client should be seen at least once a month. The best way is to get to know their routines — when they are out seeing wholesalers, when they get into the office, how late they stay, etc. — so that a servicing routine can be established.[2]

Author Durfey set up a "semi-official" route to see certain clients once every other week, rather like a floating appointment schedule. Six or eight clients could be seen by strolling from one to another within a geographical area or neighborhood where the car could be parked. The next day he scheduled another neighborhood. One old customer would even exclaim, "Didn't I miss you last Thursday?" By scheduling regular "floating appointments," the station helps its clients look forward to seeing their advertising expert.

Selling is a process, an activity that must be done. Approach sales with all the gusto possible! Be enthusiastic, even when you make only one or two sales out of ten calls. Keep going. Maintain perseverance. Anyone who enjoys working with people will love selling. A good order is when both the client and the station win. A win-win situation occurs when the client gets more business and makes more profit, and when the station has a classy schedule of nice ads that amuse and sell.

If the salesperson cannot believe that a win-win deal can be produced time after time, that person needs to change stations or get into another line of work. Moving products and services for clients is what American broadcasting is all about. Whether radio and television stations were invented to be advertising and marketing tools or not, that is what broadcasting in America has become. The system has taken form and is solidified. There is little one person could do to change it. So an understanding of the nature of selling air time helps young management talent to get a true perspective on the business of broadcasting.

Summary

Christian stations should be especially careful to pay their bills on time and not leave a bad reflection on our Lord or His Body. To do that means selling air time as programs or as advertising. If the station is operating on advertising income, a top-notch sales manager and staff is imperative. Some aspects of being a good sales person are inherent, such as personality, charm, and being able to gain quick rapport with others, but other aspects may be learned. These include the six or seven phases of making a sale: prospecting, qualifying, preparing, presenting, taking care of objections, closing, and servicing accounts. Perhaps the most important qualities a good salesperson needs are perseverance and belief in one's self and in the station.

Notes

[1] Zig Ziglar, *The Secrets of Closing the Sale* (Old Tappan: Fleming H. Revell, 1984).

[2] Much of the material in "Anatomy of a Sale" has been adapted from Charles Warner's *Broadcast and Cable Selling* (Belmont: Wadsworth Publishing Co., 1986), chapters 4, 5.

Chapter 14
Other Aspects of Broadcast Sales

Other aspects of the broadcast sales field need to be considered: choosing a sales staff, audience information, and competitive media. Prospecting and qualifying clients are discussed more in depth in this chapter, also. Because the sales function is so important to broadcasting, the sales staff is most important to a station. People who desire to enter the field should look for certain characteristics in themselves. Personnel managers looking for prospective employees also should consider these factors a priority. Does the applicant like working with people and have leadership abilities? Does he (or she) have purpose, patience, empathy, perseverance, and drive? Is the eventual goal to become manager or owner? Is making money a prime consideration?

Take the smallest possible radio station as an example. If sixteen prospects are called on with high quality presentations each week, three or four should become clients after the salesperson gets the hang of the job. At about fifteen clients a month for three months, the station should have close to fifty clients running on the air. If it is a small market where each client can only afford to spend about $150 per month, that amounts to $7,500 billing. Smaller stations pay ad salespeople 20 percent, so the person would be earning $1,500 a month to start. At $18,000 annually, that is substantially more than an announcer at a small station makes and more than the program director. That is not bad for a first job, although it may take six months to reach that billing rate. At larger stations, of course, the dollar figures are higher for all staff members.

The amount each client buys can be increased on about 20 percent of the accounts by careful servicing. Such servicing and excellent salesmanship require knowledge — knowledge of broadcast advertising and knowledge of the clients' lines of business. The salesperson must remember that it is not a broadcast signal being sold, but the audience that is tuned to it! In other words, the benefit that audience can bring to a client's business is the sales product. One prerequisite for the salesperson is to know as much as possible about that product: the station's audience.

Audience Information

Audience survey companies provide some elementary statistical information about your station and most of the stations in the market. This information is called "the ratings." "Rating" has a specific definition: it is the percentage of the population in the ratings-area listening to a particular radio station. For television stations, it is the percentage of all television households in the ratings-area viewing a particular station at one time. Rating implies the percentage of all people in a certain category within the base population. If it is an average rating, it is the rating taken every quarter-hour for all the quarter-hours involved, divided by the number of quarter hours.

An eighteen-to-thirty-four age group average quarter-hour rating would be the number of people in that age group listening to the station for at least five minutes in the average quarter hour divided by the number of people of that age group in the ratings area. The "Total Survey Area" (TSA) includes all the counties covered by at least two of the radio stations from the central city. The "Metro Survey Area" (MSA) includes the more compact close-in metropolitan area and is more often the most useful to advertisers. Most of the stations licensed to a city cover the entire MSA.

The number of persons using radio at any given moment is called "Persons Using Radio" (PUR). PUR is usually at its peak during morning drive hours. For viewers, the "Homes Using Television" (HUT) is the number of homes with the television turned on. The HUT level is highest in television's prime time, 7 to 11 p.m. More people listen to prime-time radio (morning drive time) than watch prime-time television, according to the Radio Advertising Bureau.

Other Aspects of Broadcast Sales

The number of people tuned to a station divided by the PUR (or, for television, the HUT) is called the "Share." This is always bigger than the rating. The sum of all the shares for a given market in a given time slot should equal 100 percent, or all the people using radio. Shares can be used to sell a client time to deliver a large block of a special audience. Take outdoorsmen who listen early Saturday mornings when most other people are asleep. If a station has big shares early Saturday mornings, then that station may be an excellent buy for a recreational vehicle dealer or a fishing tackle store — the kinds of clients who try to reach Saturday early morning risers.

To get "Gross Rating Points" (GRPs), the station's average quarter-hour ratings are multiplied by the number of spots in the schedule. Agencies use GRPs to evaluate the overall effectiveness of a station's buy. The average number of people listening to a station per quarter hour times the number of spots in the schedule gives the "Gross Impressions," the total of all the exposures to people in an advertiser's schedule.

The total unduplicated audience in a given time period is called the "Cumulative Audience" (CUME). As many people tune around the dial, a different audience may be tuned into the station in the 7 to 8 a.m. slot than in the 8 to 9 a.m. period. People get up, get in their cars, drive to work, and shut off the radio. Then another segment of the population gets out of bed and starts the cycle all over. Of course, it is taking the pattern to the extreme to say that a completely new audience is generated every hour. Usually, many people are listening to the same station for several time periods in a row.

In its pop-music heyday, however, WABC in New York City was described by its program director as having a new audience every half hour! Beautiful Music stations tend to have shares of average persons about equal to their CUMEs. The typical News-Talk station, however, tends to have CUMEs much higher than its average person shares. That is, many different people listen for relatively short periods of time.

The average number of times the average listener, or the average television household, hears or views a commercial is called frequency. Sometimes it is called "average frequency." The concept is important because it refers to the number of times the average viewer or listener is exposed to the ad. Frequency is the gross impressions divided by the CUME, or the average quarter-hour audience times the number of ads divided by the net unduplicated audience. "Reach" is the same as the station's CUME and refers to the total number of persons reached during a schedule week.

Use ratings to calculate the cost per thousand (CPM). Simply take 0.001 times the gross impressions and divide into the cost of the weekly schedule. This number varies from $1 to $10 depending on how specialized an audience is involved. CPM-reach is the cost of the weekly schedule divided by a thousandth of the CUME persons.

In addition to knowing the demographics of the audience, it is necessary to know the lifestyle priorities of the listeners, or the psycographics. What are the typical listeners' or viewers' habits? How many cars does each typical family own? What is the average income per household? Where do they shop? How often do they eat out? How often do they go camping or fishing or mow the lawn? What brands do they buy? How many children do they have in school?

Qualitative information that the station has about its audience will help sell advertising. Marketing classes of nearby colleges may be interested in conducting a study to determine the lifestyle habits of a given area. WHVW, Hyde Park/Poughkeepsie, New York, had the question asked of their listeners: What newspapers do you subscribe to and/or read frequently? More than half the radio station's audience never read any newspapers. Armed with this statistic, the general manager looked up the largest local business which advertised exclusively in the area daily newspaper and solicited a slice of its ad budget. His sales pitch was that the client, by advertising on radio, could reach the other half of the people in the area, people they were missing with the paper.

Competitive Media

Another area that broadcast sales people need to become knowledgeable about is competitive media.

Radio has the greatest reach: people use radio alarm clocks, car radios, earphone sets while jogging, and so on. Almost everyone listens to the radio at least once a week. People select the format that appeals best to them in a broad range of demographic groups. CHR, AC and Country are the most popular formats.

Television is America's most persuasive medium. Most of the station's viewership is tied to the success of the network with which it is affiliated. Also, television ads cost more than radio.

Newspapers, however, are just ahead of television in ad revenue. Newspaper circulation has declined in the last decade, while the cost per column inch has gone up. The Radio Advertising Bureau notes that newspaper cost per thousand has risen at a dramatically higher rate than in broadcast media. In most metro areas, only about 30 percent of the homes receive a newspaper. While newspaper ads may have huge spaces to list individual items and prices, the medium lacks the excitement of the broadcast media. "Shoppers" are free newspapers containing almost all advertising and with a smaller readership than regular newspapers.

Dr. Daniel Starch of Westchester County, New York, does ad readership studies — the Starch Reports. The typical quarter-page newspaper is seen or noted by only about 18 to 20 percent of the publication's readers and completely read by fewer than 9 percent of the readership. RAB has rundowns of Starch Reports for most daily newspapers. These can be of great value in selling broadcast schedules to heavy newspaper advertisers. RAB has done extensive studies that show the effectiveness of combination media buys — taking some of the print budget and placing it in radio. The media mix of 50 percent print and 50 percent radio nearly doubled the sales for a Cleveland department store, according to an RAB classic study.

Magazines are sold by subscriptions and on newsstands or distributed by controlled circulation, free to qualifying agents of specific industries. Most magazines exhibit national advertising — usually to specific interest groups. Magazine ads are expensive, but they focus on specific target audiences.

"Out of home" advertising includes transit cards and billboards. Outdoor advertising gets only about seven seconds of reading time and the messages that communicate best have fewer than ten words. Most have three or four. They are good reminders but not good ads for product descriptions.

Direct mail is expensive, even with computer driven messages and mailing lists. Lists cost from $25 to $70 per thousand names, and postage keeps going up. Broadcast salespeople can make good cost-per-thousand comparisons with direct mail.

The *Yellow Pages* of the telephone directory are good for reaching people who are in the process of making purchase decisions, but these ads are getting expensive fast!

Still another area of a broadcast salesperson's knowledge should be in the client's area of interest. Each area of interest has its magazine or house organ, from *The Furniture Retailer* to *The Lumber Cooperator* to *The _____ Car Dealership*. Good clients can get the salesperson's name on the mailing list of the specialty magazines so the sales representative can study the problems faced by the client's business.

Most of these specialized publications have marketing sections so, except for the special sections, most of the magazine can be skimmed. Through one of these magazines, author Durfey learned of special hardware marketing thrusts for women to fix up their homes. He photocopied the article for use in a presentation for a substantial buy from a home center lumber and hardware dealer. Trends may be picked up faster from these specialized publications than from the general media.

One of the favorite topics of conversation for the owner or manager of a business is *his* business. If the salesperson has learned some of the special terms and trends involved in that business, intelligent questions can be asked and particular concerns probed. Listen attentively, learn the client's views on these trends and problems. The knowledge gained will place the salesperson in a much better position to deal with retailers in each line of business. Each such retailer will enjoy these in-depth discussions and will respect and like the salesperson much more. All this information gives a new depth to the meaning of prospecting.

Prospecting Ideas

The top prospects for a station are those whose marketing needs intersect with the audience's lifestyle characteristics. If the members of the audience enjoy planting vegetable and flower gardens, spring is the time to call on nurseries, seed companies, and lawn and garden equipment firms. If significant numbers of listeners in a lake or river area go fishing, perhaps a special program series with boat dealers, marinas, restaurants, campgrounds, and real estate advertising could be a match up. Does the station have a large audience of farmers? Then sell agricultural reports and detailed weather forecasts. Commuter-auto related businesses can be matched up with traffic report segments. Whether it is seasonal or not, prospect by matching the marketing needs of potential clients to the lifestyle needs of the audience.

Another way to prospect is by selling packages. Each local area has its interests, even passions. In northeast Oklahoma, it is football! In this kind of area, one possibility is to make up sports booster packages that sponsor local results and "Coaches' Corner" shows. The key is to make the tariff what the local retailer can afford, perhaps $100 to $200 a month for the three-month season. Cold canvass everyone in the area of influence of the school team, using a one-page flyer/contract that has a graphic of a player in action. The flyer can have game information on it as well as the contract items and a place for the business to sign up. Go door to door telling businesses about the sports booster package. Three or four sales should be made out of every ten calls. The trick is to see a lot of people! From 10 to 20 percent of those signed will continue to advertise on the station regularly if the service remains good.

Other promotional sales campaigns similarly may be built around the safety of school children, graduation, blood drives, community days, and county fairs. Each time an account is closed, even for special packages, send the client a thank-you card. Make service calls and keep on prospecting through selling. Another place to prospect is at the local service clubs and chambers of commerce. It takes time for the sales representative to get to know the merchant members and for them to get to know him. At least, the salesperson can get to know something of the members' businesses and can probably get an appointment with individuals from the club much easier.

The sales manager may point out an inactive advertiser file as a base for prospective sales. People on that list should be called upon regularly, three a week or so, mixed in with other prospects. Perhaps the only reason these people are not on the station is because no one has asked them to advertise lately!

Qualifying Techniques

Qualifying a potential client could result in closing the sale. Radio sales consultant Jason Jennings builds an entire sales method around a qualifying call. After an appointment for the call, Jennings has the salesperson interview the potential client. The questions have to do with the details of the client's business: How long have you been in business? How long have you been at this location? How did you get into this business? Jennings then has the salesperson find out the advertising details, such as what advertising media the business uses and what budget is alloted. Finally comes the question the salesperson is really after: What business problem do you have that, if you could wave a magic wand and make it go away, you would seek to solve first?

If it is a furniture store and the manager complains that carpet specialty shops have taken all the profit out of his once lucrative carpet business, the salesperson should sympathize with him but not stop at that. Ask what problem he would solve that something could be done about now. Suppose he admits that too many colonial-style beds have been purchased and fifty or sixty are sitting around taking up space. Ask how much moving all those beds out would be worth to him, and ask what the price per unit would be. Write this down and terminate the interview tactfully, casually saying something like this: "If we can come up with any ideas on how to move these beds, I'll call you."

Now the salesperson knows what kind of budget the business has to work with, and he has enough information to write ad copy. He can go back to the station and have the production crew make up the best straight copy and best humor copy that can be generated and cut it on a cassette tape. He can make up a written proposal for the amount of money the furniture store manager stipulated, say $1000, for a two-week saturation campaign at the station's lowest unit rate. Package the presentation, wait four days to a week, then call for an appointment.

Say, "We have been thinking about you since we talked the other day, and we believe we have come up with a way you might move those beds. When can we sit down and discuss it?"

Chances are he will be interested enough to confirm an appointment. When you meet with him, go over the proposal and play the two ads. Ask which one he prefers. If he says the humorous one, say, "I'm really surprised that you chose that one. I was sure you would choose the other one." (Say that no matter which one he chooses.) Then wait to hear how he sells himself on the one he likes. He will probably balk at spending the entire $1000 at once, but gently remind him that it is the amount he stipulated to get the problem solved. This saturation scheme, with up to three ads per hour, will work on most stations, because the entire CUME audience gets several impressions during the campaign. Use multiple versions of the same script theme to keep listener interest up. Once the client moves those beds, he will become one of the station's better advertisers.

One problem in qualifying clients is determining the media budget of a potential client. One help is that newspaper and outdoor agencies display their ads for broadcast salespeople, as well as the general public to see. Start a tally book to list clients alphabetically with the newspaper column-inch insertions recorded daily. Tally the space up weekly, then multiply by the applicable rate. Add this up monthly, noting big sales and pushes. At the end of a year, you will know a lot about a number of newspaper advertisers' budgets. The same scheme works for big users of outdoor advertising. Keep tallies on those also.

Keep a card file of all prospects. Get their birth date, anniversary date, grades of their children, and any special interests, such as sports preferences, political activity (if any), service club activity, and favorite charity. Then, if there is an advertising promotion for election results or football coverage, the salesperson can look over the cards and generate a list of clients who may be interested in the special event.

Set up a modular presentation sheet system. Get a cabinet with several shelves 9 by 12 inches per section to hold 8½-by-11-inch paper. Put rate card, coverage map, survey results, and station programming summary sheets in separate shelf areas. Whenever a client gets good results, have him write a letter describing his successful experience with the station's advertising. WHVW had about sixteen of these really great letters and placed four on a page, reducing the page to one 8½-by-11-inch sheet of paper with four letters on each side. Thus two sheets of paper provided eight success letters to feature in proposals. It would be difficult to put too much stress on how valuable letters of this kind can be in presenting the case for the station.

Such letters can take away most of the fear of failure that might block a closing. A prospective client sees that other businessmen have benefited, so he can too. Catalog all the success stories by business categories so they can be referred to in answering objections. Many clients benefit from broadcast ads but, for one reason or another, would not write a letter. Although a letter would be better, the salesperson can still tell the story of their success.

Develop an illustrated presentation paper for special events and seasons. Use a newspaper clip-art book to get flower borders for spring buys, harvest motif corners for fall buys and so on. This ready-made artwork dresses up, romanticizes, and makes timely the visual presentation sheets. Scale the proposed schedules to the amount the business can afford, then nearly double the amount as Plan A. Plan B is about what the salesperson feels the business can afford, and Plan C is about 60 percent of B. Do not propose any plan that would not work for the client! After a while, the salesperson will get to the point where he can tell how many ads a week it will take to get results for a client. Do not propose a schedule any smaller than this minimum.

If the clients are qualified carefully, their interests can be matched with specific ad positions such as news or sports or special music programming. Some stations prepare special programs to fulfill such interests — a homemaker's show for a sewing center, a recipe corner for a supermarket, obituaries for funeral homes, or birth announcements for diaper services. A station's program director may not like "too much clutter," but the smaller the station, the more likely such programs will generate income from local advertisers. Each merchant will feel that he has something special on the air. Get the client to commit for a full year if special programming such as this is created.

A seasoned professional takes about an hour to prepare the customer proposal sheet; select referral letters, coverage map, rate card, and station blurb and collate them into a binder; and create the copy for the speculation tape. It will take twice as long for the beginner to assemble and write these materials. Bill Payne, owner and manager of KTFX (FM), Tulsa, told author Durfey of a system he learned about at a national broadcasters meeting.

Payne said he keeps a thick spiral-ring notebook with him at all times. He writes down every phone call and every contact, and he makes notes on every interview — like an extensive diary — and he keeps a running account of the date and time with each entry. Durfey tried the system and found that when he was waiting for a doctor or dentist appointment or for a client, he could use a page or two to write spec copy or proposal packages. This uses time efficiently. Studies show that people waste more than five hours a week waiting in lines, in offices, or sitting in boring meetings. This is time that could be otherwise productive, and working on such a notebook is a great way to utilize this time.

The results of this couple of hours time will look to the client as if the salesperson spent a week or so just getting ready for the sales call. Concentrate on the client. Listen to him. The written proposal, the neat grooming, and the professional dress will give the salesperson an instant credibility. By courteous listening and well-paced explanation of the facts, trust is built. To paraphrase a Ziglar aphorism, "When people know how much you care, then they will care how much you know." The salesperson must let a client know that his position is understood and his success desired; the prosperity of his business, not just the selling of advertising, is your goal.

All of these preparations take time. Three preparations a day take six hours for the beginner. Allow an hour and a half for each interview. Use about five hours between 9:30 a.m. and 2:30 p.m., including a luncheon appointment. Make appointment calls between 8:30 and 9:30 a.m. Make service calls between 2:20 and 4:20 p.m. If an appointment is missed, make it up with an unscheduled call later. Preparations can be made evenings and weekends. The salesperson can plan to work sixty to seventy hours a week for the first year. After he gets the client list established, he can relax with a forty- to fifty-hour week.

Summary

With knowledge, stamina, and patience, in three years, the salesperson should either own a station, be making

$70,000 to $80,000 annually as a sales manager, or be managing a small station at about $40,000 a year plus perks. For someone who wants to become a manager or an owner, there is no better way than to create sales. In choosing a staff, the sales manager should look for leadership ability, a genuine desire to meet people, the ability to make a good impression, purpose or ambition, patience, and perseverance.

In addition to the above qualities, a good salesperson must "know the territory," as the salesman in *The Music Man* says. That includes information concerning the station audience's lifestyle, the competitive media in the area, ideas on how to find clients, and knowledge of qualifying techniques.

Chapter 15
Closing the Sale

All the preparation for a sale is worthless if the sale is not closed. How much is the commission on an "almost closed" sale? After the material is presented to the client, close! Along the way there are usually objections. The client may want to stall his decision, find a reason to buy, or show resistance so people will not think he is a pushover, or he may know almost nothing about what is being sold. People will buy something when they want it more than they *do not* want to spend money.

Zig Ziglar says there are five main reasons people do not buy anything: "These are no need, no money, no desire, no hurry, and no trust."[1] Need, desire, and trust must be proven to the client during the presentation. If objections arise in these areas, there are several ways to handle them. One way is to ignore the objection, particularly if the answer is included in the proposal.

The reply might be, "We will be coming to that point soon in the material you have in your hand," or "If we could hold that thought for just a little while until we get to the appropriate place, that would be fair, wouldn't it?"

Another way to meet objections is to turn them into questions, then answer the questions. "So your question is . . . ? Is that right?" If he says, "Yes," then answer the question. If the client is dogmatic, ask him to repeat his objection: "I'm glad you raised that question. To make absolutely certain I understand what you are saying, would you mind repeating it?" This calms the client down. Try to answer questions with facts and examples.

Another way to handle an objection is to ask the client if that is the only objection he has, or if there is another reason why the schedule could not be started soon. Then, when both objections are answered, close. A similar technique may be used when it seems the client has an unstated objection behind the one he is voicing. Perhaps his wife does not approve of any more advertising, or perhaps he wants to advertise some loser merchandise that he is stuck with and doesn't want to tell you about.

If you ask, "What other reason can you think of that would keep you from buying the package," the client will either blurt out the real reason or swallow the hidden problem and go ahead and buy. If the client is still adamant about a certain point, say, "I know just how you feel. Some of our better advertisers felt the same way until they learned the facts. And the facts are . . . ." Answer his objection with another example.

If he has tried the medium which is being presented, perhaps on another station, and had bad results, *do not knock the other medium or the other station!* Tell him, "Mr. Client, you are a smart merchandiser who knows the right items to offer at the right price and at the right time, and if you knew or if I knew that any single form of advertising would be 100 percent effective every time, we would both be millionaires, now, wouldn't we?" (Do not forget to keep smiling all through this presentation.)

Tell the client that there is no iron-clad guarantee that the medium will be successful for him this time, but say "Last year, Mr. So-and-So Advertiser sold out . . ." — and give him a success story as an example.

One final technique for objections is to turn them into reasons to buy.

"This is our slow season."

"I realize that, Mr. Client, but wouldn't this be an ideal time to get some people in here to reduce your inventory before you put out next season's goods?"

The ABC's of selling are: A = always, B = be, and C = closing. Always be closing. This refers to the technique of using trial closes. The first imperative is the salesperson's enthusiasm and expectation. *Expect* the client to buy. Go in knowing he is going to okay one of the proposed schedules, or more. Throughout the interview, picture the client enjoying the benefits of the station's advertising. Talk benefits, and say, "*When* those customers come in . . . " instead of "*If*" they come in. Paint a mental picture for the client of the benefits he will enjoy from the advertising.

Often the *assumptive close* is just a question such as, "We'll start your schedule Monday, then?" If he says, "Yes," hand him the pen. Or use a *choice close* with the assumptive close. "Should we start your schedule Friday or Monday?" When the choice is made, the client has bought. It is always better to give him a choice between something and something than between something and nothing. Ask if he would like Plan A better than Plan B, if he would like the straight or the humorous copy, thirty or sixty seconds, morning or afternoon drivetime, news or sports, and so forth.

The hardest close is when the client wants to stall. To prevent the stall of "I have got to talk to my wife," or to "my partner, boss, or accountant," ask up front in the interview if he is the person with authority to approve the proposal. If he says, "Yes," then answer, "I assume if you like what you see and hear and believe your business will benefit from what we have to show you, then your approval is all that is needed. Right?" If he answers, "No," to either of these questions, reschedule the appointment to a time when both parties can be present. Sometimes when a rescheduling is requested, the client will rethink his authority. After that agreement has been reached, the client cannot use this dodge at the end of the interview to stall or delay a decision.

Ziglar has a terrific response for the stall. It goes something like this:

"Efficiency experts and business people agree that the best time to make accurate decisions is when you have the necessary facts that are unclouded with any other issues of the day. This way you can be more certain that your thought processes are aimed at making the right decision, based on factual information which is fresh in your mind. Confused information or forgotten facts will almost always lead to a faulty decision. With this in mind, could we reason together for a minute to make certain you arrive at the correct decision. That is what you want, isn't it, Mr. Client?"

Other closing strategies include:

The summary close. This involves presenting a summary of the major benefits and the proposed schedule after the written proposal and the presentation. End with, "Shall we go ahead and schedule you for Plan A?" Sometimes this technique is combined with *the silent close*, which is not saying anything after asking for the order. Just sit silent, and after a while, the client will speak first, if only out of embarrassment. He will take the offer about half the time. The rest of the time the client will voice an objection, often in the form of a proposition. "I would buy your package if I could get the entire schedule to run on Saturdays only." The salesperson's answer should be, "Then I understand that if we schedule all your ads for Saturdays only, you will okay so many spots weekly for thirteen weeks at such-and-such price each?" If he says, "Yes," get the order signed!

The *I'll-see-if-I-can-get-you-on close* works when selling advertising time for an event or special, such as football games or sports booster slots, and several salespeople are selling the package. Ask to use the client's phone. Dial the station and ask for the traffic director. "Hello, Edna. This is Mike. I'm at Mr. Client's and he is interested in spots during the game Saturday. How many do we have left?" Pause, look at the client, and cover the phone. "She's looking it up!" Smile and uncover the phone. "Okay, Edna, hold that till I get back, will ya?" Then turn to the client and say, "I can save it until 4:45 for you. What do you say? Shall we have you as one of our exclusive sponsors?"

The *minor point close* involves trying to get the client's approval on a minor point in the presentation, for example, skipping Tuesday in the schedule and spreading the ads out on the weekend. If approval is forthcoming on this point, hand him the contract and pen and show him where the agreed upon choice is listed.

The *Ben Franklin close* involves summarizing the benefits of the package on one side of a piece of paper and all the reasons supporting the client's objections on the other. Use the prospect's help to fill in the paper: "You can see that the reasons to buy outweigh the reasons not to buy. That's fair enough, isn't it?"

The *Columbo close* is taken from the TV character played by Peter Falk, of course. Remember how the detective would complete an interview at a suspect's home, seemingly not getting what he came for? Then, with his coat over his shoulder and heading for the door, he would stop with his hand on the door and turn back. He would smile and say, "Oh, I forgot. Just one more thing!" The salesperson can do the same thing. If the prospect is not showing signs of closing, pack up and head for the door. With a hand on the knob, turn back, smile, and say, "I almost forgot. You like football! We have one more sponsor position left, and if you give me your okay today, we can fit you in!" Of course, with this close in mind, the topic of football sponsorship would not be mentioned during the interview. This close works twenty to thirty percent of the time, and that makes it worth trying.

A variation on the Columbo Close is the *What-did-I-do-wrong close*. To use this one, the salesperson reaches the door, turns, smiles, and says: "I respect your opinion, and I feel I could learn from this experience. Do you mind if I ask you one more question? Would you mind telling me what I did wrong? Where did I lose the sale?" The prospect more than likely will not be able to resist explaining. In which case, he will be open to be sold by answering whatever his objection was, or he will be more susceptible next time.

In getting the client's signature, do not use the words "sign" or "signature." People *sign* death warrants or *sign* for a loan. Ask the client to "okay the schedule here" or to "okay the schedule at the check mark."

Radio sales consultant Pam Lontos teaches a technique that uses a lot of questions in the presentation. Instead of telling the station's demographic target, Lontos has the salesperson ask the client what demographic the business needs to reach. Let us say that a bicycle shop is thinking about advertising. The prospect says that the company is advertising on a Hot Hits station to reach the teenagers, but the station the salesperson represents is Adult Contemporary and reaches the parents of the teens who use the bikes. Lontos believes that if the salesperson were to simply explain the demographics of the AC station, the sale would be lost. Instead, she says, the salesperson should ask who usually comes to shop for bikes. The client answers that the parents come in with the teens. Then ask who selects the bike. Usually the teenager. Finally, ask who pays for the bike? Usually the parents. Say, "Then the parents have something to do with the purchase of the bike?" When the client answers, "Yes," it is a perfect opportunity to say, "Wouldn't it make sense to attract parents? Why not tell them to shop in your store when their child wants a bike? Why not keep your schedule on the rock station but augment it with a schedule aimed at parents?" When the client agrees, only the details need to be worked out.

If the qualifying question already has been asked, the prospect is ready to be closed. Use more questions. "Would you prefer thirties or sixties? Start filling out the contract. Would you prefer a Monday through Friday schedule, or do you want to run on weekends, too?" "Would you feel that our Total Audience Plan (TAP) would fill your needs, or would you prefer only drive time?" Continue to fill out the schedule. Total it up, and when the contract is filled out, summarize in this manner: "Now, you said that you would like sixties in drive time, three a day Monday through Friday and five on Saturday, at four hundred dollars a week. Is that right, Mr. Prospect? Would you like to start those sixties on Saturday or Monday?" Put a start date on the contract and ask him to okay the schedule!

It is not possible to summarize all the great sales motivational material available to enquiring minds. Ziglar's book, *Secrets of Closing the Sale*, is a must for every aspiring salesperson or sales manager. A new book by Charles Warner, *Broadcast and Cable Selling*, is a good background in broadcast sales. The Pam Lontos videotape series of lessons on radio sales costs more than the books involved, but the techniques covered — when mastered — can earn many times the cost of the videotaped lessons in commissions during the first year! Jason Jennings has audio cassette material, and there are several other good broadcast sales consultants' materials and courses available. The successful broadcast salesperson is constantly studying to become better at a constantly changing and challenging profession. (Contact the Radio Advertising Bureau for information about these training materials.)

Broadcast Cooperative Programs

Broadcast co-op is a share-the-payment plan for retailers and manufacturers and distributors. The manufacturer or distributor pays all or part of the bill for ads that feature products made or distributed by the co-op entity. Facts on which manufacturers and distributors participate in co-op plans, and to what extent and with what restrictions, are contained in *Co-op Guides*. These guides are available from the Radio Advertising Bureau and its TV counterpart, the Television Advertising Bureau (TAB). The information these agencies provide is very valuable to the local salesperson. The usual co-op percentage is 50-50. That is, the manufacturer pays half and the local retailer pays half. These deals usually involve special copy being used that primarily sells the manufacturer's product, "available at such-and-such a store, address, city."

If this is the product the client wants to sell anyway, then this is a good deal for him. Most co-op plans are based on how much of a manufacturer's product a retailer purchases. Such a plan might reimburse a retailer for fifty percent of the cost of his broadcast flyte, a series of ads sold as a package, up to a limit of five percent of the cost of the product purchased by the client's business within a given period. Therefore, if an auto parts store orders $20,000 in parts from a major automobile manufacturer, the company will reimburse the local dealer for half the cost of local ads up to $1,000.

Co-op programs vary greatly. Some offer 100 percent reimbursement for local ads merely mentioning the product;

some offer only 25 percent on ads that are mostly for the product and have only a seven-second local address tag. Some offer reimbursement levels based on a percentage of purchases. Some have a fixed amount per unit sold, such as $200 per automobile allowance or five cents per box of soap, etc. Some plans are only for newspapers, some only for broadcast media, others for many media in a media mix. That is why a current co-op handbook is necessary to look up the present plan for each product. Often merchants have co-op packets from suppliers that they have never opened! The station salesperson may be the sole source of information on co-op plans for the clients, who actually may double their schedules during certain flytes.

The servicing required of the station is expanded with co-op clients. The usual billing procedure requires a copy of the script used, an affidavit of performance showing when each spot aired (with the copy which was used attached), and sworn to before a notary by the station manager. The bill also must be notarized. Some clients will want a higher rate billed to the manufacturer or supplier in order to get the reimbursement to cover the entire cost of the ads. This practice traditionally is called "double billing," but *stations lose their licenses for this practice, which the FCC calls "fraudulent billing"*!

Billing is complicated further when an advertiser, say a camera shop, legitimately combines several flytes during one time period for different product suppliers, such as Kodak processing and film, Cannon cameras, Nikon cameras, Vivitar lenses, and Bessler products (many of which have 75 to 100 percent reimbursement). In advertising like this, the bills must be handled separately for each supplier, as if this were individual company advertising for the period, each according to its own co-op plan.

The retailer must take care not to spend more of his co-op dollars than he has accumulated in his accrual account at the suppliers. The supplier may be contacted to give the accrual amount, based on a percentage of purchases. The retailer often has special claim forms to accompany the station's bills to send in for the reimbursement funds. In the meantime, the retailer should pay the entire bill to the station.

Co-op money can increase the billing for a conscientious salesperson and help increase a station's revenue.

Summary

There are a variety of methods to use for closing a sale. Experience will help a salesperson decide which closing method to use in a given situation; no close works with every prospect. Regardless of the method, the salesperson should *always be closing.* The "almost closed" sale is like the big fish that got away — neither one puts any food on the table or trophies on the wall. Cooperative programs provide a good source of potential revenue when the salesperson takes the time to study the *Co-op Guides* and apply the options to the local market.

Notes

[1]Ziglar, p. 28.

Chapter 16
Broadcast Sales Management

The sales manager is one of the most important people on the station's management team. The chief engineer provides and maintains the signal, the program director conceives and delivers the programming and promotions to create and sustain an audience, and the sales manager provides the income to drive the system by linking an audience to advertisers. The price to charge advertisers for each ad is printed on the station's rate card, and that price is arrived at through a circuitous route.

Rates and Rate Cards

There are various schemes for the construction of a rate card, but each card type lists its lowest unit rate, which is the lowest rate per ad charged to the station's most preferred advertisers. Establishing the lowest unit rate is the first step in creating a rate card. If the station has been operating for a time and the monthly operating expenses are fairly well known, then divide the monthly expense figure by 30 to obtain the daily operating expense, or the break-even point. For example, let us say it takes $500 a day to operate a modest-sized FM station that is on the air twenty hours a day. Divide $500 by 20 to get $25 per hour, the average operating break point. Now let's say that the programming department believes that no more than ten ads can be sold in any given hour without jeopardizing the audience retention factors. Thus at a lowest unit rate of $2.50 per ad ($25 divided by 10), the sales department would have to sell the station out, that is, sell every ad spot just to break even.

In practice, a station seldom sells more than 80 percent of its inventory (the total number of ads it wants to sell in a time period), because the station's need to sell certain ad positions may not fill the advertising needs of a potential client. Meeting the needs of advertisers with midday and evening positions is not as probable as selling out drive times. Therefore, a station should have no ad on the air priced less than $2.50 divided by 0.8 or $3.13 net. By net, we mean the price the station gets after all commissions are paid. To be safe on discounts and occasional agency commissions, that rate should be rounded off to $3.50.

If $3.50 is the lowest unit rate for a station with a $500 daily operating budget, the published rate must be higher. There is an old adage in radio broadcasting: Make nut by 10 a.m.!" The "nut" is the basic expenses for the day's operations. Let's say that gives four hours of drive time and forty availabilities, or spots for ads. This adds up to about $12 to $18 for each ad so that forty ads 80 percent sold out on any given day will add up to the "nut."

Nonpreemptible guaranteed position drive-time spot orders probably ought to go for $20 each, but perhaps these clients could be given a bonus of a $4 ad at 9 p.m. bringing the average spot price down to $12 and making the client feel better about the deal. Afternoon drive time could sell for a little less, say $12 each, with bonus spots at $4 each in the midday, giving an average spot price of about $9.

The critical question is: "What are the other stations in the area asking and getting for their ads?" If the merchants and agencies are conditioned to paying $40 to $80 per 30-second ad in this market, a $12 to $20 fixed position drive-time rate is not going to look like a bad deal, even on a "new" station. What is the cost per thousand? A quarter-hour audience of 4,000 to 10,000 listeners is needed to sustain these rates.

Simpler operations have a one-price rate card. At the $500 a day "nut" example, the one price probably would be $10 per ad, and every client would pay $10 regardless of where the ads are placed. Obviously, however, 6 to 9 a.m. and 4 to 6 p.m. will fill up first on a station. That would be fifty ads sold and the $500 nut reached.

The premise with a one-price card is that the station sales staff will be able to find advertisers who really want and need ads in time slots other than drive time. If the station has twelve to twenty-four year olds listening from 6 p.m.

to midnight, then record stores, concerts, jeans, colleges, and fast-food places may pay a flat rate to reach this audience. If young housewives listen between 9 a.m. and 4 p.m., then soap manufacturers, grocery stores, second-car dealers, fine restaurants, and clothing stores might pay the flat rate. Flat-rate cards tend to encourage the radio drive time to fill up first, then the middays and evenings with all sales out of drive time essentially more difficult to make. The flat-rate card is not designed as an aid in inventory control — that is, filling up all hours uniformly with sold ads.

Grid Cards Versus Traditional Cards

There are two popular alternatives that use the station rate card as a tool to make selling of various time periods easier. One is the grid card and the other is simply a traditional rate card. The traditional card charges more for drive times, less for midday, and much less for evenings. This card essentially maintains the cost per thousand and, as the listenership goes up or down, so does the price. Also, the quantity discounts and contract length discounts are figured in. For example, see Figure 16.1 for a sample rate card and notice that the more spots in the contract, the less each costs.

The alternative — the grid card — is operated by its inventory control aspects. The concept is that the lowest rate card or grid of prices is used during November and December in selling contracts for the following year to clients who commit to an entire year. Grid 1 (lowest prices) are used until about 50 percent of drive time is sold (and this is usually timed to occur between Christmas and New Year), then Grid 2 (with somewhat higher prices) kicks in. Station salespersons tell potential clients, "Better get your schedules in soon. As the number of ads per hour get scarcer, the price keeps going up. We are in Grid 2 already, and in a few weeks, the price will be going up again." Approximately 20 percent more is sold during January. The last week of January, another grid step is announced and, on February 1, the new, higher prices are charged for ten-month contracts. Approximately another 20 percent of inventory will be sold at these

Religious Broadcast Management Handbook

K+CR
TOTAL COMMITMENT RADIO
AM 1530

Wagoner
485-5153

P.O. Box 219 • Wagoner, OK 74477

Coweta
486-5827

RATE CARD # 2
JULY 1, 1985

COMMERCIAL RATES

Times/week	30 seconds	60 seconds
5	$8.00	$14.00
10	7.00	12.00
15	6.00	10.00
20	5.00	8.00

ADD 15% for NEWS or WEATHER

PROGRAM RATES

Times/year	15m	30m	60m
52	$25.00	$40.00	$80.00
260	20.00	35.00	70.00

GENERAL RATE POLICY

15% Agency Commission Paid to Recognized Agencies.

Minimum 3 month contract on all orders of programs.

Time run in a given month is billed the first of the following month, payment is expected by the 10th of that month.

higher Grid 3 rates. The rest of the year will be on Grid 4 and, just before Christmas, Grid 5.

The grid-card system for a station with a substantial audience tends to be an incentive for ad agencies and bigger advertisers to hustle up their fifty-two-week fixed availability spot buys so that the first grid rates will apply. For small market stations, the grid card is unduly complex. In all sizes of markets, the card will not bring in more per spot than clients are willing to pay or can afford to pay.

For television stations, the concept is the same as for radio, except that the price premiums are not on drive time but on the 8 p.m. to 11 p.m. period. The same cost-per-thousand-home concepts are true, in that the more viewers there are, the more the spot costs.

Regardless of the grids and station needs, the rate card cannot exact more from clients than "the market will bear." The economic conditions of the marketplace and the viability of advertising in that particular market will tend to settle media prices at a range where clients are comfortable with the rate and stations are operating reasonably profitably. Your station must seek to operate within that range to maintain saleability of ads and programs.

Co-op Management

Some manufacturers will share the cost of advertising with local merchants in co-op agreements.

In order to direct a sales department effort in co-op sales, a station needs to compile a sufficient supply of co-op information. This information would include the parameters of different co-op plans, such as the percentage of the local ad bill paid; percentage of accrual purchases that count toward the local ad pool for each merchant; and the dates the accruals start and stop; the name, address and telephone numbers for the contact person at the manufacturer's co-op coordinating location; a copy of the forms necessary for the merchant to collect his portion of the funds; and information on restrictions on scripts or specific copy that has to be used to qualify for the plan's rebates.

The sales manager may appoint a co-op coordinator. In smaller markets, the sales manager handles the co-op programs for the sales staff. The first step is to start a co-op information library (shelf) with the information cited above as a starting point. Buying a co-op encylopedia is a start toward building a co-op library; or, if a station belongs to the Radio Advertisers Bureau, that station will receive the latest information from a co-op encyclopedia to monthly co-op updates, including names and even success stories. The cost for a subscription to the bureau runs between $1,000 and $10,000 a year, depending on the billing of the station. The Television Advertising Bureau (TAB) has a similar service for TV stations at slightly higher costs. TAB and RAB will do about half of the co-op coordinating work for the station, but the other half must be done locally.

The local half of the co-op coordination involves an interface between the announced co-op programs and the local merchants. The sales manager or co-op coordinator goes over the library information and matches the published plans with the applicable area merchants. Sales people need to talk to clients concerning the brand names they carry. Also, clients should be asked if any co-op lists have been sent to them from product companies. If so, the salesperson can ask to borrow them and copy the important parts, especially the scripts. Discuss the accrual each client has with each supplier, and — if the client does not know these balances — one possibility is to make an agreement with the client to act as an adviser for him and handle his co-op advertising. The salesperson can offer to "handle all the paperwork" involved. To do this, however, he has to get the client's merchant number.

Once a survey of all the brands sold and a correlation is run determining the merchants who sell the various brands with the co-op plans, a list may be made for each merchant. Perhaps a clothing merchant has a T-shirt supplier, one or more jeans suppliers, socks and underwear suppliers, shoe suppliers, etc. who can support a modest schedule for each supplier, tagged with the client's address. By running four or five ads a day, one for each type of merchandise, and a couple of other ads — paid locally and not on the co-op — to extol the idea that all these types of clothing are available at one location, the co-op ads could be tied together.

The advertiser typically would pay half of the cost for the four ads — which would be the same as the price for two ads — and would pay the full price for the other two ads, meaning he actually gets six ads for the price of four. These co-op deals work well on four- to six-week flytes for a combination such as the one described above. The local merchant must want to advertise with the combination agreed upon and have the co-op accruals to cover the supplier's portion of the bills. He also must be willing to work out the details about three months in advance so the paperwork can be organized by air time.

Before air time, the salesperson will need to call suppliers' co-op agents and determine accrual amounts, check scripts and flyte dates, then verify conversations by letter with a carbon for the station files. On some occasions special scripts must be written and submitted to the co-op checkers and mailed back after approval. All this special approved copy must be produced before air date.

One organization that is a good source of co-op information, including approved copy and, in many cases, approved production of copy, is Kwikee Radio Broadcast System (KRBS), P.O. Box 786, Peoria, Illinois 61652 (Phone: 309-692-1530). This is a division of Multi-Ad Services, which also supplies clip art to newspapers and TV ads to television stations. The material is free to small radio stations and contains success stories, approved copy, co-op plan information, and contact names for co-op and advertising accrual information. The Kwikee kit contains only the national brands who have contracted with the system but really is a great starting point for small stations just beginning a co-op service for their advertising clients.

Advertising Agencies

Larger advertisers often have an agency to take care of all their advertising needs. The agency discusses a budget with the client at the beginning of the year (or the quarter) and then plans multimedia campaigns for the client. In working with agencies, stations need to get the proposals for clients to account executives and agency time buyers in advance, sometimes before budget review time rolls around, in order to get the flyte(s) approved and included in the budget for the client. Some agencies have absolute control once the overall budget amount has been set; other agencies go to the client with every change or difference in an iron-clad plan.

The process, at any rate, takes time and agency buyers seldom place buys on the salesperson's first call. Agencies measure buys against ARB's, or Neilson or Burch ratings and try to buy the least cost per thousand for the target demographic that they can accomplish for the client. They need a good reason to buy on a particular station. This means a station must be making presentations three to four months in advance of the season of the flytes — even more than a year ahead, in some cases — such as in November for ad flytes occurring during the following year.

A station needs a good rating or, at least, decent shares of target demographics, because agencies tend to buy only three or four stations deep in the ratings. This usually means, for radio, that they buy the top Contemporary Hits, top Adult Contemporary, top News-Talk, or Beautiful Music, and Country or some specialized format station that meets their client's demographic and/or programming needs. For television, it usually means buying the three network local stations and the top independent in the market. If a station is not described in the "safe buys" listed above, then the station representative has to get to know the buyers and account executives and find out what special promotion catches the fancy of the advertiser and his agency that could be included in the advertiser's budget.

Some station managers believe that if they do not have the ratings to be included in top demographic agency buying plans, then the effort at agency sales is not worth the trouble. Small stations in the suburbs have such low rates that the agency's 15 percent commission on the buy placed on these stations is not worth enough to the agency for its trouble.

The trend of the 80s is for several suburban stations that ring a metro area, each with only a fraction of the ratings of the group to band together in an *unwired network* that has much better suburban demographics than most of the metro stations. This network involves six to eight stations that team up to sell total audience plan spots from 6 a.m. to 6 p.m. The spots are sold at average local rates times the number of stations involved. This allows the unwired network to sell a package of spot on each of the stations for about the same price as one of the stations closer to the top of the ratings pack. Sold as "the best way to reach the affluent suburban population," the suburban unwired network may well be a much better approach to ad agencies than any single suburban station proposal.

Agencies take 15 percent off the monthly bill before they send the radio station the 85 percent that is left. Agencies also demand an affidavit billing procedure that includes a script of the copy used, a statement listing exactly when each spot was broadcast, and a notarized bill attesting to the price and placement of each spot.

Sales managers usually call on local advertising agencies and occasionally agencies within a hundred-mile radius. Many important products have advertising agencies in large metro centers, however, such as New York City, Los Angeles, or Dallas. It would not be practical for station sales managers to call on distant agencies, of course.

The National Representative

The national representative acts as a salesperson in distant cities, representing a number of stations to advertising agencies, usually in New York. Some representatives are members of a firm that has offices in every large city where big advertising agencies have set up shop. These organizations sell "their" stations in most agency cities, and the individual station's sales manager has the task of keeping the rep firm informed about station activities, promotions, publicity, scoops, awards, and trends. The sales manager discusses potential buys with the representative and helps him select rates, placement, and special programming for target products.

The sales manager supervises the billing procedures which are similar to the agency billing. Photocopies of approved copy (scripts), affidavits of performance listing the times for each ad during the preceding month, and notarized bills must be processed and sent to the agency and to the representative or his firm. When the bill is paid, usually with a check from the representative's firm, it will be decreased by the 15 percent agency commission and a 15 percent commission to the representative. For example, out of every $100 of the bill, the rep firm will receive $85 and retain 15 percent of the $85, or $12.75, and send $72.25 of every $100 billed to the station. Many stations charge $14 for a $10 ad "national rate" to compensate for the commissions that are deducted by agencies and station representatives.

Small stations cannot usually secure a national representative. Their billing and audience is too small to be worthwhile for representatives. Many national representatives think that $50,000 a year is the least they can bill on a given station (in their normal business placements) in order to make money on that station. Therefore, some of these unwired networks of suburban stations are banding together to retain a national representative. Their combined billing would be equal to a major station in the metro area, perhaps even equal to the largest metro stations in the center city.

The Sales Team

Where do salespeople come from? One of the most important tasks of a station sales manager is to recruit and train salespeople. One of the best places to find a broadcast salesperson is from a smaller station. Other sources of broadcast sales personnel include other sales fields. At least, that makes sure that the representative can sell something! Insurance debit-book salespeople usually do well in selling advertising because they have become accustomed to merchandising intangibles. In Oklahoma, soft-drink route salesmen are considered excellent candidates for broadcast sales due to their experience in competitive marketing. In Texas, former grade school teachers have proven to be good broadcast sales people, presumably due to their ability to communicate. Whenever you get your recruits, only about one in ten of those interviewed will be truly enthusiastic about selling ads for the station. About one in five can be trained to be a reliable professional addition to the sales force.

Various sales consulting firms determined in the late 1970s that female sales personnel make better performers than male recruits and recommended that radio stations should hire women. One way to attract applicants is to put an ad on the station itself. Something like: "Start an exciting career in broadcast sales. If you like listening to this station, then why not learn how to sell air time. Sales background helpful. Generous commission plan — or generous draw, salary, or commission. Bring resume in person to KAAA and fill out an application." The station receptionist accepts resumes and hands out applications and tells applicants that the sales manager will get back to them. He then looks over the applications, selects the most eligible, and invites them to a testing session at the public room of a local motel or a classroom at a school. The rest are written a "not at this time" letter. Only half of those invited will come to the "test."

The sales manager should tell the group about long hours, facing rejection, and so on, then announce that a qualifying test is going to be given. He also should announce that, if anyone feels this is too strenuous to consider, he or she should just go ahead and leave with no hard feelings on either side. At this point, one or two people probably will get up and leave. Then the test is administered. It should be a psychological preference profile test that measures aptitude for working with people. With the four or five who remain, schedule interviews for later in the week to judge the most suitable sales candidates.

Once the recruit is hired, the process of training begins. The Pam Lontos videotapes, mentioned in chapter 15 are useful, as well as the Ken Greenwood system of sales training. While in training, recruits should be encouraged to prospect new accounts, possibly from among friends or acquaintances. The recruits must learn the rate card, the meaning of coverage and ratings, and the details of the broadcast business — spot lengths, scheduling schemes, rates, promotions, contests, and special programming. The sales manager usually goes out with the new recruits on sales calls. The recruit usually is given a prospective sponsor or two to work up a package for each with script, proposal, etc. Then the manager goes along on the appointment to help close.

Sales training sessions should include mock pitches, or opportunities for trainees to try to sell advertising to a client played by the sales manager or a veteran salesperson from the station. The manager should have the sales crew keep a time diary with mileage notations, as well as a record of what was presented, what was asked, and what was sold. The asked column is the amount of weekly ads offered to the client and the sales column is the amount actually sold. The diary can be used to advise the trainee on how to better use his or her time. The same is true of mileage reports, which also are valuable for Internal Revenue Service records, and the presentation, asked, and sold numbers, can be of value to the station in increasing billing. A record of what is presented, to whom, and when is necessary so that the station can keep appropriate records. The asked-to-sold ratio indicates the competitive position of the station and the effectiveness of the sales team.

Training, in the form of regular sales meetings, should continue as long as there is a sales staff. One function of the sales manager is to raise the efficiency of the sales organization. The second leading cause of failure in the sales profession is the improper utilization of time. The sales manager presumably is the most experienced salesperson on the staff and the person to suggest better sales time utilization. The following breakdown has been proven effective for time management: prospecting, 10 percent; research and targeting, 15 percent; qualifying, 15 percent; presenting, 40 percent; servicing, 20 percent.

Each salesperson must make three to five presentations a day in order to close enough sales to make enough commission to be valuable to the station and support himself or herself. In order to make enough presentations, the salesman must prospect, research, target, and qualify the client; and, after closing, must service the accounts sold. The sales manager should have specific knowledge about the local market and each salesperson involved so as to adjust the priorities on time use for each area of sales production.

Sales Meetings

Part of the sales meeting should consist of training, no matter how sophisticated the sales crew has become. Let the people who have closed some sales tell of their success. Let one "big one that got away" story be told, and have the rest of the staff comment on ways that could have been used to close that account. Discuss prospecting observations such as new construction, sales signs seen, other media information, and stories in the marketplace. This will bring out all aspects of the market rapidly. Trade accounts. If one salesperson has tried five to seven times to get a certain client to close, see if another salesperson might have a better rapport. Perhaps that salesperson has a difficult client of his own with which to reciprocate. Use sales meetings to explain upcoming promotion campaigns and/or contests to the staff. Sometimes sales personnel input can help perfect a promotion and make it easier to sell. The sales manager collects the report sheets, comments on data generated, and tells the crew of any new developments.

Sales Ammunition

It is usually the sales manager's duty to design and reproduce material that helps explain how the station can help clients. In addition to the rate card and coverage maps, the sales manager needs to prepare a statement concerning the scope, goals, and philosophy of the station. This statement should be brief but describe the background of the owner and management people, the target demographic group, and the audience characteristics — or a profile of a typical listener. The statement should summarize recent contests and promotions and give a brief statement of results for the station. Also of value to sales is a breakdown of audience figures, a demographic breakout, audience numbers, cumulative audience figures, and turnover rate. If a general statement on reach and frequency can be constructed, the page could be very useful to clients in buying schedules on the station.

The sales manager also may design special promotional packages to accompany the other basic material. Packages should have artwork that illustrates the concept, the number of ads, the fundamental statement of the concept, and the cost for participating, along with the places to sign for the schedule and to make copy notes or to write the script. Station success letters should be continually recruited by the sales manager and arranged for salespeople to make up presentations from the appropriate letters and the pieces listed above.

Record Keeping

The sales manager should keep records of all potential advertisers and, of course, of all advertisers after the contracts are completed. The cards should be retained. Records often are kept on file cards. Various colors of cards are used to designate types of businesses, and tabs are used to indicate salespersons. A card should contain the birthdate of the client's representative, business anniversary date(s), his children's names and birthdates, key personnel's birthdates, the principal owner or manager's anniversary date and spouse's name, and the interests of the client — politics, sports, recreation, religion, and hobbies. Some notes on his style of doing business also could be indicated.

If this material is contained in a micro computer, sorting of birthdates and anniversaries can be done so that greeting cards may be sent on time. File cards should be indexed by political parties to organize any debate sponsors and "get out to vote" announcements. Sports interest cards should be indexed to get good prospect lists for selling sporting events, and other specials. Also all past sponsors of special packages, contests, and promotions will provide a ready prospect list for future sales of such specials. Without a computer, the sales manager needs to sort through all the cards to provide the information lists described above. He then makes these materials available to the sales staff in the meetings and checks up on personnel to make sure thank-you notes are sent after buys are scheduled and that special occasion cards are sent.

Collect the success stories, promotions and contests, and station prospects, put them together with projected plans for promotions, program specials, etc., and type up a one-page newsletter to distribute with the billing each month. This is to inform but also can be used as a sales tool to tell clients about specials they can add on to their present or regular schedules. Add a line suggesting that the regular salesperson be called for news of these specials. It is surprising how many customers will call for specifics.

Summary

The sales manager has one of the most vital jobs at a broadcast station: generating the revenue to keep the rest of the system operating. The job includes preparing the rate card which best suits the station and its advertisers, preparing ammunition for the sales staff to use with clients, and hiring, training, and motivating the sales staff. Other duties involve coordinating sales through cooperative programs, advertising agencies, and national representatives.

Sales managers from small suburban stations are finding that they can have more clout with advertising agencies by banding together in "unwired networks" to sell total audience plan ads. The sum is greater than the individual parts.

Chapter 17
Noncommercial Operations

Noncommercial/educational broadcast stations are licensed to schools, universities, and nonprofit organizations, and often are on specially designated frequencies. FM stations on the low end of the dial — from 88.1 to 91.9 MHz — are designated as noncommercial/educational stations.

Any nonprofit organization that believes it needs an educational station can apply for one on a frequency-find basis. If a search of the 88.1 to 91.9 MHz band shows that an FM station would fit in a particular area, the nonprofit organization can file an application for it.

Certain TV channels in the FCC TV Table of Assignments are marked by an asterisk indicating use by noncommercial/educational stations only. In many communities, UHF channels are still available for noncommercial/educational stations.

As the name indicates, noncommercial stations generally broadcast without commercials. Although the FCC recently has relaxed its rules concerning messages on noncommercial channels, the traditional concept of not running commercials on noncommercial stations still stands. The relaxed rules allow for a commercial identification of a donor business.

Raising Money for Operational Expenses

There are several ways to generate revenue for the operational expenses of a noncommercial station. The most obvious way is to ask for money on the air, but this technique can be overdone. Successful noncommercial stations have found that requests for donations once an hour in otherwise excellent programming that serves the needs of the community seem to be appropriate. WNET, Channel 13, in New York City, has used a sixty-second music filler after programs but before the top-of-the-hour station identification with a slide on the screen reading "Music to Write Checks By." WCIE, a 100kw Christian noncommercial powerhouse in Lakeland, Florida, also confines solicitation announcements to once an hour. Using too much of the program day to make requests for operational expense donations can backfire. Listeners and viewers who ordinarily would be contributors easily can be repulsed by excessive begging.

Many noncommercial stations reserve the extended appeals programming to annual or semi-annual telethons or talkathons. A UHF TV station in Portsmouth, Virginia, aired a fund raiser with the owner-manager as host some years ago. This led to the format of Pat Robertson's *700 Club*, where 700 people were asked to send operations contributions monthly. The viewers enjoyed the format so much that they asked that the ingredients of the program, minus the fund raising, be continued during the rest of the year.

Fund-raising events require an enormous amount of preparation, starting with a good mailing list. Offering booster club discount cards or program guides can be an excellent way to generate a substantial mailing list for the station's computer. Frequent use of request lines for music or prayer lines at Christian stations also adds names to the mailing list.

Prior to the telethon/talkathon, a direct-mail campaign and on-air promotions can attract attention to the special programming. Extra talent and crew must be lined up to produce the live shows. Often political figures and celebrities act as co-hosts with the station's air personalities. Christian stations may call in pastors from large area churches to be co-hosts. A tally board usually is set up, and the running totals and goals are broadcast often. Most noncommercial stations believe the long hours involved in organizing and executing telethons or talkathons are well worth it.

Some stations use an auction format for all their fund raising, while others have a telethon/talkathon in the fall and an auction in the spring. In an auction, merchandise is solicited from area merchants and celebrities to be auctioned off over the air to raise operating funds. Sometimes the auction is held in conjunction with a local charitable service organization, such as the Junior League, which supplies the considerable labor involved in soliciting for merchandise, collecting and delivering the merchandise, and completing a variety of auction-day jobs. Christian stations can draw on church members from around their communities to help, and they may get access to the churches' mailing lists, as well.

Under the revised FCC rules, noncommercial stations may describe the merchandise and tell the business names, locations, and slogans of those who supplied the items. This provides a greater incentive for area businesses to participate. As with telethons/talkathons, auctions should be promoted with direct mail and on-the-air promotions. Participating service organizations should also mail promotional material to their constituencies.

The day the auction is over is the day work starts on the next year's auction, with merchandise collection, indexing, and storage spread throughout the year. Some stations have a full-time executive to coordinate the auction effort.

Development Directors Find Underwriters

Instead of a sales manager, most noncommercial stations have development directors who "sell" the station to foundations and government bureaus. Sometimes the production costs of special programs of interest to segments of the population can be "sold." For instance, aviation weather forecasts could be presented on a grant from the Federal Aviation Agency, or an agricultural information program on a grant from the area agricultural cooperative merchants. News is often presented on a grant from area banks, financial market reports on a grant from a local brokerage house, and so on.

Many development directors package program production grants with print advertising in the station program guide. Such a guide might read: "This financial news program has been produced on a grant from the Merrill

Lynch Pierce Fenner & Smith, Inc., office at One Williams Center, with financial planning and assistance for every investor." The combination of the print listing and the broadcast identification of the grant source is essentially sold for informational programming that probably would be broadcast anyway.

This process is called underwriting, and the cost of production includes the cost of the station's operation for the time slot during which the program being underwritten is broadcast. If all the station's programming is similarly underwritten, then all the operating budget is covered by the various grants.

It is possible for a station to have all of its operating budget underwritten, but it is not probable unless it is a religious station. Religious noncommercial stations that broadcast a lot of teaching tapes are not allowed to sell air time to the participating ministries, but they may prorate the operating budget throughout the number of hours of broadcasting for the month.

For example, let us say that the operating budget, including debt retirement and equipment depreciation schedules, is about $21,000 per month or $252,000 per year. At thirty days per month, that amounts to $700 per day, and with a broadcast schedule of twenty hours per day, the prorated cost to broadcast one hour is $35. Therefore, for the month in question, a ministry with a half hour program would be charged $17.50 a day for the program, plus tape handling and postage charges — probably about $20 per day for the broadcast of each half-hour program. If five hours of the broadcast day features taped programs, then 25 percent of the operating budget is covered by the taped programs. Thus, if $69,000 is raised in the auction, $60,000 comes in from the talkathon, and $63,000 comes from the taped programs, then about $60,000 or $5,000 per month needs to be raised through underwriting in our example.

At religious noncommercial broadcast stations, some of the underwriting may come from Christian merchants and from the area's larger fellowships or church organizations.

Perhaps blocks of popular Christian music programming could be underwritten by some of the area's larger church youth groups, with members being interviewed and acting as deejays. The church's activities could be mentioned every day during that time slot.

The bottom line is that these methods raise operating capital to support the station's expenses, but the noncommercial station has *grants* instead of *sales, underwriters* instead of *sponsors, program guides* instead of *promotional pieces.*

Development directors need marketplace experience just like commercial sales managers need street experience in sales. Involvement with religious organizations such as the Full Gospel Business Men's Fellowship International or service organizations such as the Rotary Club and Chamber of Commerce is a good way for development directors to get to know potential underwriters and volunteers for fund-raising events.

Dealing With Volunteers

Some noncommercial broadcasters recruit church members, college students, or housewives to volunteer as crew members for television or as announcers, deejays, or newscasters on radio. In many instances, you get what you pay for. It is difficult to compete with slick commercial stations with a noncommercial radio sound that has different voices and personalities in a haphazard, whenever-they-have-time schedule. TV camera and studio crews need time to coalesce as a group, and training is apparent on the air. For a professional look and sound, hire people who are committed to be part of a professional team, people who will give the station a competitive edge even though it is a noncommercial station.

Keep volunteers in the mail room, helping the receptionist, answering the phones, calling people to ask them to participate, helping with the computer, moving scenery, and generally helping employees. Volunteers often are reliable as news stringers, especially if they regularly attend certain meetings anyway. They also work well as school or church reporters.

If a volunteer maintains a long-standing relationship with a radio station and wants to move into more professional duties, then a special pretaped program might be appropriate.

Many large noncommercial stations have volunteer coordinators to act as managers of the unpaid help. The largest of such organizations have application forms. They develop references and a file on each potential volunteer to determine the character and background of each applicant and to screen out any with undesirable behavior patterns. This is especially helpful if volunteers are to handle prayer line or counseling line telephones. Generally, volunteers need to be trained for their duties, oriented to the goals and purposes of the station, and given a list of management personnel to understand how the chain of command works. Volunteers can be an excellent extension of a broadcast ministry when recruited and managed with care.

Summary

Noncommercial/educational stations do many of the same things as commercial stations, but they are called by different names. Noncommercial stations have *grants* instead of *sales*, *underwriters* instead of *sponsors*, *program guides* instead of *promotional pieces*, and so on. Operational expenses for noncommercial stations are raised by soliciting donations, conducting auctions and telethons/talkathons, underwriting programs, and prorating to outside programs. Volunteers can be a great asset to a noncommercial station if they are recruited with care and trained well.

Part Six

Management: Behind the Scenes

Chapter 18
Personnel and Program Management

Broadcast stations are licensed by the federal government in the public interest. The FCC has determined that failure to be an Equal Employment Opportunity employer is against the public interest and can be hazardous to your health!

Equal Employment Opportunity (EEO) implies a very carefully implemented hiring-recruiting procedure. Most EEO programs have an on-going recruitment regimen. Many stations regularly send out general letters to colleges and universities with curricular programs related to the employment skills sought in new employees. These letters tell the academic department chairpersons that the station is an EEO employer and that the station from time to time solicits applications for certain positions. These are described along with the qualifications desired for each. When an opening arises, stations announce the opening and qualifications to each academic department and solicit applications for that specific opening. Such letters are sent to community centers in minority communities and to any ethnic schools or colleges within the listening area of the individual station. A complete record of all letters sent, to whom, and any applications received, must be kept on file to demonstrate compliance with the FCC's EEO measuring stick.

FCC Guidelines for Minority Hiring Practices

The FCC guidelines for minority hiring practices apparently are based on the ethnic population data for the area the station serves. Let us say a given broadcast station serves the "Metro City" area. The latest U.S. Census Department figures show the area's population demographics as 15 percent black, 12 percent Hispanic, 3 percent Asian-American, 5 percent "other," and 65 percent Caucasian. The

EEO employer ideally is supposed to have the percentage of minority employment equal to the percentage of that minority within the population of the station's coverage area. What is more important is that the government expects *at least half of these minority employees to be in management positions!*

Management positions in broadcasting include traffic director, music director, program director, promotions director, productions director, news director, public affairs director, film director, and chief engineer. The word "manager" often is used interchangeably with the word "director" in the foregoing titles. Most directors or managers are paid on an "exempt-salary" basis, that is, other than hourly. Exempt or salary employment status is defined by the U.S. Department of Labor as those supervisory employees who spend more than half their work week supervising the work of others, and whose work week varies in the number of hours spent working, and who are not eligible (or are exempt from) the overtime pay provisions of the labor laws.

Exempt personnel must be paid at or above a minimum rate. Although the amount escalates from year to year through inflation, in the mid 1980s the threshold level was $155 per week. The work week usually would not exceed 45 hours, but it could be much shorter. Small market stations must be very wary of these exempt rules in assigning duties to supervisory employees who have exempt status. One of the possible problems involves radio program directors who are also disc jockeys. These people should have deejay shifts shorter than twenty hours a week but should have more than twenty hours a week operating in the program director role in order to comply with the Labor Department rules. Also, in smaller market TV stations, the chief engineer may not be an operator or switcher more than half the work week.

Referring back to the Metro City demographics, if a station in that area has twenty employees, three should be black, two or three should be Hispanic-Americans, one or two should be Asian-Americans, one should be an "other," and the rest should be Caucasian. Of the seven to nine minority employees, about four should have exempt supervisory positions to meet the guidelines.

Until quite recently, the FCC has required stations to file an Employment Report Form enumerating the number of employees in various broadcast categories and the number of minorities in each category. Stations that failed to meet the guidelines (quotas) were in jeopardy of being designated for a hearing on why their licenses should be renewed or, at least, they were asked for an explanation.

As recently as 1979, the FCC required all transmitter operators to have passed a rigid examination for a "Third Class License With Broadcast Endorsement" in order to sign the transmitter log. The Element 9 test, or Broadcast Endorsement exam, was so difficult that only about half of those taking the test passed it the first time. When minority group applicants were screened for most radio jobs, they were told, "You must have the FCC license. Go and pass the test." Those with poorer educations flunked the test in greater proportion than the overall dismal pass rate for the test. Thus, when stations were admonished by the commission for not having enough minority employees, the stations replied, "You require employees to have a special license in order to be employed, and no minority applicants have met the commission's own qualifications."

In the FCC's political wisdom, the requirements for operators have been relaxed so that the applicant merely needs to sign a registration card and send it to the FCC in order to be certified to operate transmitters. Now it is up to the management of each station to ensure that each operator knows how to read meters, knows applicable rules and regulations, and knows how to keep the logs or records necessary for compliance with the station's mode of operation. The qualifications of employees therefore are up to the individual station's discretion and no longer subject to FCC testing. Let the employer beware!

How to Interview Applicants

Suppose a program director has a deejay opening coming up and has sent out recruitment letters to minority organizations and colleges in the area. Now the interviewing process begins. He may ask all applicants for a resume, photo, and audition tape (an air check is best). In this way, the program director may be able to determine whether the applicant is a minority without asking for race on an application. The difference between an air check and an audition tape is that an air check should be an unedited tape taken right off the air, but with most of the music edited out, while an audition tape is a showcase piece, well edited and perfect. If an audition tape is submitted full of mistakes, the person's work attitude is severely in question, as are his or her abilities!

The EEO station should have a sign or poster explaining that the station is an equal opportunity employer displayed in plain sight in the reception area. The application forms should not ask the age, race, or religion of the applicant! The interviewer can estimate the race and age by inspection at the interview but may not use that information for discriminatory purposes.

After listening to the audition tapes, the best three or four applicants are called in for the program director to interview. The program director cannot ask female applicants whether they are planning a family or how they plan to juggle career and mothering duties; or, if they have children, he may not ask what their day-care plans are. Questions like that are out of bounds at an equal opportunity interview. The program director may, however, ask career development plans such as, "We are a smaller station. How long in your career plan do you see yourself at this market level before you will need to progress to a larger station?"

Since the program director may not ask questions concerning religion, how does a Christian broadcast station assure that its employees are believers? One large well-established Christian broadcasting organization asks the usual prehiring and job-related questions, then asks, "Now, John or Mary, tell me about yourself. What are the most important things in your life?" This is an opportunity for the applicant to give a testimony or to be a witness. If the applicant misses the cue, the next candidate of equal performance criteria who does not miss it is hired!

In its pop music heyday of the late 1960s or early 1970s, WHVW in Poughkeepsie had a fantastic sound with energetic, enthusiastic young announcers whose talent often shone through as if it were a 50kw metro station, although it was only a 500w daytimer. There was a secret to how such good talent was recruited and retained. WHVW established a reputation for general excellence, good ratings, and recognition as a nationwide trend setter in innovative programming for the size of the station. The contests were fun, and the listeners loved the station. When there was a vacancy, nearly a hundred tapes would pour in. The program director interviewed the brightest up and comers with little experience but the greatest "smarts" and most dedication to the industry. He would tell them that the pay was just a little better than the market average starting pay, that the format was strict, but the opportunity to learn the intricacies of the format was great. Career planning was discussed at length. The "graduates" of the program were discussed, such as Johnny Donovan of WABC, New York. Then the program director asked, "Where do you want to go from here?"

After that, an unofficial bargain was struck with the best applicant: "If you will stay here without looking for another job for one full year, and study programming and develop your talent to its very finest, we will find you a bigger job in a larger market." Dozens of bright young talents gave their very best. Some stayed for two years, but all were placed in better positions in bigger markets when management and the applicant agreed the time was right for a move.

The station positioned itself in the industry as an excellent training ground for enthusiastic young talent on the way up and thus received the benefit of the excellence and enthusiasm on the air that electrified the listening audience and continually propelled the station into high ratings and saleability. Stations with such a hiring perspective and policy with regard to the career goals of potential employees may well attract and employ the best help.

Small-Market Exemptions and Training

Once hired, the new employee must be paid at least minimum wage and time-and-a-half for any hours more than forty a week, except in "small-market stations" where control-board help may be paid at the regular wage. This arrangement is called "the small-market exemption." Many smaller radio stations have enjoyed this exemption for announcers by being outside the top hundred markets, but recently have been included in the expansion of a metro market to surrounding developing counties. When the county in which the station is located is contained in a Standard Metropolitan Statistical Area (SMSA) rated in the top one hundred SMSA's, the station loses its small-market exemption, although it may be located in "an adjacent county to the big city." Many small-market exemptions have been lost in this manner.

Some rural and/or smaller broadcast operations may carry the training aspects of giving beginners some experience a step farther than the WHVW illustration. These training arrangements involve cooperation with various agencies. Your state Department of Labor may have a special program for hiring the handicapped. A large part of most broadcast operating positions involves sitting at a switching center and pushing buttons on a time sequence pattern and occasionally talking. Such operators might well be wheelchair-confined providing that the operating positions are accessible to the wheelchair. In such instances, the government has been paying between 50 and 100 percent of the cost of training handicapped persons in a program that will lead to employment — and that percentage includes the salary of the trainee.

Another aspect of the Labor Department's training program is training of school dropouts and the chronically unemployed. If participating in these programs, broadcasters must be very careful to accept potential employees who have the best aptitudes and attitudes for broadcasting and to be certain that the station's expanding staff can absorb the employment of such applicants.

Another source of trainable employables is cooperation with area college and university internship programs. These internships vary in many aspects. Some programs prohibit the student being paid, while others encourage putting the student on the payroll. It is usually beneficial to meet with school officials and discuss the requirements of having interns at the station. When junior and senior students are involved, the station may be able to use them in news, production, programming, or sales roles, as well as in operating roles. In many operations, it is not necessary nor is it even the policy to hire any of these interns after graduation, but the self-selection process of observing and evaluating the interns may turn up some excellent possibilities for later hiring. Christian stations located near Christian colleges with communications programs are especially fortunate if they can cooperate in internship programs where the students are predisposed to the objectives of Christian broadcasting.

Employee Files and Forms

No matter how the employee, trainee, or intern is recruited, and whether or not that person is paid, the first thing the program director or group leader needs to do is establish an employment file for that person. Included in the individual employee folder should be the original application for employment, training, or internship; the W-4 form from the Internal Revenue Service, which includes the employee's selection of the number of deductions and Social Security number; and information on time cards and sick days, in case any are job related. If any illnesses are job related, they must be summarized and reported periodically for the Occupational Health and Safety Administration (OHSA) using forms provided by the agency. Keeping such information in each employee's file enables the station to file or post the proper OHSA forms correctly when required each January.

Accurate payroll records also must be maintained for both IRS and Labor Department purposes. The deduction of a little more than 7 percent from the employee's gross pay is matched by an equal "contribution" from the employer for Social Security. A chart with the pay levels and number of claimed deductions gives the amount of federal tax to be withheld from the gross pay and a similar chart is used for deducting state tax from the gross income. The typical employee's paycheck is 15 to 20 percent lighter than the gross pay and, by the time the employer pays for unemployment assessments and matches Social Security deductions, the employee ends up costing the station about 15 percent more than the gross pay. These depositories, as the payments from employers' accounts to the correct government accounts are called, must be made by the fifteenth or by the end of the month following the month in which the paychecks were written.

It also pays to have performance reviews in the employee folders as well. This not only includes notes taken from the control room discrepancy reports, but also special commendation memos. All notes of mess-ups as well as triumphs should be in the pertinent employee folder. In a smaller station, employee advancement is usually obvious, but in larger operations, only carefully maintained files will sometimes allow supervisors to discern the proper advancement for the appropriate people. One source of data involves the completion of the program director's report forms for radio.

Report Forms: Technical and Personnel

The program director's report form is divided into several sections: music, news, public affairs, personnel, and technical sections. The technical section of the form provides a system for informing the chief engineer and the manager about equipment malfunctions. What better monitoring of equipment performance is there than to have deejays and newspeople note when machines misfire or string tapes fail to play or records skip or sound bad? These are written up on a "discrepancy sheet" which the program director scans a couple of times a day. Many of the problems involve a minor adjustment or cleaning and are easily rectified by the program director.

Each operator should clean all the cart heads — and at a religious broadcast station, all the tape heads — when going on duty. Engineering should provide the solvent, cotton swabs, and instructions for this exercise and note the entries in the discrepancy sheets as to who has performed this detail. The operator or program director must occasionally clean the rubber pinch roller on a slow running cart machine, repack a wayward cart with tighter winding, or adjust the stopping mechanism inside a "stuck" cart. Occasionally, surface dirt and junk must be cleaned from a phonograph needle to clear up the sound from the turntable. In nearly half the technical discrepencies, the problem is solved with some cleaning or minor adjustments.

Maintenance details should be noted. Problems that center on certain machines repeatedly or on given personnel shifts in any pattern may point out to management and engineering that certain machines should be replaced or that certain personnel are harder on equipment than others. But, above all, the technical portion of the report forms provides a conduit of communications to the engineer. One chief engineer told his program director, "I couldn't fix it if I didn't know it didn't work!"

The personnel section of the program director's report form gathers the attendance and sickness information on all of the employees in the program department. The manager will transfer this information to the employee files.

Summary

When station management understands the intricacies of minority hiring rules, the possibilities of screening out inefficient employees through proper interviews, the possibilities of receiving legitimate aid with training salaries, the importance of keeping equipment clean, and the vital importance of keeping proper records in all these areas, station management is then well on the way to achieving a successful, well-run establishment in compliance with FCC guidelines.

Chapter 19
Office Management

The key to internal communication effectiveness is an efficient and professional station office staff. At a very small station, the office staff also may be the station operators, either while they are disc-jockeying or while automated programming is on the air. In larger stations, the office staff may be more numerous than the on-air staff. The areas that must be properly attended to at any broadcast station are: (1) telephone messages, (2) copywriting, (3) accounts payable, (4) payroll, (5) traffic, (6) accounts receivable, (7) maintenance.

Telephone Messages

The success or failure of a station can literally turn on the staff's ability to take good telephone messages.

Few things are more frustrating to a salesperson or sales manager than to get a message that reads, "One of your clients called." Which client was it? What is the telephone number? Was a problem mentioned? What person from the client company called? The sales staff usually is out on the street, so the people who take telephone messages need to find out who is calling and what the call is about before telling the caller that the salesperson is out. "May I tell him who is calling and what it regards?" would be a good phrase to use. Then tell the caller, "Mr. Salesman is out right now. If the problem needs immediate attention, we will try to locate him and relay the message." This is why each person on the sales staff should leave the best possible itinerary with the office staff, or wear an electronic pager.

Copywriting

One of the critical roles of the office team is copywriting. At some stations, salespeople write their own scripts, while in others there is a staff copywriter. The copywriter's duties include taking the copy notes from the sales staff and writing copy for either live delivery or for production. Some stations have the production manager write the copy for produced ads because he or she knows where appropriate production music and sound effects cuts are located and is familiar with their content.

The rule of thumb in writing copy for production is to get the idea or premise of the spot, then look for production elements to fit the idea. Once the music bed with the right mood and tempo is located and/or the appropriate sound effects found, then the ad is written with the tempo and timing of these elements in mind.

Straight copy uses 60 to 70 words for a 30-second ad and about 125 words for a 60-second ad. Sound effects take time, and the word count must be reduced to accommodate the time to include these sounds. Also each music bed has its own distinct staging. If the music has a pleasant, mood setting opening you want to emphasize, you may not want words covering it. The same thing applies if the ending of the music is strong. Therefore, even with music beds, the number of words in the copy must be reduced when music emphasis is desired.

The most effective ads are written to communicate on both the logical and emotional levels. Unless the ad is deliberately zany and off-beat, it must make logical sense to the audience. The listener or viewer must be told how to save money, enjoy product benefits, get relief, attain prestige, or meet needs.

The copy also should have an emotional appeal, which is often achieved by matching the mood of the music bed or by injecting humor into the copy. Sometimes the emotions can be touched by using a short drama for the ad. Romantic emotional appeals can be achieved by matching the tempo of the words with the tempo of the music. Think emotional. Use emotional words. Use alliteration and rhyme. Use a romantic voice. The voice, copy, and music create a romantic emotional appeal, while the words state a logical reason for the listener or viewer to buy. Extreme contrasts between mood and logic can yield effective humorous cuts.

Sometimes when writing for production, the writer needs to listen to the music over and over again while writing and editing the copy for a spot. At first, it will probably take about an hour to write a spot. Later on, after a copywriter has some experience, the copy for a script will flow out of the typewriter every few minutes. Even the experienced copywriter needs to establish a premise or copy platform on which to stage the details of the persuasion. There is a certain mood to the copy and a good copywriter needs to know the lifestyle of the listeners and viewers in order to paint a picture in their minds of themselves enjoying the benefit of the sponsor's product or service.

Copy on a station needs to exhibit a variety of styles and approaches so that the total station sound includes dry copy, music bed productions, minor cuts, testimonials, dialogue and skit copy, as well as various announcer's voices on the air. Copywriters and producers need to keep track of the music beds and effects used in each ad and also record this information in the client's file, so that when a given client asks for different copy on the same music bed or on one with a similar effect, the station can find the sounds easily. Sometimes a log book is kept in the production room for this purpose.

Copy for local TV is written essentially the same as radio copy, except that the visual element also is kept in mind. The copy is written and produced as a radio spot and dubbed onto a videotape then appropriate pictures are edited to the audio.

The quality of production is one aspect of a great broadcast station. Cleaner copy, excellently executed, gives sales personnel an extra dimension of value to sell. Some stations sell well-produced schedules with the stipulation that the ads can be used for a unified campaign on other stations. Often the production *and* the ad flyte on the producing station cost less than the price of production at a specialized production agency. Several small radio stations have added some graphic arts capability and TV production equipment to their creative copy departments and become full-service agencies for their better clients. A great copy and production department is a tremendous asset to a station.

Accounts Payable

The accounts payable department varies in size from a few duties added to the job of a secretary, receptionist, or office person to a full-sized staff in bigger stations. Accounts payable refers to the station's organization for paying bills. Almost every station has bills for ASCAP, BMI, and SESAC fees, utilities, lease or property payments, insurance, printing, and debt retirement, as well as electronic or engineering parts and labor. These bills are sent at varying times, some with penalty fees, some without. Someone needs to be responsible for paying these bills on time but not too early. Paying just at the end of the thirty-day grace period allows the station's collections to build up.

Payroll

The payroll is a bit more complicated. The hourly wage multiplied by the number of hours worked (up to forty) yields the gross pay for each employee. One and one-half times the hourly rate is added for each hour worked more than forty in the standard work week. The gross pay for each employee is entered into the payroll records. Then the employee's Federal Insurance Contributions Act (FICA) percentage (also called Social Security) is deducted and the federal withholding tax is calculated from a chart with the gross pay and the number of dependents listed. A similar chart is used to deduct state income taxes. These charts use the dependent information listed by each employee on an Internal Revenue Service (IRS) W-4 form. Also list any other deductions authorized by the employee, such as optional group insurance or savings bonds. The gross pay less all the above deductions yields the net, or take-home, pay.

A time of reckoning comes once a month when the Federal Depository must be paid. Due on or before the fifteenth day of the month for the preceding month, the Federal Depository 941 check includes the employee FICA deduction plus the employer's portion of the FICA tax along with the federal income tax for each employee. Accompanying this check should be a Federal Depository form that has the company name and identification number. It also should indicate which taxes are being paid and for what time period. The check and the form should be taken to your bank, which acts as the depository for the government. Be sure to get a photocopy of the form and check to prove you paid the taxes. The bank forwards the funds to the government.

At the end of each quarter, the IRS sends a form that looks a little like a personal income tax form, but it is for reporting the 941 and the 940 Federal Unemployment Tax Administration (FUTA) taxes. Most small stations only need to pay 940 taxes once a quarter using a form like the 941 tax form. The report summarizes the payroll deductions for federal withholding taxes for each quarter. There are fines and penalties for paying late or filing the form beyond the deadline.

Each state has separate payroll deduction methods and instructions. Many states have a state income tax and employer fees for unemployment insurance. These are separate quarterly report forms for most states.

Instead of handling payroll in-house, some stations arrange for their banks to take care of all the payroll functions for a small fee. Some stations hire a certified public accounting firm to do the payroll and a summary of accounts receivable and a corporate balance sheet each month.

Traffic

The person responsible for traffic at the station has the task of taking each contract from the sales staff and seeing that the clients' ads appear on the station schedule, or log. The log is a daily listing of programs and advertisers in chronological order. The air personnel use the log to determine the order of elements to program. After each ad is aired, the announcer usually checks off the sponsor's entry in the log. At the end of each month, traffic goes over the logs and tallies up each advertiser's number of spots aired for the month for accounts receivable.

Accounts Receivable

Traffic determines the number of spots aired, which is compared to the contract to verify that the client got all the agreed-upon spots aired. Then accounts receivable prepares a bill to send to the client on the first of the month following the month during which the ads were aired. Any amount still owed from ads airing in months previous to the month normally being billed is listed on the bill as being past due. Once the bills are mailed, the traffic person looks for checks to arrive and credits each client's account when the money arrives.

This billing process gets more complex when affidavits are required. Co-op and agency accounts must have a listing of exactly which times each ad ran. The listing of the exact run times is typed on a special station form called the "Affidavit of Performance," which must have the notarized signature of an official of the station. Also included are a script of the ad and a statement certifying that the ad ran on the station at the times indicated on the attached affidavit. This copy is also signed and notarized. Usually two or three copies of the bill, the affidavit, and the notarized copy are sent to the client or the agency involved. These must be sent on the first or second of the month following the billing month.

Some stations have been known to mail their billings on the tenth or fifteenth of the following month and then wondered why their collections were slow. Businesses tend to pay bills in the order they arrive, so it is important to get the billings mailed on time.

Most broadcast stations solve the problem of an end-of-the-month crunch by using a computer system to configure the logs and process the billing, complete with affidavits. Joel Rosenblum of Generic Computer Systems says the usual time needed to enter information into the system is about five minutes per contract. Each time a contract comes in, the sales manager enters the information into the system. At the end of the business day, the sales manager presses a computer key or two to produce the next day's log in about ten minutes. This is less time than it takes to photocopy a typed master log. According to Rosenblum, it takes only about a day for the computer to type out all the bills at the end of the month, and this includes affidavits for co-op and agency accounts.

With a Generic Computer System, it costs about $2,600 for the software to program a computer acquired locally by the broadcaster. About $5,000 would set up a station with the hardware (the computer, hard disc, and printer) and the software. Generic has software systems designed for both Apple and IBM computers.

A number of other companies offer specialized software for broadcasters, including Sunspot, Rocky Mountain Software, Datacount, and Omnisoft.

The real payoff in computer traffic system usage is in the sales reports and the aging sheets. Sample print-outs of a program log, invoice, invoice with exact time, affidavit of performance, accounts trial report, expiration report, sales hourly breakdown, accounts receivable aging report, billing summary, sales commission summary, and revenue projections appear in Appendix 5.

An hour of the sample log page shows the schedule printout with space for the announcer to write the actual times for station identifications and announcements just as in the old manual systems. The Generic System will sort on program type or on product code. Each product is assigned a code, and if management wants to know where all the automobile-related ads are located on the log, a product code sort will reveal this type of information by listing advertisers according to product category.

The station invoice can be typed so that the address will fall in the window of a window envelope, and forms are available that can be printed with the station logo on them. The computer also can print a promo line across the bottom of the bill.

Another kind of invoice lists the exact times the spots ran. A slight alteration of the invoice with the times becomes the Affidavit of Performance form. Generic designed this affidavit printout with the input of some of the biggest advertising agencies in the country, and the form has been in use for five years.

The account trial balance report for each salesperson shows accounts that owe money for thirty, sixty, and ninety days so the salesperson can collect the accounts that are in arrears and get the commissions. The expiration report helps sales staff keep accounts renewed. All of the station's accounts are listed on the accounts receivable aging report (rather than listed by salesperson) so that management can keep track of all station accounts that owe money.

The preliminary billing report gives management a quick summary of what the bills will look like so that the billing information can be edited *before* the bills are made ready for sending to the clients. The computer system is most efficient when all the accounts in its memory are correct and up to date and the computer prints bills calculated in an uninterrupted billing run.

The sales commission summary reports the billing collected for accounts credited to each salesperson and the total commission due each salesperson for the month covered by the report. This report is given to payroll for commission calculations so that the checks may be written.

The projected revenues form will take a station's sales at any given moment in a month and project the total billing for the month based on the contracts sold up to the date of the projection.

These computer-generated reports show how even the smallest station can have more comprehensive information for better decision making than has been available in the past. With the fast pace of change, today's competitive broadcast managers need to have the right data available to make the proper adjustments.

Accounts receivable becomes more complicated when excellent salespeople probe deeper into the market and the station begins to fill up with ads. More clients will be added to the slow pay list — the busier the station, the longer the list. Management needs to pay close attention to this list and make positive efforts to collect delinquent accounts. Some stations put vinyl stickers as warnings on overdue bills. These stickers work in 10 percent to 20 percent of the delinquent cases. Often a client will pay if a manager stops by and asks for the check.

If the client pays nothing after running up a ninety-day delinquency, it is time to take the client off the air. Once the client is off the air, however, the possibilities of collectability go down drastically.

One method of collecting this sometimes substantial amount is to go to the client and get an agreement that the client actually owes the amount in the bill. If there is any discussion concerning the actual amount due, the amount should be discussed and agreed upon. Then the station manager should ask the client to sign a standard loan agreement certifying that he and the business actually owe the station the agreed amount and that an agreed upon amount will be applied against this principle and interest balance each month. If the business is going bankrupt, this instrument will move the station up into the preferred creditors before the court, next to mortgage and lien holders. Author Durfey's late father, Carlton Durfey, perfected this business method and collected more than half of the delinquent accounts he encountered.

Maintenance

General housekeeping and building and grounds maintenance fall under specialty management at larger stations. At smaller stations, the general housekeeping is often passed out to various staff members. At one station in New York, the program director cleaned the production studio/office and emptied the wastebasket in that area. The news director did the same for the newsroom, the music director cleaned the main control room, the chief engineer cleaned the transmitter room and shop, the traffic director/secretary cleaned the general office and reception room, and the station manager cleaned the management office.

Because the public visits the station, general buildings and grounds maintenance needs the attention of management. For smaller stations, contract labor such as plumbers, electricians, roofing contractors, and gardening/lawn care contractors (who may even trade the service out) are found to be a good source of buildings and grounds maintenance, especially when the choice for many stations would be to have a management team member attempt this maintenance. The station would make more money hiring a specialized subcontractor and sending the management team out to sell where they are much more efficient!

Summary

Efficient, professional management methods will help any station make the most of its potential in the market. When each area is operating smoothly, there is more time for everyone on the staff to do the little things that separate an ordinary station from an exceptional one.

Chapter 20

Management From a Biblical Perspective

Anyone who has ever worked for an organization has experienced a "management style." Some organizations are characterized by an authoritative, almost dictatorial style of management, while others seem to have a special, open, easy, and participatory style.

Douglas McGregor in his best-selling book, *The Human Side of Enterprise,* first labels three styles of management as Theories X, Y, and V. He describes Theory X as management through power, actual physical power in pre-twentieth-century times, and today through moral authority ("the work ethic") and monetary pressure. In contrast, his Theory Y operates on the premise that people have wants and needs that can be used to entice them into complying with authority. Theory V focuses on the acts of the manager and "managee."[1]

If all this sounds rather manipulative — it is!

Suppose that management is the art or science of getting other people — for the purposes of this book, broadcast subordinates or station employees — to do whatever is necessary to meet the goals of an organization. Let us break down the various styles of management and see the pros and cons of each by assuming that they can be outlined in a continuum from dictatorial to consultive.

Management Styles

Dictatorial. This is a management style characterized by assumption of absolute control by upper management, with one-way communication — from the top brass down to the troops who wait for orders in a fashion similar to well-trained soldiers on the edge of a battlefield. Official procedures are dictated in committees dominated by top management and written in procedural manuals with the only additions being orders from headquarters. In such management systems, there are no suggestions or input from workers, in fact, no upward communications. Top management is surrounded by yes-men, people who unwaveringly agree with everything the executives believe and say.

This style of management does not foster excellence in the field of media affairs. The only time it might be of value would be in a time of extreme emergency when threats to life, limb, and property are eminent.

On the evening of November 9, 1965, author Durfey was on a hill overlooking the mid-Hudson Valley in New York when the lights began going out block by block. A check with New York City radio stations (only a few were on) revealed that a full-scale power blackout was under way. It was the onset of the greatest power failure in history, which affected thirty million people in most of seven states and Ontario. Durfey's station was a daytime-only station and normally off the air after sundown, but management decided that traffic snarls and possible panic and/or fear would warrant news updates and information provided to the public on the situation. The telephones still worked, so a call to a local contractor brought a gasoline-powered electric generator to the station, then Durfey called technicians and announcers back to the station. Having been a consulting engineer, Durfey knew how to rewire the station so that it could operate on emergency power and was able to tell technical employees exactly what to do. A temporary studio was set up and a wire sent to the FCC explaining the emergency setup. All of this was accomplished in less than two hours. Seeking opinions or input from the troops would only have held up the operation.

Application of this management style in media, however, probably should be limited to those rare emergency occasions when the short-run efficiency achieved warrants the adoption of a dictatorial style.

Authoritative. A highly structured management style that is slightly less rigid than the dictatorial, an authoritative system reserves authority to a management elite who make up a management team. Members of this team have the power to make decisions; workers are deemed too stupid to make any. Committees abound, each with a member of the management team as head, and decisions usually follow traditional patterns of precedents already set. Often the authoritative style of management follows the dictatorial style when a leader dies or retires. Things are done in a certain way, often by a procedural manual, or action may be postponed until a management conference can be held. The leadership hierarchy ranges from the elite down through various levels of junior management. There is a chain of command with most communications coming down through it and little progressing back up the chain. With little communication coming back up from the employees, there usually is a suggestion box.

Many times the employees have their own management chain in unions whose representatives negotiate with the representatives of the organizations. These organizations are characterized by union jurisdictions that define job tasks and the number and type of workers that must be present for each kind of job. The influence of the unions impresses a second communications channel on the organization. Thus, often a worker would communicate with the shop steward and union leaders rather than with the corporate managers. In broadcast communication organizations, the older companies seem to have evolved into the authoritative management system.

Participative. This style of management is characterized by a two-way communications system, through which the suggestions of the workers are sought after and valued. Many of the aspects of the authoritative management system can still be present, with the exception that managers operating according to this kind of system usually solicit ideas and suggestions from employees. For example, managers will present a project to a group of workers and ask for suggestions as to how the goal can be met most easily and efficiently. These suggestions are often used by the managers to shape the entire project; however, the creation of the project is left for management to decide. Employees in such an atmosphere feel free, and are even encouraged, to go to superiors with an idea or a suggestion. They know that their opinions will be well received and thoughtfully considered. Therefore, many procedures are more often developed by employees involved with the actual work than set down in procedural manuals. Of course, these procedures must be approved by management; but few plans that work well are discarded under this system.

Participatively managed companies tend to have higher employee morale than in organizations that stress more authoritative management styles. Many great broadcasting stations have operated with this style of management. These tend to be the larger stations with experienced management and junior management with experience from other operations.

Consultative. This is an even more open style of management. In this system, the input of the employee is sought for all areas of decision making. All levels of workers are consulted in setting company goals and priorities. If any decision impacts a given employee, then he or she usually is consulted before the decision is finalized. Once the employee has been consulted, however, the actual decision is made by management who considers all input and then "sells" the final decision to the worker or workers. Since the employees have, in most cases, helped shape the decision and/or goals or scope of a project, the plans usually are adopted with full cooperation.

A personal example of this style of management from author Durfey's experience as chairman of a department at a large university involved a way to handle more students each semester. He approached two teachers, one of television courses and one of radio, with the idea of splitting beginning courses into lecture and lab and hiring another junior instructor to teach the lab. The radio teacher embraced the idea as the best way to instruct more students; but the television courses teacher felt a more traditional method he had developed should be given a longer trial. Durfey honored both ideas and hired an assistant instructor to teach radio and news labs instead of TV labs. This way a larger number of students could be taught, and the method developed by the TV teacher and his colleagues would not be jeopardized.

Servant Style Management. This is a style of management that seeks to hire the very best employees for every task — the best trained, the best educated, the most experienced, the most professional "self-starters." Management's primary responsibility is to find the very best team members, both in competency and in compatibility. All must be team players, that is, each person must be willing to pull for the good of the group at no thought to personal aggrandizement or special recognition. Management has a goal-setting session with the team, and all agree on the goals. Then the manager steps back and becomes a facilitator and cheerleader or exhorter for the team. If the team needs special equipment, the manager supplies it, also serving as mediator if any disputes arise. The manager works to keep morale high.

Biblical Examples of Management Styles

Human nature apparently tends to follow the same patterns throughout history, for there are examples of these types of leadership throughout the Scriptures. In Daniel 2:1-13, Nebuchadnezzar *commanded* his wise men to explain a dream to him that he did not even remember! Their response was that he was making unfair and unreasonable demands. Then the king became furious and threatened to put them to death. Usually, "off with their heads" is the first reaction of management operating in a dictatorial style to those objecting or disagreeing, no matter how reasonable the objections.

The first king of Israel, Saul, exemplified an authoritative style of leadership. He was a decisive king, using his authority and position to motivate people to follow him into battle (1 Sam. 11). He became too self-important, however, and overstepped his authority by performing priestly duties, an area that had been set aside by God for those designated as priests (1 Sam. 13). In the end, Saul's pride and authority complex cost his life and that of his sons (1 Sam. 31:6). This is one of the possible dangers of dictatorial and authoritative management styles — prideful authority which blinds the leader to the effect his decisions can have on others.

Often university management professors define management as "getting work done through others." This world-view of management gives business leaders the ego-building concept of the right to control, exploit, or manipulate those working under them. (Many men run their families the same way!) It is tragic that many Christian broadcast managers have accepted this worldly philosophy of management. When the mother of John and James, the sons of Zebedee, asked Jesus to place her sons on the throne next to Him, He told her that He had no right to say who would sit where. But when the other disciples became indignant at the "Sons of Thunder," Jesus called them together and said:

> **Among the heathen, kings are tyrants and each minor official lords it over those beneath him. But among you it is quite different. Anyone wanting to be a leader among you must be your servant. And if you want to be right at the top, you must serve like a slave. Your attitude must be like my own, for I, the Messiah, did not come to be served, but to serve, and to give my life as a ransom for many (Matt. 20:25-28 TLB[2]).**

The apostle Paul often exercised a consultative style of leadership. He had messengers who reported on the needs of a given community of Christians, and then he would write and specify the right corrective spiritual behavior needed in that particular assembly. Paul always mentioned specific problem areas unique to that fellowship and focused his comments on those problems.

In Acts 6, we have an example of consultative-style leadership. The Greek-speaking Jews pointed out to the apostles that their widows were not being cared for as well as the widows of the native Hebrew Christians. The apostles' solution was to have seven men chosen to handle the charity distribution of the early Christian community, which freed the apostles to handle the duties of spreading the gospel while reserving the right to review the work of the seven and make final decisions.

Jesus used all of the forms of leadership during His ministry. He used dictatorial management when He drove the money changers out of the temple (John 2:13-16). In verse 16, He said that they were desecrating His Father's house, therefore it was His business, and it called for immediate strong action not requiring consultation with the disciples.

Jesus used the authoritative style when He delegated authority to His disciples traveling to various villages (Matt. 10:1-15) and when He delegated His authority to His Body on earth (Matt. 28:18-20).

Jesus exercised a servant style of leadership during the Last Supper when He washed the feet of His disciples (John 13:1-17). The group had walked at least a couple of miles from the Jerusalem suburb of Bethany around the Mount of Olives to the south-Jerusalem house where they had reserved space to celebrate the Passover. As Jesus and His disciples were in a private room and not strictly the guests of the owner, no servants were available to serve them. In that culture and time, servants met guests of a householder and washed their feet partly as a courtesy because of the dusty, dirty roads and partly to keep the house floors clean! Since no such servants were available on this occasion, Jesus set an example by serving the others.

"The" Right Management Attitudes

There is no absolutely correct style of leadership that will cover all situations. Various styles permit the proper application of management skills to fit the appropriate situation, although the servant and consultative styles are best for managing creative people.

In broadcasting, each team member must feel that he or she is making a creative contribution to the whole in order to feel useful. If a great broadcasting station is to build and maintain a loyal and tremendous audience and attract and sustain abundant advertisers, it must keep a competent team. Each air personality, each news person, each sales person must make a total effort toward excellence and professionalism, using all the creative abilities at their command to achieve the high goals of the station.

Authoritative and dictorial styles of management tend to stifle creativity, giving rise to stations with an automated sound, although in reality, they are operating live. Under this style of operation, the worker tends to live in fear of encountering the displeasure of the manager's whims or rule book. The spirit of fear stifles creativity. Such stations have a high turnover of help and only the "formula" keeps the place together. People are not happy working there, and eventually the air sound projects this.

Getting the right team together in the first place constitutes the largest component of the management system selection. Finding creative people who are not temperamental and are good team players is not always easy. The reputation of the station within the industry has something to do with the ability to attract and retain creative team players. The way the manager begins to build an operation is to set the tone in person — to show excellence in news, in the deejay portions of the broadcast time, and in being a sales representative. Then a manager should try to hire people who sound better on the air or perform better on the sales field than he does. In the hiring process, management should make clear the amount of participation expected of new employees, hold brainstorming sessions to solicit ideas from all employees, and schedule briefing sessions to communicate the goals of the organization and tell how the ideas are being implemented within those goals. Give credit to those who contribute ideas for projects. Management should produce promos for each air person and get traffic to schedule them. This shows management appreciation for each team player, as well as building the station's audience.

Even in a communications business, internal communication at individual broadcast operations may not be as excellent as they should be. God used communications as an example of organizational strength when He disrupted the communications system of those who attempted to build the Tower of Babel.

> Now the whole world had one language and a common speech. As men moved eastward, they found a plain in Shinar and settled there.
>
> They said to each other, Come, let's make bricks and bake them thoroughly. They used brick instead of stone, and tar instead of mortar. Then they said, Come, let us build ourselves a city, with a tower that reaches to the heavens, so that we may make a name for ourselves and not be scattered over the face of the whole earth.
>
> But the LORD came down to see the city and the tower that the men were building. The LORD said, If as one people speaking the same language they have begun to do this, then nothing they plan to do will be impossible for them. Come, let us go down and confuse their language so they will not understand each other.
>
> So the LORD scattered them from there over all the earth, and they stopped building the city. That is why it was called Babel — because there the LORD confused the language of the whole world. From there the LORD scattered them over the face of the whole earth (Gen. 11:1-9 NIV[3]).

In order to build an organization (that the Lord said would succeed), the people developed an organization with unity, an effective communication system, and commitment to work on a goal. Only the fact that they were not doing the will of God brought the project down! God shut down their project by disrupting their communication system, which made the unity and commitment to a common goal dissipate rapidly.

Care must be taken to maintain good two-way communication — especially because we are in the communications business. Sometimes management in broadcasting takes its internal communications for granted. This is always dangerous and can lead to inefficiency, stress, or expensive mistakes, because others on the team do not know what is on the manager's mind until something is said or communicated.

Summary

Christian broadcast managers must learn to inspire unity, to establish team goals, and to maintain good internal communications. They must serve the Lord in all of these while accomplishing and sustaining organizational success with consultative, participative, and servant management styles that train new team members, include workers in goal-setting meetings, and continue to meet the needs of creative employees, as they work at making and keeping their broadcast station a success.

The bottom line is to take the authority necessary to achieve the purpose of the station while operating in all areas according to the commandment Jesus said summarized all others: "In everything, do to others what you would have them do to you" (Matt. 7:12a NIV).

Notes

[1] Douglas McGregor, *The Human Side of Enterprise* (New York: McGraw-Hill, 1960).

[2] *The Living Bible* (TLB). Copyright © 1971 by Tyndale House, Wheaton, Illinois.

[3] *The Holy Bible, New International Version* (NIV). Copyright © 1973, 1978 by the New York International Bible Society.

Appendices

Appendix 1

FIELD INTENSITY MEASUREMENTS

RADIO STATION KTCR, WAGONER, OK. 1530 KHZ

RADIAL AZIMUTH : N 315 E

Point Number	Distance from Antenna in Miles	Field Intensity in MV/M
1.	0.2	920
2.	.33	560
3.	.42	420
4.	.54	310
5.	.9	190
6.	1.2	140
7.	1.5	110
8.	1.7	94
9.	2.7	56
10.	2.9	omit
11.	4.0	25
12.	5.6	24
13.	7.1	15
14.	8.5	12
15.	9.9	10
16.	11.3	6.1
17.	12.2	8.4
18.	12.8	6.2
19.	13.2	3.8

Appendix 1

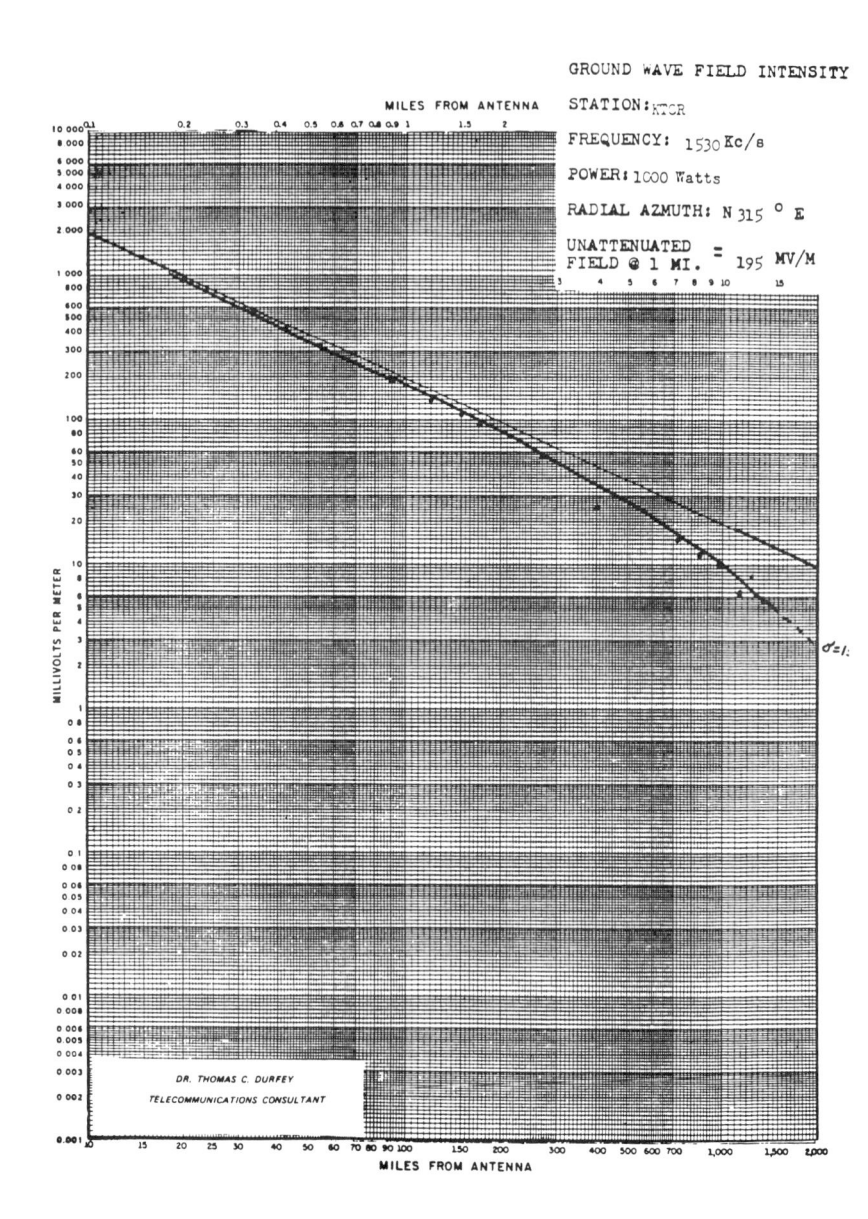

GROUND WAVE FIELD INTENSITY

STATION: KTCR

FREQUENCY: 1530 Kc/s

POWER: 1000 Watts

RADIAL AZMUTH: N 315 ° E

UNATTENUATED FIELD @ 1 MI. = 195 MV/M

DR. THOMAS C. DURFEY
TELECOMMUNICATIONS CONSULTANT

Appendix 1

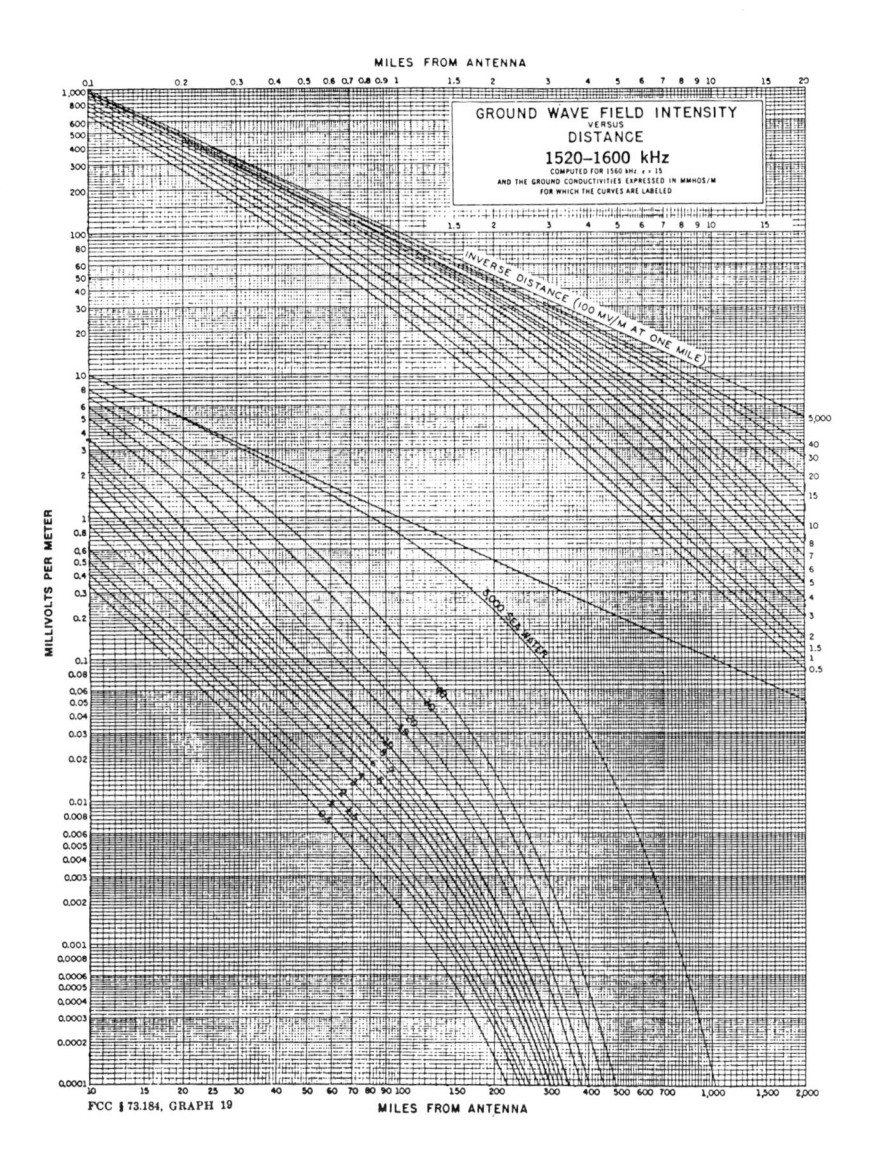

Appendix 1

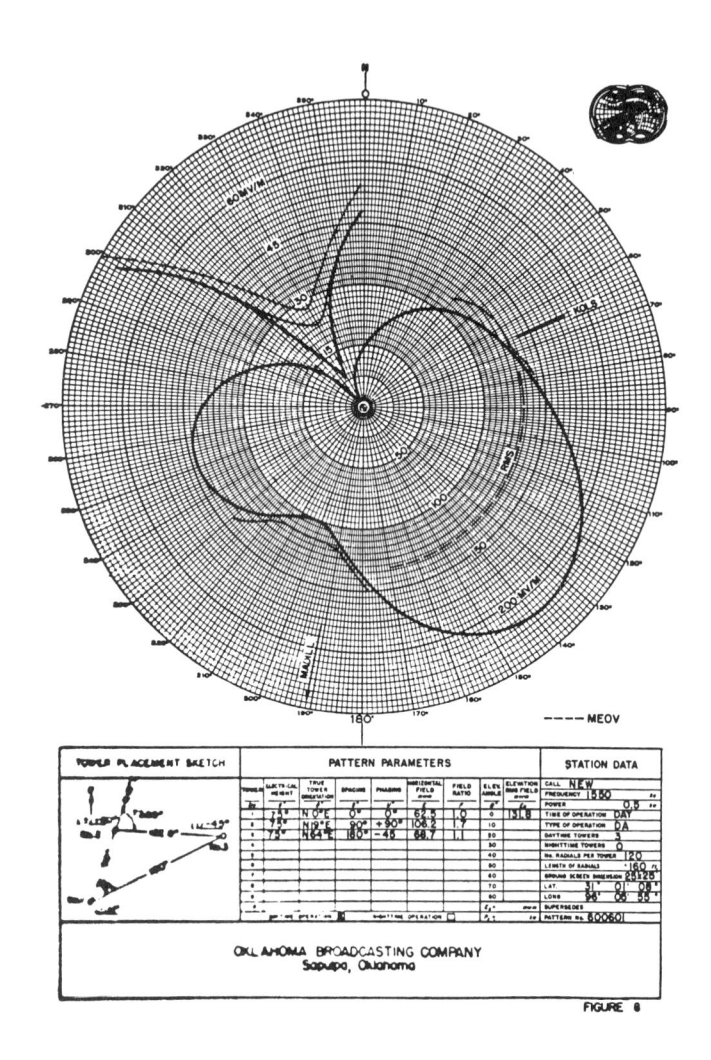

Appendix 1

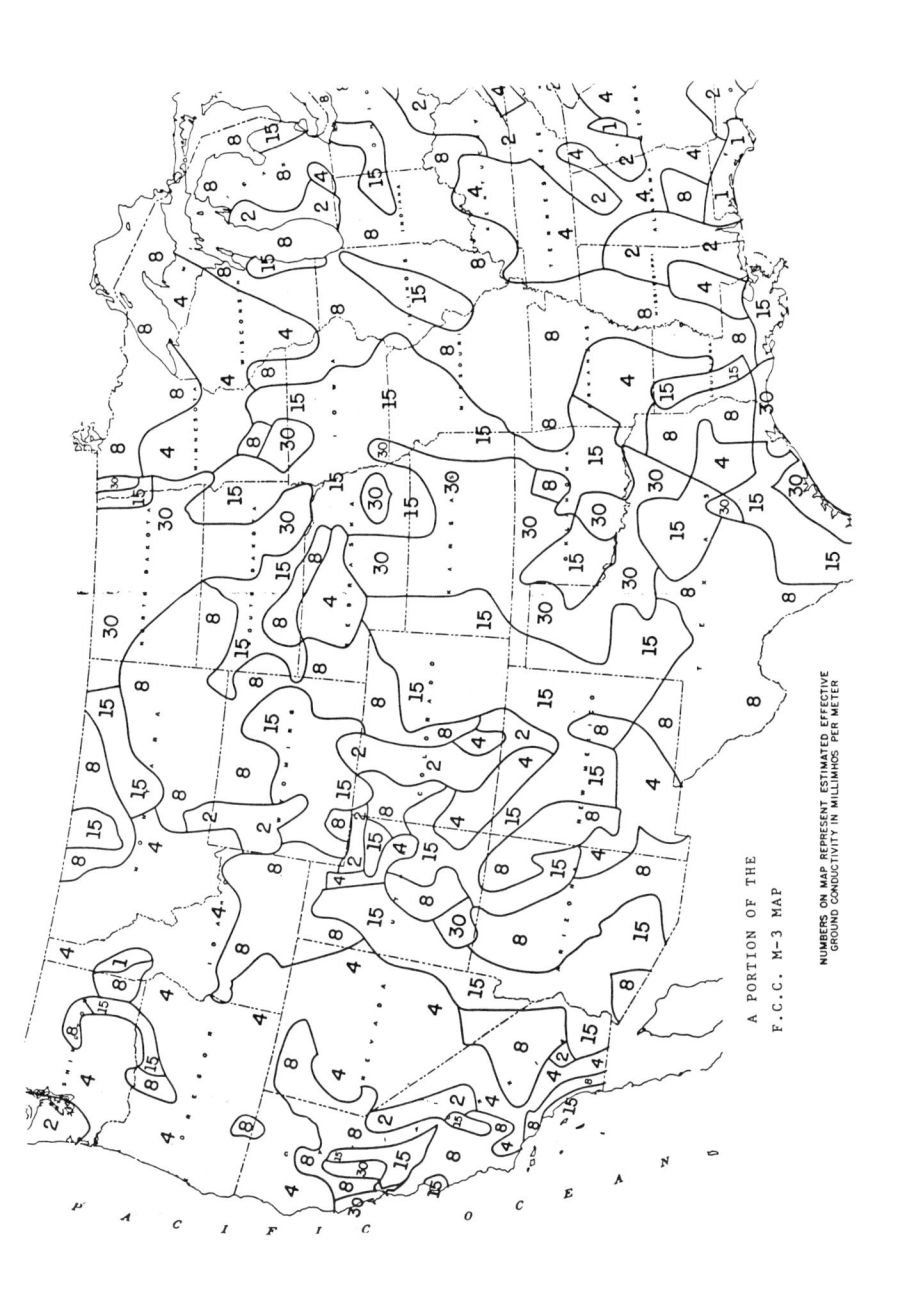

A PORTION OF THE
F.C.C. M-3 MAP

NUMBERS ON MAP REPRESENT ESTIMATED EFFECTIVE
GROUND CONDUCTIVITY IN MILLIMHOS PER METER

Appendix 1

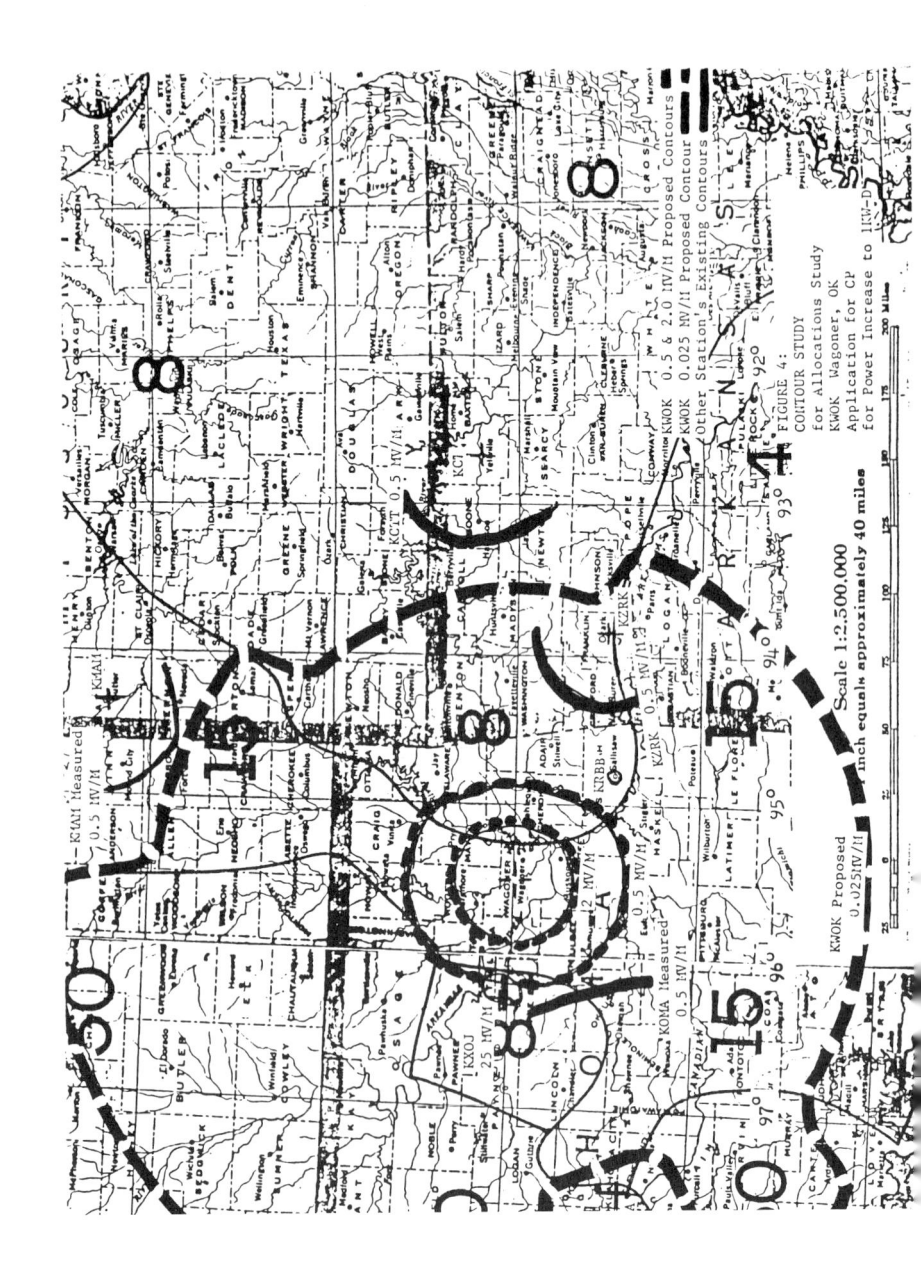

Appendix 2
Tenderability Defects

[A] Form 301 older than 1982.

[B] No name or address — I, Item 1.

[C] Community or channel of allocation omitted — I, Item 2.

*[D] No certification re 47 U.S.C. 310(b) — II, Item 3.

*[E] No exhibit provided if response to II, Item 3(b), is YES.

*[F] No response re multiple ownership — II, Item 6 or 8.

*[G] No exhibit if reponse to II, Item 6 or 8, is YES.

*[H] No financial certification — III, Item 1 or 2.

[I] Community to be served omitted — V-B, Item 2.

[J] Channel of allocation omitted — V-B, Item 3.

†[K] Coordinates of antenna, V-B, Item 4, missing or do not match V-G, Item 1.

[L] Effective radiated power not specified — V-B, Item 5.

[M] Radiation-center height omitted — V-B, any of Item 6.

†[N] Radiation-center height in V-B, any of Item 6, conflicts with antenna sketch, V-G, Item 6 (Exhibit).

[O] Failure to respond re directional antenna — V-B, Item 7.

[P] No exhibit provided if response to V-B, Item 7, is YES.

[Q] Overall structure height omitted — V-B, Item 9.

†[R] Overall structure height, V-B, Item 9, conflicts with antenna sketch, V-G, Item 6 (Exhibit).

[S] Map showing community to be served, distance scale, and signal contours omitted — V-B, Item 10 (Exhibit).

Appendix 2

†[T]   Topographic site map with scale of distance, coordinate markings, and contour lines per Public Notice 4/5/85, Mimeo 3693 not supplied — V-B, Item 13 (Exhibit).
†[U]   No V-G provided.
†[V]   V-G incomplete excluding Item 4.
†[W]   Antenna sketch omitted of V-G provided — V-G, Item 6 (Exhibit).
†[X]   Structure height, V-G, Item 5, conflicts with antenna sketch, V-G, Item 6 (Exhibit).
*[Y]   No public-notice certification — VII.
 [Z]   Applicant's signature missing — VII.
†[AA] No site-availability certification.
*   Not applicable to minor-change applications.
†   Not applicable where minor-change application proposes no change in site or in supporting structure.

Appendix 2

United States of America
Federal Communications Commission
Washington, D.C. 20554

Approved by OMB
3060-0027
Expires 12/31/84

For Commission Use Only
File No.

APPLICATION FOR CONSTRUCTION PERMIT FOR COMMERCIAL BROADCAST STATION
(Carefully read instructions before filling out Form— RETURN ONLY FORM TO FCC)

Section I — General Information

1. Name of Applicant: WELDEN, BREVOORT, HICKMAN, INC.

   Street Address: BOX 219

   City: WAGONER   State: OK   ZIP Code: 74477   Telephone No. (Include Area Code): 918-485-5153

   Send notices and communications to the following named person at the address below:

   Name: KENDALL DURFEY

   Street Address: BOX 219

   City: WAGONER   State: OK   ZIP Code: 74477   Telephone No. (Include Area Code): 918-485-5153

2. This application is for: ☐ AM   ☒ FM   ☐ TV

   (a) Channel No. or Frequency: 264 A

   (b) Community of license:

   City: UTICA   State: NY

   (c) Check one of the following boxes:

   New Station ☒

   Change in existing station — Major ☐   Minor ☐

   Amendment to pending Application ☐

   Modification of Construction Permit ☐   Call Letters: _____ - ___   Give reference No. _____

NOTE: It is not necessary to use this form to amend a previously filed application. Should you do so, however, please submit only Section I and those other portions of the form that contain the amended information.

3. Is this application mutually exclusive with a renewal application?

   ☐ YES   ☒ NO

   If Yes, state: Call letters: _____-___   Community of license: City _____   State ___

FCC 301
January 1982

Appendix 2

Section II   Legal Qualifications

Name of Applicant   WELDEN, BREVOORT, HICKMAN, INC.

1. Applicant is: *(check one box below)*

   ☐ an individual   ☐ a general partnership   ☒ a corporation

   ☐ a limited partnership   ☐ other

2. If the applicant is an unincorporated association or a legal entity other than an individual, partnership or corporation, describe in Exhibit No. _____ the nature of the applicant.

Citizenship And Other Statutory Requirements

	YES	NO
3. (a) Is the applicant in compliance with the provisions of Section 310 of the Communications Act of 1934, as amended, relating to interests of aliens and Foreign governments?	☒	☐
(b) Will any funds, credits, etc., for the construction, purchase or operation of the station(s) be provided by aliens, foreign entities, domestic entities controlled by aliens, or their agents?	☐	☒

If yes, provide particulars as Exhibit No. _____

4. (a) Has an adverse finding been made, adverse final action taken or consent decree approved by any court or administrative body as to the applicant or any party to the application in any civil or criminal proceeding brought under the provisions of any law related to the following: Any felony, antitrust, unfair competition, fraud, unfair labor practices or discrimination?	☐	☒
(b) Is there now pending in any court or administrative body any proceeding involving any of the matters referred to in (a)?	☐	☒

If the answer to (a) or (b) above is Yes, attach as Exhibit No. _____, a full disclosure concerning the persons and matters involved, identifying the court or administrative body and the proceeding *(by dates and file numbers)*, stating the facts upon which the proceeding was based or the nature of the offense committed, and disposition or current status of the matter.

Appendix 2

Section II (page 2)　　　　　　　　　　Legal Qualifications

Applicants are reminded that questions 5 through 7 of this Section must be completed as to all "parties to this application" as that term is defined in the instructions to Section II of this form.

Table I Parties To Application

5. (a) Complete Table I with respect to all parties to this application.

(Note: If the applicant considers that to furnish complete information would pose an unreasonable burden, it may request that the Commission waive the strict terms of this requirement with appropriate justification)

INSTRUCTIONS: If applicant is an individual, fill out column (a) only. If applicant is a partnership, fill out columns (a), (b), and (d), stated as to each general or limited partner *(including silent partners):* (a) name and residence, (b) nature of partnership interest *(i.e., general or limited),* and (d) percent of ownership interest. If applicant is a corporation or an unincorporated association with 50 or fewer stockholders, stock subscribers, holders of membership certificate or other ownership interest, fill out all columns, giving the information requested as to all officers, directors and members of governing board. In addition, give the information as to all persons or entities who are the beneficial or record owners of or have the right to vote capital stock, membership or owner interests or are subscribers to such interests. If the applicant has more than 50 stockholders, stock subscribers or holders of membership certificates or other ownership interests, furnish the information as to officers, directors, members of governing board, and all persons or entities who are the beneficial or record owners of or have the right to vote 1% or more of the capital stock, membership or owner interest, except that if such entity is a bank, insurance company or investment company *(as defined by 15 U.S.C. §80a-3)* which does not invest for purposes of control, the stock, membership or owner interest need only be reported if 5% or more.

Name and Residence *(Home)* Address(es) (a)	Nature of Partnership Interest or Office Held (b)	Director or Member of Governing Board YES	Director or Member of Governing Board NO	% of: Ownership (O) or Partnership (P) or Voting Stock (VS) or Membership (M) (d)
PHYLLIS FREY 44 NORTH PITTSBURG TULSA, OK 74115	PRESIDENT	X		51% VS
KENDALL DURFEY BOX 219 WAGONER, OK 74477	VICE PRESIDENT	X		25% VS
NELSON DURFEY 224 NORTHWEST STREET APT. #202 STILLWATER, OK 74075	SECRETARY	X		24% VS

FCC 301 — Page 3
January 1982

Appendix 2

Section II (page 3) Legal Qualifications

	YES	NO
5. (b) Does the applicant or any party to this application, own or have any interest in a daily newspaper or cable television system?	☐	☒
(c) Does the applicant or any party to this application have an interest in an investment company, bank, or insurance company which has an interest in a broadcast station, cable system or daily newspaper?	☐	☒
(d) Is the applicant or any party to this application an officer, director or partner of an investment company, bank, or insurance company which has an interest in a broadcast station, cable system or daily newspaper?	☐	☒

If the answer to questions 5(b), (c) or (d) is Yes, attach as Exhibit No._____, a full disclosure concerning persons involved, the nature of such interest, the media interest and its location.

Other Broadcast Interests

6. Does applicant or any party to this application have any interest in or connection with the following:

	YES	NO
(a) an AM, FM or TV broadcast station?	☒	☐
(b) a broadcast application pending before the FCC?	☐	☒

7. Has the applicant or any party to this application had any interest in:

	YES	NO
(a) a broadcast application which has been dismissed with predjudice by the Commission?	☐	☒
(b) a broadcast application which has been denied by the Commission?	☐	☒
(c) a broadcast station, the license of which has been revoked?	☐	☒
(d) a broadcast application in any Commission proceeding which left unresolved character issues against that applicant?	☐	☒

(e) if the answer to any of the questions in 6 or 7 is Yes, state in Exhibit No. L 1 , the following information:

    (i) Name of party having such interest;
    (ii) Nature of interest or connection, giving dates;
    (iii) Call letters of stations or file number of application, or docket number;
    (iv) Location.

	YES	NO
8. (a) Are any of the parties to this application related to each other *(as husband, wife, father, mother, brother, sister, son or daughter)*?	☒	☐
(b) Does any member of the immediate family *(i.e., husband, wife, father, mother, brother, sister, son or daughter)* of any party to this application have any interest in or, connection with any other broadcast station or pending broadcast application?	☒	☐

If the answer to (a) or (b) above is Yes, attach as Exhibit No. L 1 , a full disclosure concerning the persons involved, their relationship, the nature and extent of such interest or connection, the file number of such application, and the location of such station or proposed station.

FCC 301 — Page 4
January 1982

Appendix 2

APPLICATION FOR CONSTRUCTION PERMIT
NEW FM STATION UTICA, NY
WELDEN, BREVOORT, HICKMAN, INC.
JANUARY 1986
EXHIBIT L 1

Kendall Durfey and Nelson Durfey are brothers, each own 10% of Telemonde Corporation, owner of KTCR-AM, Wagoner, OK. Telemonde Corporation was formed in the summer of 1983 to purchase the Wagoner station. Kendall is full time program director and officer of Telemonde Corporation, Nelson is a fulltime student in broadcasting at Oklahoma State University and chief engineer of KVRO-FM, Stillwater, OK.

Appendix 2

Section II (page 4)　　　　　　　　　　**Legal Qualifications**

Ownership And Control

	YES	NO
9. Are there any documents, instruments, contracts or understandings relating to ownership or future ownership rights *(including, but not limited to, non-voting stock interests, beneficial stock ownership interests, options, warrants, debentures)*?	☐	☒

If Yes, provide particulars as Exhibit No._____.

10. Do documents, instruments, agreements or understandings for the pledge of stock of a corporate applicant, as security for loans or contractual performance, provide that (a) voting rights will remain with the applicant, even in the event of default on the obligation; (b) in the event of default, there will be either a private or public sale of the stock; and (c) prior to the exercise of stockholder rights by the purchaser at such sale, the prior consent of the Commission *(pursuant to 47 U.S.C. 310 (d))* will be obtained?　　☒　☐

If No, attach as Exhibit No._____, a full explanation.

Section III　　　　　　　　　　**Financial Qualifications**

NOTE: If this application is for a change in an operating facility do not fill out this section.

1. The applicant certifies that sufficient net liquid assets are on hand or are available from committed sources to construct and operate the requested facilities for three months without revenue.　　☒　☐

2. The applicant certifies that:

　(a) it has a reasonable assurance of a present firm intention for each agreement to furnish capital or purchase capital stock by parties to the application, each loan by banks, financial institutions or others, and each purchase of equipment on credit;

　(b) it can and will meet all contractual requirements as to collateral, guarantees, and capital investment;

　(c) it has determined that a reasonable assurance exists that all such sources *(excluding banks, financial institutions, and equipment manufacturers)* have sufficient net liquid assets to meet these commitments.　　☒　☐

FCC 301 — Page 5
January 1982

Appendix 2

Section IV Program Service Statement

For AM And FM Applications

1. Attach as Exhibit No. P 1, a brief description, in narrative form, of the planned programming service relating to the issues of public concern facing the proposed service area.

For Television Applications

2. State the minimum amount of time, between 6:00 a.m. and midnight, the applicant proposes to normally devote each week to the program types listed below *(See definitions in instructions)*. Commercial matter, within a program segment, shall be excluded in computing the time devoted to that particular program segment, e.g., a 15-minute news program containing three minutes of commercial matter, shall be computed as a 12-minute news program.

	Hours	Minutes	% of Total Time on Air
News	_____	_____	_____
Public Affairs	_____	_____	_____
All other Programs *Exclusive of Sports and Entertainment*	_____	_____	_____
LOCAL PROGRAMMING	_____	_____	_____

3. State the maximum amount of commercial matter the applicant proposes to allow normally in any 60-minute segment:

4. State the maximum amount of commercial matter the applicant proposes to allow normally in a 60-minute segment between the hours of 6 p.m. to 11 p.m. *(5 p.m. to 10 p.m. Central and Mountain Times)*:

   (a) State the number of hourly segments per week this amount is expected to be exceeded, if any:

5. State in Exhibit No._____, in full detail, the reasons why the applicant would allow the amount of commercial matter stated in Questions 3 and 4 above to be exceeded.

FCC 301 – Page 6
January 1982

Appendix 2

APPLICATION FOR CONTRUCTION PERMIT
NEW FM STATION UTICA, NY
WELDEN, BREVOORT, HICKMAN, INC.
JANUARY 1986
EXHIBIT P 1

PROGRAM SERVICE STATEMENT

A diligent continuing effort will be maintained to discern the problems and concerns of the greater Utica community and to air the citizen's comments about these problems in a series of five minute community interviews to be presented in prime time. The format chosen for the station will seek to further diversify the style of stations in the area.

Appendix 2

Section VI   Equal Employment Opportunity Program

1. Does the applicant propose to employ five or more fulltime employees?   ☐ YES   ☒ NO

   If the answer is Yes, the applicant must include an EEO program called for in the separate 5 Point Model EEO Program.

Section VII   Certification

1. Has or will the applicant comply with the public notice requirement of Section 73.3580 of the Commission's Rules?   ☐ YES   ☐ NO

The APPLICANT hereby waives any claim to the use of any particular frequency as against the regulatory power of the United States because of the previous use of the same, whether by license or otherwise, and requests an authorization in accordance with this application. *(See Section 304 of the Communications Act of 1934, as amended.)*

The APPLICANT acknowledges that all the statements made in this application and attached exhibits are considered material representations, and that all exhibits are a material part hereof and incorporated herein.

The APPLICANT represents that this application is not filed for the purpose of impeding, obstructing, or delaying determination on any other application with which it may be in conflict.

In accordance with Section 1.65 of the Commission's Rules, the APPLICANT has a continuing obligation to advise the Commission, through amendments, of any substantial and significant changes in information furnished.

**WILLFUL FALSE STATEMENTS MADE ON THIS FORM ARE PUNISHABLE BY FINE AND IMPRISONMENT.
U.S. CODE, TITLE 18, Section 1001.**

I certify that the statements in this application are true, complete, and correct to the best of my knowledge and belief, and are made in good faith.

Signed and dated this _29th_ day of _January_, 19_86_.

Welden Brevoort Hickman Inc
Name of Applicant

Phyllis Ross Frey
Signature

President
Title

**FCC NOTICE TO INDIVIDUALS REQUIRED BY THE PRIVACY ACT
AND THE PAPERWORK REDUCTION ACT**

The solicitation of personal information requested in this application is authorized by the Communications Act of 1934, as amended. The principal purpose for which the information will be used is to determine if the benefit requested is consistent with the public interest. The staff, consisting variously of attorneys, accountants, engineers, and application examiners, will use the information to determine whether the application should be granted, denied, dismissed, or designated for hearing. If all the information requested is not provided, the application may be returned without action having been taken upon it or its processing may be delayed while a request is made to provide the missing information. Accordingly, every effort should be made to provide all necessary information. Your response is required to obtain the requested Permit.

THE FOREGOING NOTICE IS REQUIRED BY THE PRIVACY ACT OF 1974, P.L. 93-579, DECEMBER 31, 1974, 5 U.S.C. 552a(e)(3)

Appendix 2

APPLICATION FOR CONSTRUCTION PERMIT
New FM-Utica, N.Y.
Welden, Brevoort & Hickman, Inc.

Engineering Statement

I have been engaged to help prepare an application for a construction permit for a new FM station, assigned in the Table of FM assignments to Utica, New York in the Docket 80-90 proceedings, by Mrs. Phyllis Frey and my sons Kendall and Nelson, d/b/a Welden, Brevoort & Hickman, Inc. The applicant proposes to build and operate this class A FM facility on 100.7mhz (Channel 264A) in Utica, N.Y.

Arrangements have been made to side mount the one-bay proposed FM transmitting antenna on one leg if the self supporting tower used by WNYZ (FM), formerly WIBQ on Smith Hill Road, at a point up the tower such that the Height Above Average Terrain (HAAT) for the proposed operation will be 500 feet (152.5 meters). This cooresponds to a point 114 feet (34.8 meters) above the base of the tower. These figures were determined using the terrain calculations filed by the consulting engineering firm of Gautney and Jones in December 1965 for the construction permit of WIBQ originally proposed for channel 235 (94.9 MC) later modified to 98.7 Mhz and found in the WIBQ application Section V-B, page 2 dated December 2, 1968 and signed by George Gautney. Reasonalble assurance has been obtained from Teamworx New York, Inc., owners of this tower site, through their agent, Jim Ashton, that the applicant will be leased the 114 foot (34.8 meters) level on the existing WNYZ tower.

The Effective Radiated Power from the 500 foot HAAT (152.5 meters) was necessarily less than the 3KW from 100m,(320 feet) authorized for class A stations and was determined to be 1.1 kw from the 500 foot (152.5 meters) HAAT. Using the FCC 50-50 curves, the distances to the 70 DBU (3.16 MV/M) contour and the 60 DBU (1 MV/M) contour were determined and tabulated in Section V-B (page 3) of the application in paragraph 15.

These distances to contours along the 8 radials have been plotted on an air sectional with scale of miles, site, city boundries, area and 1980 census population count within the 60 DBU contour (237,819 people) displayed as Exhibit E-1.

Exhibit E-2 shows the proposed transmitter location on the entire 7½' topo to show the latitude and lognitude clearly with the scale of miles included. On the next page, Engineering Exhibit 3 (E-3) outlines the applicants' belief that no interference will be caused by a grant of this application.

Section V-G also is included in this application, although applicant is applying to attach an antenna to an already existing tower. A vertical plan sketch for this tower attachment is included as Engineering Exhibit 4 (E4) for the Commission's convience.

The qualifications of the Engineer making these calculations and exhibits is included in the affidavit attached.

Respectfully submitted,
Thomas C. Durtey
Dr. Thomas C. Durtey
Technical Consultant

Appendix 2

EXHIBIT E

State of Oklahoma) ss:
County of Wagoner)

Thomas C. Durfey, being duly sworn, states:
That he is a Telecommunications Consultant with offices at Route 1, Coweta, Oklahoma 74429.

That he has been employed as a radio or television engineer in operation, research, construction, and consulting since 1955, that he had held a first class radio-telephone operators license (#P1-10-31264) for over 25 years. That he received a degree of Bachelor of Science in Physics from Union College of Schenectady, New York in 1957, and a Master of Arts degree from Dartmouth College in Engineering-Physics in 1960 with a thesis on "Vertical Incidence Polarization Effects of the Ionosphere". That he taught Physics and Communications-Electronics at Mohawk Valley Technical Institute and Dutchess Community College of the State University of New York. That he earned the degree of Doctor of Philosophy from New York University in 1978, in low-power broadcast aspects of Television Translators, that he currently is teaching in and department chairman of Telecommunications at Oral Roberts University in Tulsa, Oklahoma. That since 1955, he has designed many directional antennas, performed the calculations and/or measurements to obtain coverage and interference contours as well as broadcast allocations work. That he prepared the design of the first broadcast directional array on a computer to be submitted to a commission hearing, which resulted in a grant. That he has prepared previous broadcast applications which have been filed with and granted by the Federal Communications Commission.

That he is a qualified and experienced Radio and Television consultant whose qualifications are a matter of record with the Federal Communications Commission.

That the calculations and/or measurements and exhibits in the accompanying report were made by him personally or under his direction, and that all facts contained herein are true of his own personal knowledge or belief; and on such statements made on belief, they are believed to be true.

Thomas C. Durfey
Affiant

Subscribed and sworn before me this 30TH day of January, 1986

Notary Public

MY COMMISSION EXPIRES JULY 25, 1988

Date of Commission Expiration: _____

Appendix 2

Section V-B FM Broadcast Engineering Data

Name of Applicant: WELDEN, BREVOORT, HICKMAN, INC.

1. Purpose of authorization applied for:

   ☒ Construct a new station   ☐ Install Auxiliary system

   Change:
   - ☐ Effective radiated power
   - ☐ Frequency
   - ☐ Antenna height above average terrain
   - ☐ Transmitter location
   - ☐ Studio location outside community of license
   - ☐ Other *(Summarize briefly the nature of the changes proposed.)*

2. Station location:
   - State: NEW YORK
   - City or Town: UTICA

3. Facilities requested:
   - Frequency: 100.7 MHz
   - Channel No.: 264
   - Class: ☒ A ☐ B ☐ C

4. Geographic coordinates of antenna (to nearest second)
   - North Latitude: 43° 08' 38.5"
   - West Longitude: 75° 10' 44.5"

5. Effective radiated power:

Polarization	Horizontal Plane	Maximum (Beam tilt only)
Horizontal	1.1 kW	kW
Vertical	1.1 kW	kW

6. Height of antenna radiation center:

	Average terrain (HAAT)	Mean Sea Level	Ground
Horizontal	152.5 M 500 ft.	402.6 M 1321 ft.	114 ft. 34.7 M
Vertical	152.5 M 500 ft.	402.6 M 1321 ft.	114 ft. 34.7 M

7. Is a directional antenna being proposed?   YES ☐   NO ☒

   If Yes, attach as Exhibit No. _____ an engineering statement with all data specified in Section 73.316(d) of the Commission's Rules.

FCC 301 - Page 11
April 1985

Appendix 2

Section V-B (page 2) FM Broadcast Engineering Data

8. Transmitter location: State NEW YORK   County ONEIDA

    City or Town: DEARFIELD TWNSHIP NEAR UTICA
    Street Address (or other identification): ATOP SMITH HILL ON SMITH HILL ROAD

9. Overall height of complete structure above ground (without obstruction lighting).   293 ft.   89.3 M

    ALREADY EXISTING STRUCTURE (WNYZ-FM)

10. Attach as Exhibit No. E_1_ map(s) (Sectional Aeronautical charts or equivalent) of the area proposed to be served and show thereon:

    (a) Proposed transmitter location and the radials along which the profile graphs have been prepared;

    (b) The 3.16 mV/m and the 1 mV/m contours predicted;

    (c) On the map(s) showing 3.16 mV/m contour, clearly indicate the legal boundaries of the principal community proposed to be served;

    (d) Area (sq. mi.) and population (latest census) within 1 mV/m contour;

    (e) Scale of miles.

11. Will the proposed 3.16 mV/m contour completely encompass the principal community, without major terrain obstruction?   YES ☒   NO ☐

    If No, please submit justifications.

12. If the main studio will not be within the boundaries of the principal community to be served, attach as Exhibit No. _____ a justification pursuant to Section 73.1125 of the Commission's Rules.
    MAIN STUDIO WILL BE WITHIN THE UTICA CITY LIMITS AT A LOCATION YET TO BE DETERMINED.

13. Attach as Exhibit No. E_2_ map(s) (7.5 minute U.S. Geographic Survey topographic quadrangles if available) of the proposed antenna location showing the following information:

    (a) Proposed transmitter location accurately plotted with the latitude the longitude lines clearly marked and showing a scale of statute lines.

    (b) Transmitter location and call letters of all AM broadcast stations within 2 miles of the proposed antenna location.   NONE

14. If there are any FM or TV stations within 200 feet of proposed antenna or non-broadcast radio stations (except amateur & citizens band), established commercial and government receiving stations in the general vicinity which may be adversely affected by the proposed operation, attach as Exhibit No. E_3_ the expected effect, a description of remedial steps that may be pursued if necessary, and a statement from the applicant accepting full responsibility for the elimination of any objectionable effect on existing stations.

FCC 301 - Page 12
April 1985

Appendix 2

Section V-B (page 3)   FM Broadcast Engineering Data

15. Tabulation of Terrain Data. *(Calculated in accordance with the procedure prescribed in Section 73.313 of the Commission's Rules utilizing 7-1/2 minute topographic maps, if available).*

Radial bearing (degrees true)	Height of antenna, radiation center above average elevation of radial (2-10 mi) Feet	Predicted Distance To the 3.16 mV/m contour Miles	To the 1 mV/m contour Miles
0°	416ft 126.8 M	7.4 mi 11.9 KM	13.3 mi 21.4 KM
45°	336ft 102.4 M	6.6 mi 10.6 KM	11.9 mi 19.2 KM
90°	126ft 38.4 M	4.0 mi 6.4 KM	7.2 mi 11.6 KM
135°	716ft 218.2 M	9.8 mi 15.8 KM	17.2 mi 27.7 KM
180°	396ft 120.7 M	7.2 mi 11.6 KM	12.9 mi 20.8 KM
225°	716ft 218.2 M	9.8 mi 15.8 KM	17.2 mi 27.7 KM
270°	766ft 233.5 M	10.1 mi 17.2 KM	17.7 mi 28.5 KM
315°	531ft 161.8 M	8.4 mi 13.5 KM	14.9 mi 24.0 KM
(.)			

(.) Radial over principal community if not included above. Do not include in Average.

16. Environmental Statement, See Part I, Subpart 1 of the Commission's Rules.

Would a Commission grant of this application be a major action as defined by Section 1.1305 of the Commission's Rules?   ☐ YES ☒ NO

If Yes, attach as Exhibit No. ENV, a narrative statement in accordance with Section 1.1311 of the Commission's Rules.

If No, explain briefly. Tower is already in existance. The applicant will attach antenna at a midway point up the tower.

I certify that I represent the applicant in the capacity indicated below and that I have examined the foregoing statement of technical information and that it is true to the best of my knowledge and belief.

January 29, 1986
Date

Dr. Thomas C. Durfey
Name

Signature *(check appropriate box below)*

Box 50-U, Rte. 1, Coweta, OK 74429
Address *(include ZIP Code)*

918-486-5059
Telephone No. *(include Area Code)*

☐ Technical Director
☒ Technical Consultant
☐ Registered Professional Engineer
☐ Other *(Specify)*
☐ Chief Operator

FCC 301 · Page 13
April 1985

Appendix 2

APPLICATION FOR CONSTRUCTION PERMIT
NEW FM-UTICA, N.Y.
WELDEN, BREVOORT, HICKMAN, INC.

EXHIBIT ENV.

STATEMENT CONCERNING ENVIRONMENTAL CONSIDERATIONS
PURSUANT TO SECTION 1.1311 OF THE FCC RULES
ANSI RADIATION LIMIT

TOWER IS ALREADY IN EXISTANCE. THE APPLICANT WILL ATTACH ANTENNA AT A MIDWAY POINT UP THE TOWER.
THIS SITE IS NOT A WILDERNESS AREA, WILDLIFE PRESERVE, NATURAL FLYWAY FOR BIRDS, OR SITE OF SCENIC, CULTURAL, HISTORIC, ARCHITECTURAL, ARCHEOLOGICAL, OR RECREATION AREA, IT IS AN ANTENNA FARM.
THERE HAVE NOT BEEN AND IT IS PRECEIVED THAT THERE WILL BE NO ADVERSE ENVIRONMENTAL EFFECT BECAUSE OF THE POPOSED ANTENNA ATTACHMENT.

ACCORDING TO THE ANSI RF RADIATION GUIDELINES THIS INSTALLATION MEETS AND EXCEEDS THEIR COMPLIANCE WITH C95.1-1982 EXPOSURE GUIDELINES ANYWHERE ON THE GROUND.

Appendix 2

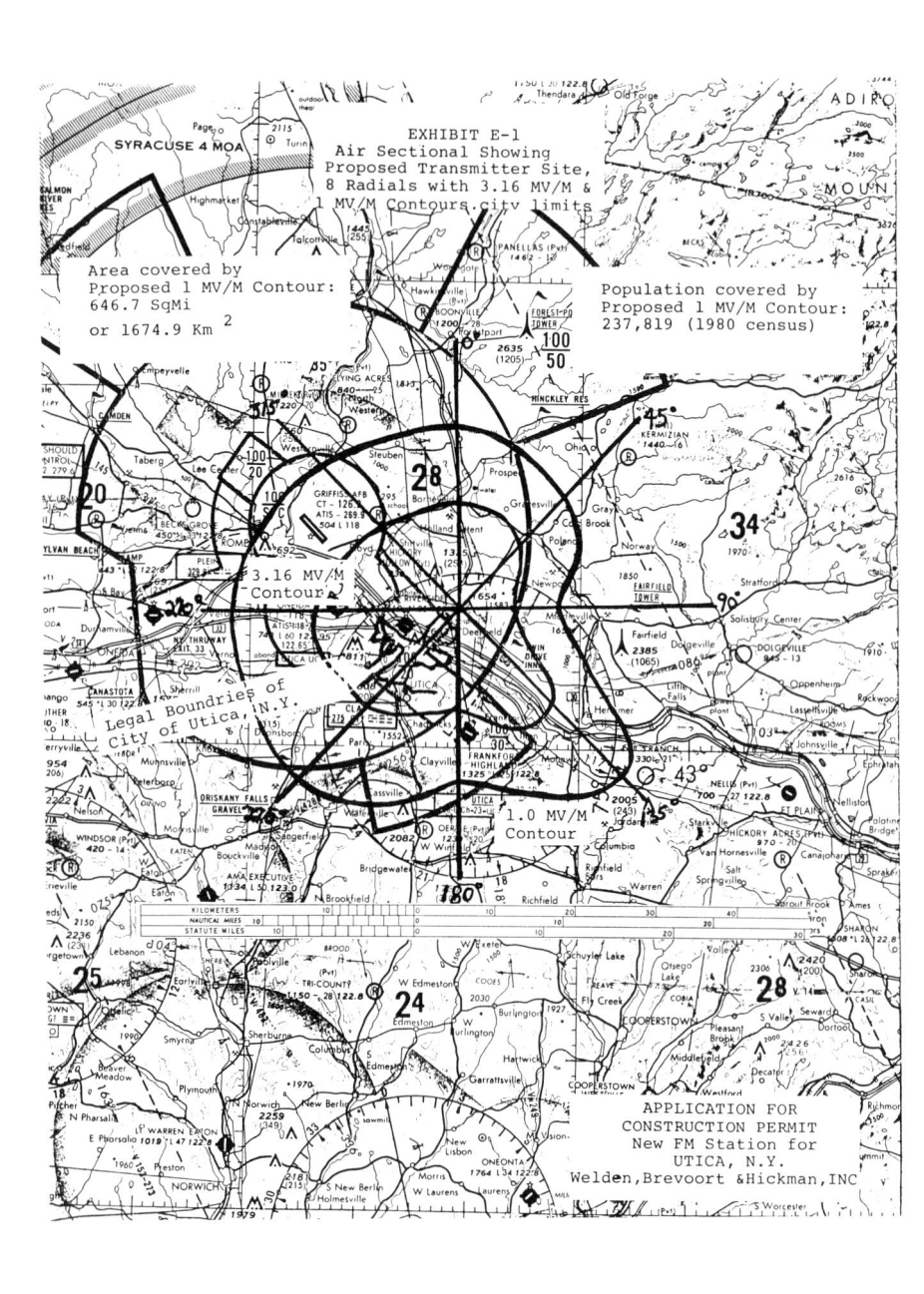

Appendix 2

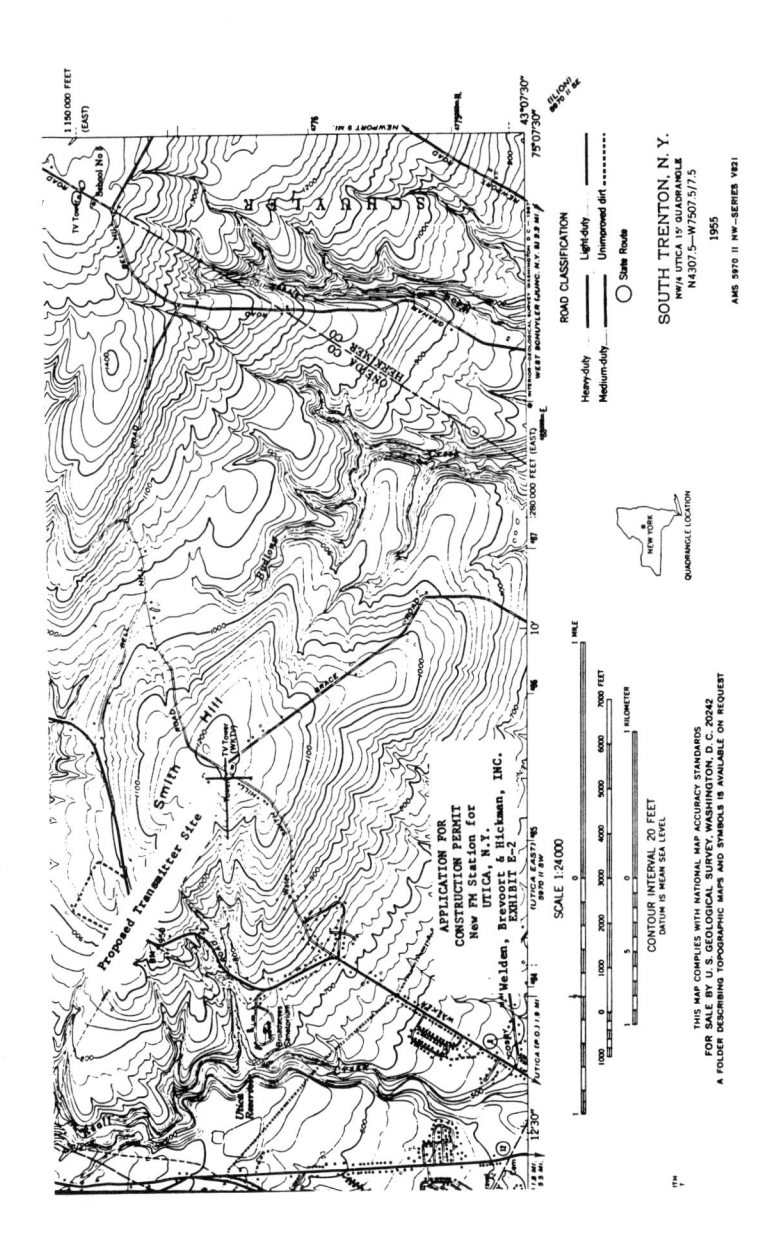

261

Appendix 2

EXHIBIT E 3

VB (P2) #14

The tower on which the proposed Class A station is to attach their antenna was constructed for FM broadcast station WNYZ (formerly WIBQ (FM)) 25kw on 98.7 mhz. The WNYZ 5 bay antenna occupies the top mast of the tower. Several short wave operations also are attached on the tower including: KEG 618, KZB 58, KA 74893, KFZ 577, KFF 722, KDJ 755, KLS 597, as well as the GE Service Company at 464.8 mhz transmitt-469.8 mhz receive and Dearfield Fire Company on 154.98 mhz, simplex. The applicant takes full responsibility for adding a 1.1kw 100.7mhz signal to the tower and will take whatever remedial steps that might be necessary for the elimination of any objectional interference that might be caused by the addition of the proposed station.

APPLICATION FOR
CONSTRUCTION PERMIT
NEW FM STATION FOR
UTICA, N.Y.
WELDEN, BREVOORT, HICKMAN, INC.

Appendix 2

```
                              TOM DURFEY                              PAGE  1
                              COWETA, OK

                  FM STUDY (NEW RULES ADOPTED 3/1/84)       JANUARY  7, 1986

JOB TITLE : UTICA, NY STUDY
CHANNEL 264A
COORDINATES : 43-08-38   75-10-44

                   This product is provided by DW, Inc. dba DATAWORLD,
                        solely for the standard business uses of
                                       TOM DURFEY
                   and is not to be duplicated for other purposes or provided
                        to others without written permission of DW, Inc.

                                  ALL RIGHTS RESERVED

                               Copyright (c) 1986, DW, Inc.

        Disclaimer: DW, Inc. assumes no liability for any errors or omissions
        in the information hereby provided, and shall not be liable for any
        injuries or damages (including consequential) which might result from
        use of the said information.

CALL      CITY                     CHANNEL   ERP-W/KW   LATITUDE    BEARING    DIST.     REQ.
STATUS    STATE    FCC FILE  #     CLASS     EAH-FT     LONGITUDE              (KM)      (KM)
----------------------------------------------------------------------------------------------

WRVO      OSWEGO                 *  210       24.0     43-25-14     286.1     114.31    16.0
 LIC      NY                        B          430     76-32-08                98.31  CLEAR

WRCU-FM   HAMILTON               *  211       1.90     42-48-38     218.0      46.95     8.0
 LIC      NY                        A          155     75-31-58                38.95  CLEAR

PRM       WOODSTOCK                 261                42-00-18     145.2     153.48    27.0
          NY    DOC-85-338          A                  74-07-12               126.48  CLEAR

ALLOC     DELHI                     262                42-16-48     167.3      98.33    27.0
          NY    DOC-84-231          A                  74-55-00                71.33  CLEAR

CBOB-FM   BROCKVILLE                262        100     44-38-25     348.2     169.96    98.0
 LIC      ON                        C1         440     75-37-08                71.96  CLEAR

ALLOC     WARRENSBURG               263                43-29-24      70.9     120.70    64.0
          NY    DOC-84-231          A                  73-46-06                56.70  CLEAR

WVOR-FM   ROCHESTER                 263       50.0     43-02-05     267.0     183.15   105.0
 LIC      NY                        B          480     77-25-25                78.15  CLEAR

ALLOC     UTICA                     264                43-06-18     220.9       5.73   105.0
          NY    DOC-84-231          A                  75-13-30               -99.27  SHORT

WHUD      PEEKSKILL                 264       50.0     41-20-18     151.8     226.79   163.0
 LIC      NY                        B          500     73-53-41                63.79  CLEAR

CBF-FM    MONTREAL                  264        100     45-30-20      25.1     291.29   239.0
 LIC      QU                        C1         823     73-35-32                52.29  CLEAR

WEZG-FM   NORTH SYRACUSE            265       3.00     43-09-06     271.0      77.59    64.0
 LIC      NY                        A          165     76-07-58                13.59  CLOSE
```

263

Appendix 2

```
                                      TOM DURFEY                                    PAGE   2
                                      COWETA, OK

                          FM STUDY (NEW RULES ADOPTED 3/1/84)        JANUARY  7, 1986

JOB TITLE : UTICA, NY STUDY
CHANNEL 264A
COORDINATES : 43-08-38   75-10-44


CALL      CITY                    CHANNEL   ERP-W/KW   LATITUDE    BEARING   DIST.    REQ.
STATUS    STATE    FCC FILE #      CLASS     EAH-FT    LONGITUDE              (KM)    (KM)
------------------------------------------------------------------------------------------

WEZG-FM   NORTH SYRACUSE            265       3.00     43-03-33     263.4    78.49   64.0
  CP       NY   BPH-780822AN         A         235     76-08-10                14.49 CLOSE

WCDO-FM   SIDNEY                    265        .64     42-17-33     189.3    95.82   64.0
  LIC      NY                        A         570     75-22-03                31.82 CLEAR

WCDO-FM   SIDNEY                    265        .94     42-17-33     189.3    95.82   64.0
  APP      NY   BPH-851002IC         A         577     75-22-03                31.82 CLEAR

WWOM      ALBANY                    265       3.00     42-43-54     113.0   115.31   64.0
  LIC      NY                        A         300     73-52-56                51.31 CLEAR

WQIX      HORSEHEADS                265       3.00     42-12-00     233.2   173.03   64.0
  LIC      NY                        A         245     76-51-30               109.03 CLEAR

ALLOC     FORT PLAIN                266                42-56-12     116.7    51.07   27.0
           NY   DOC-84-231            A                 74-37-10                24.07 CLEAR

CHEQ-FM   SMITHS FALLS              266       47.3     44-52-55     341.7   203.83   98.0
  LIC     ON                         C1        278     75-59-37               105.83 CLEAR

ALLOC     STILLWATER                267                42-56-18      99.9   126.36   27.0
           NY   DOC-84-231            A                 73-39-13                99.36 CLEAR

                          >> END CHANNEL 264A  STUDY <<
```

Appendix 2

Approved by OMB
OMB No. 3060-0027
Expires 5-31-88

CERTIFICATION OF SITE AVAILABILITY

1. The applicant certifies that it has reasonable assurance in good faith that the site or structure proposed in Items 1 and/or 2, Section V-G, FCC Form 301, as the location of its transmitting antenna, will be available to the applicant for applicant's intended purpose.

YES X   NO _____

If no, explain fully:

2. If reasonable assurance is not based on applicant's ownership of the proposed site or structure, applicant certifies that it has obtained such reasonable assurance by contacting the owner or person possessing control of the site or structure.

____JIM ASHTON_____   (315) 736-9313
Name of Person Contacted   Telephone Number

Person contacted (check one):

Owner _____   Owner's Agent X   Other (specify) _____

Phyllis Ann Trey   _January 29, 1986_
Applicant's Signature   Date
        Pres.

265

Appendix 2

Broadcast Application	FEDERAL COMMUNICATIONS COMMISSION	Section V-G
	ANTENNA AND SITE INFORMATION	

Name of Applicant	Call Sign	Station Location
WELDEN, BREVOORT, HICKMAN, INC.	UTICA, N.Y.	NEW FM STATION ON EXISTING TOWER

Purpose of Application (Put "X" in appropriate box)	Facilities Requested
☐ New antenna construction ☒ Alteration of existing antenna structure ☐ Change in location	SIDE MOUNT ONE FM BAY ON ON WNYZ-FM'S EXISTING TOWER

1. Location of Antenna:

State	County	City or Town
NEW YORK	ONEIDA	DEARFIELD TWNSHIP NEAR UTICA

   Exact antenna location (street address). If outside city limits, give name of nearest town and distance and direction of antenna from town.
   ATOP SMITH HILL ON SMITH HILL ROAD NEAR UTICA IN DEARFIELD TOWNSHIP

   Geographical coordinates (to nearest second). For directional antenna give coordinates of center of array. For single vertical radiator give tower location.

   North Latitude   43° 08' 38.5"   West Longitude   75° 10' 44.5"

2. Is the proposed site the same transmitter-antenna site of other stations authorized by the Commission or specified in another application pending before the Commission?   ☒ YES   ☐ NO

   If Yes, give call sign: WNYZ-FM

3. Has the FAA been notified of proposed construction? TOWER ALREADY THERE   ☐ YES   ☒ NO
   If Yes, give date and office where notice was filed.

4. List all landing areas within 5 miles of antenna site. Give distance and direction to the nearest boundary of each landing area from the antenna site.

	Landing Area	Distance	Direction
(a)	ONEIDA COUNTY	5.0 mi 8.05 KM	W S W
(b)			
(c)			

5. Attach as Exhibit No. 54 a description of the antenna system, including whether tower(s) are self-supporting or guyed. If a directional antenna, give spacing and orientation of towers.

   SELF SUPPORTING

Tower	#1	#2	#3	#4	#5	#6
Overall height above ground (include obstruction lighting)	296 ft 90.2 M					
Overall height above mean sea level (include obstruction lighting)	1503 ft 458.1 M					

FCC 301 - Page 17
April 1985

Appendix 2

Section V-G (page 2)   Antenna And Site Information

6. Attach as Exhibit No. E-4 a vertical plan sketch for the proposed total structure (including supporting building, if any) giving heights above ground in feet for all significant features. Clearly indicate existing portions, noting lighting, and distinguish between the skeletal or other main supporting structure and the antenna elements.

I certify that I represent the applicant in the capacity indicated below and that I have examined the foregoing statement of technical information and that it is true to the best of my knowledge and belief.

Dr. Thomas C. Durfey
Name

[signature]
Signature (check appropriate box below)

918-486-5059
Telephone (include area code)

January 29, 1986
Date

☐ Technical Director   ☐ Registered Professional Engineer   ☐ Chief Operator   ☑ Technical Consultant

FCC 301 - Page 18
April 1985

Appendix 2

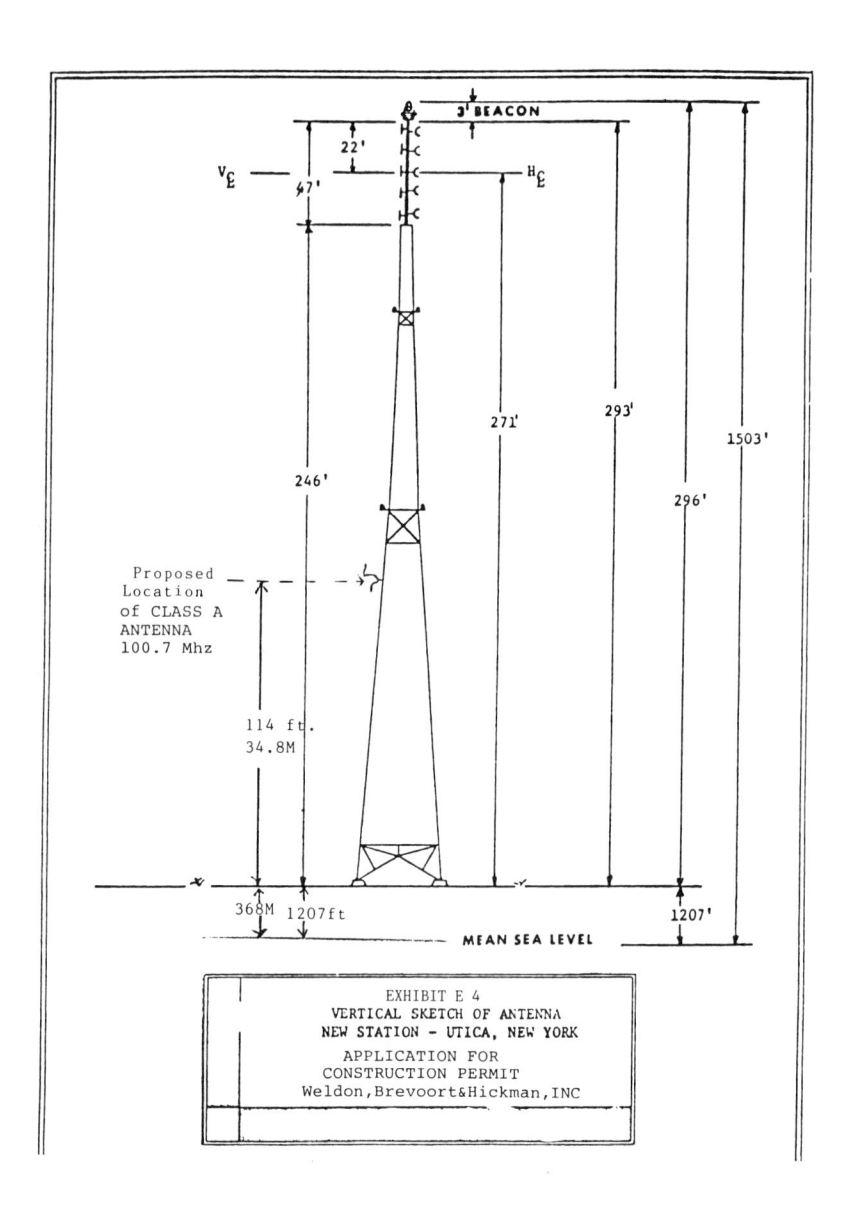

EXHIBIT E 4
VERTICAL SKETCH OF ANTENNA
NEW STATION - UTICA, NEW YORK
APPLICATION FOR
CONSTRUCTION PERMIT
Weldon, Brevoort & Hickman, INC

Appendix 2

Dr. Thomas C. Durfey
Telecommunications Consultant
Box 50-U Route 1
Coweta, OK 74429

Mr. Ralph W. Fusco, Esq.
Banker's Trust Building
185 Genesee Street
Utica, New York 13501

Dear Ralph:

Transmitted herewith is the Application for a new Utica, NY FM Broadcast station being filed for by Welden, Brevoort, Hickman, INC. . . along with the Public Notice Correspondance. Our associates appreciate having you establish a PUBLIC FILE for this application at your law offices. Please add my personal appreciation for your consideration in this matter as well.

I was pleased to find your folks well when talking to your dad on the telephone recently. . . I can't believe that over 25 years have passed since we worked with your family in establishing WBVM. We'll be in touch in the future as this venture begins to develop. Again, Thank-you for your help in establishing their Public File at your Law Office.

Cordially,

Dr. Thomas C. Durfey

Appendix 2

Dr. Thomas C. Durfey
Telecommunications Consultant
Box 50-U   Route 1
Coweta, OK   74429

Ms Pearl Adams
Legal Notice Dept.
Utica OBSERVER-DISPATCH
221 Oriskany Plaza
Utica, NY 13503

Dear Ms Adams:

Please publish the attached Legal Notice in your evening paper twice during the week of February 10-17, 1986 and twice again during the week of February 17-24, 1986. Please send one Proof of Publication from these insertions and the billing to the above address.

Thank-you for your attention to this matter.

Sincerely,

Thomas C. Durfey
Telecommunications Consultant

Appendix 2

PUBLIC NOTICE

On February 3, 1986, Welden, Brevoort, Hickman, Inc. filed an application with the Federal Communications Commission for a Construction Permit for a new FM broadcast station to operate on Channel 264A (100.7Mhz) in Utica, NY. The Effective Radiated Power will be 1.1 Kw. The studio will be located at a site to be determined in Utica, NY. The transmitter will be located on Smith Hill Road, just north of the Utica City Limits Antenna height above average terrain will be 500 feet.

The officers, directors & Stockholders of Welden, Brevoort, Hickman,Inc. are Phyllis A. Frey, Kendall C. and Nelson T. Durfey.

A copy of this application is available for public inspection during norman business hours Monday-Friday, at the Law Office of Ralph W. Fusco, 185 Genesee St.,Utica.

Appendix 3
National Religious Broadcasters' Code of Ethics

Recognizing the vital and increasingly important role played by broadcasting as an agency of mass communication — vastly extending the potential audiences of the church and the classroom — National Religious Broadcasters believes that the propagation of the Gospel by radio and television is essential to the religious inspiration, guidance, and education of the public, to the enrichment of national life and to the full use of this blessing of modern civilization in the public interest. In furtherance of this belief and of its purpose to foster and encourage the broadcasting of religious programs, and "to establish and maintain high standards with respect to content, method of presentation, speakers' qualifications, and ethical practices to the end that such programs may be constantly developed and improved and that their public interest and usefulness may be enhanced," the Association has adopted and each of its members has subscribed to the following Code of Ethics:

Program production

1. Sponsorship

Sponsorship of all programs broadcast by or in the name of the Association or any of its members shall be solely by a nonprofit organization whose aim and purpose is the propagation of the Gospel.

2. Character

The message disseminated in such programs shall be positive, concise, and constructive.

3. Production

The content, production, and presentation of such programs, including both music and continuity, shall be consistent with the program standards of the station or network over which they are broadcast and with the legal requirements and of all regulations of the Federal Communications Commission.

4. Cooperation

Persons engaging in the broadcasting of such programs shall cooperate with the station or network management by prompt appearance, courtesy, and scrupulous conformity with the limitations imposed by the physical, technical, and economic characteristics of radio.

5. Financial accountability

Appeals shall be of a bona-fide character for legitimate religious purposes and shall be presented in a dignified manner. All donors shall be promptly furnished with receipts and an accounting thereof shall be furnished on request of the Board of Directors.

Station ownership and operation

In furtherance of its purpose to operate radio and television stations with the highest degree of quality, integrity, and Christian ethics, the radio and television stations have adopted and each of its members has subscribed to the following Code of Ethics:

1. Obligation

The license granted by the FCC to operate a station is a privilege, not a right. Thus it is the obligation of each station to serve its listening constituency with programs that will instruct, uplift, and enhance their understanding of Christian principles and patriotic endeavors. We believe this is best accomplished by airing only programming which:

a. enriches the lives of the listeners in areas of education, culture, entertainment, information, and news

b. contributes to the sanctity and uplifting of the home

c. respects the rights of all people

d. protects and upholds the integrity of the United States of America

e. presents the Gospel message in clarity and fidelity.

It is also the obligation of each station to operate with the highest degree of quality by:

a. constant and thorough maintenance of equipment

b. careful logging and operational procedures

c. employment of competent and experienced personnel in both the programming and engineering sections.

2. Finance

All matters of finance, appeals for funds and negotiations with advertisers shall be conducted with dignity and integrity. All donors shall be promptly furnished with receipts.

3. Advertising

Each station operating on a commercial basis will maintain high standards in the selection and presentation of advertising.

Statement of Faith

1. We believe the Bible to be inspired, the only infallible, authoritative Word of God.

2. We believe that there is one God, eternally existent in three Persons: Father, Son, and Holy Ghost.

3. We believe in the deity of Christ, in His virgin birth, in His sinless life, in His miracles, in His victorious and atoning death through His shed blood, in His bodily resurrection, in His ascension to the right hand of the Father, and in His personal return in power and glory.

4. We believe that for the salvation of lost and sinful man regeneration by the Holy Spirit is absolutely essential.

5. We believe in the present ministry of the Holy Spirit, by whose indwelling the Christian is enabled to live a godly life.

6. We believe in the resurrection of both the saved and the lost, they that are saved unto the resurrection of life and they that are lost unto the resurrection of damnation.

7. We believe in the spiritual unity of believers in Christ.

Appendix 4

Appendix 4

DATE _____

PROGRAM DIRECTOR'S WEEKLY SUMMARY SHEET

To be filed with General Manager by noon Friday.
Total hours operation this week _____
Total amount of time devoted to program types:

	Hours	Minutes	% of Week
1. News	_____	_____	_____
2. Public Affairs	_____	_____	_____
3. Other (entertainment/sports)	_____	_____	_____

Commercials in 60-Minute Segments:

A. Up to and including 10 minutes   _____

B. 10-14 minutes   _____

C. 14-18 minutes   _____

D. Over 18 minutes   _____

If (D.) is exceeded; when:

why:

Personnel absences (reasons):

Equipment Problems (reasons):

Signed: _____
Program Director

Appendix 4

WEEKLY MUSIC REPORT

To be turned in to general manager every Friday.

Attach a play list to this report.

What new songs were added to the play list category this week?

  1.   Reason
2.
3.
4.
5.
6.
7.
8.
9.
10.

Songs removed from play list.

  1.   Reason
2.
3.
4.
5.
6.
7.
8.
9.
10.

Payola statement:

Comment on music trends from trade journals:

Other:

Appendix 4

DATE _____

WEEKLY NEWS REPORT

To be turned in to general manager every Friday by noon. Total number of minutes of news content this week _____.

Scoops (list story by topic)

What stories were aired on other stations first? and why?

State the main topics in the news this week.

State the events made to balance viewpoints in the station's covering of news events this week. Were they all successful?

Any marked public reaction to any of the stories?

How many times was the wire service fed, by whom and with what story?

List other problems — comments (equipment and personnel problems)

Attach copies of all exceptional stories.

Appendix 4

DATE _____

WEEKLY PUBLIC AFFAIRS/OTHER REPORT

To be turned in to general manager every Friday noon.
Public affairs this week in hours _____, and minutes _____.

Does this Program relate to a specific CN Survey Item — Which one? and How?	Duration	Air Date	Content Synopsis	How Program Chosen and By Whom	Comments	Tape is Filed as #

Number of PSA's this week _____   Any special work for them? _____
Featuring local agency(s) _____

Appendix 5

Appendix 5

```
PROGRAM LOG WISR   Example:              ANNOUNCER ON    TIME
                                         --------------------

                                         ANNOUNCER OFF   TIME
                                         --------------------
--------------------------------------------------------------------------------
       SCHED      ACTUAL
       TIME       TIME     PROGRAM-SPONSOR         : CART    LEN    SOURCE   TYPE
       8:00:00             STATION ID              :                LIVE     INF
       8:00:10             NEWS SPONSORED BY       :                LIVE     INF
       8:01:00               FIRST NAT'L BANK/SR   :        0:60             CP
       8:05:00             MUSIC CONTINUED                          REC      ENT
       8:05:00               MCDONALD'S/NON BREAKFAST :     0:30             CA
       8:05:30               CHRYSLER PLYMOUTH/KASING :     0:30             CA
       8:06:00               KOEPPEN ALIGNMENT SERVICE : B60 0:30            CA
       8:15:00               I C GOLDEN LAGER      :        0:60             CA
       8:16:00               CHRYSLER PLYMOUTH     :        0:30             CA
       8:16:30               PIRATES               : B133   0:30             CA
       8:17:00               PSA------------------ : A213   0:30             PS
       8:25:00               MOUNTAIN DEW          :        0:60             CA
       8:26:00               PITTSBURGH HOME SAVINGS : A240 0:60             CA
       8:27:00               CLEARVIEW TIRE        :        0:30             CA
       8:28:00             BUSINESS TRAVELER       :                REC      INF
       8:28:30               MOYER'S CUSTOM        :        0:30             CA
       8:29:00             TIME SIGNAL--1/2 HR. AM :                LIVE     INF
       8:30:00             THRU THE BIBLE BROADCAST :               TAPE     REL
       8:31:00             DR. J VERNON MAGEE      :       30:00             CP
       8:59:00             TIME SIGNAL/HR. AM      :                LIVE     INF
       8:59:00               GEORGE KERR TV        :        0:30             CP
```

Appendix 5

```
*note: this space may be used         RADIO STATION WISR
       for the station logo           P.O. BOX 151
                                      BUTLER, PA. 16001




                                    I N V O I C E
===============================================================================
                                     DATE:  10-03-841
  INVOICE NUMBER: 09840002           SALESPERSON:  03
  SPONSOR NUMBER: 011                SCHEDULE DATES: 09/01/84 - 09/30/84
  ADVERTISER:  BUTLER SHEARER HARDWARE   REVENUE CLASS:  CASH
  REFERENCE:                         TERMS:  NET 30 DAYS
                                     CONTACT:  Lorraine Laconi
         BUTLER SHEARER HARDWARE     TELEPHONE:  412 283 5300
         153 NORTH MAIN STREET
         BUTLER,              PA  16001

-------------------------------------------------------------------------------
           ORDER      LGTH      UNITS        UNIT COST      GROSS AMOUNT
-------------------------------------------------------------------------------
>fold    AM/0040      :30        14            $6.00           $84.00
 here    AM/0041     60: 0        4           $50.00          $200.00
         AM/0042      :30         4            $5.00           $20.00




===============================================================================
TOTAL SPOTS     TOTAL CHARGES      AGY COMM      SALES TAX      AMOUNT DUE
    22              $304.00         $.00           $.00          $304.00
-------------------------------------------------------------------------------
      ******** We Insure Sales Results (or any comment you want) ********
===============================================================================
```

Appendix 5

```
                              STATION WISR-AM
                              BOX 151
                              BUTLER           PA 16003-0000

                              I N V O I C E
=================================================================
  INVOICE NUMBER:  11840097   DATE:  11-30-84
  SPONSOR NUMBER:  0231       SALESPERSON:   05
  ADVERTISER:      HI HO      SCHEDULE DATES:  11/01/84 - 11/30/84
                              REVENUE CLASS:   CASH
                              TERMS:      NET 30 DAYS
                              CONTACT:  L. LACONI
              BOB MARTO      TELEPHONE:  412-283-1500
              RT 8 SOUTH
              GIBSONIA       PA  15044-0000

=================================================================
              EXACT COMMERCIAL TIMES:  date, time, length
=================================================================
11/08 09:21   :30   11/08 14:25   :30   11/08 14:45   :30   11/08 15:27   :30
11/08 15:06   :30   11/09 07:25   :30   11/09 14:06   :30   11/09 14:45   :30
11/09 15:29   :30   11/09 15:09   :30   11/10 06:25   :30   11/10 08:16   :30
11/12 09:21   :30   11/12 13:55   :30   11/12 14:16   :30   11/12 15:13   :30
11/12 15:26   :30   11/13 07:36   :30   11/13 13:35   :30   11/13 13:45   :30
11/13 15:26   :30   11/13 15:40   :30   11/14 08:25   :30   11/14 14:06   :30
11/14 14:45   :30   11/14 15:17   :30   11/14 16:17   :30   11/15 15:17   :30
11/15 16:17   :30   11/15 13:11   :30   11/15 14:11   :30   11/15 06:17   :30
11/20 06:35   :30   11/20 13:29   :30   11/20 14:55   :30   11/20 15:11   :30
11/20 15:26   :30   11/22 06:36   :30   11/22 13:36   :30   11/22 13:55   :30
11/22 15:12   :30   11/22 15:08   :30   11/24 06:16   :30   11/24 13:25   :30
11/24 14:57   :30   11/24 15:29   :30   11/24 15:50   :30   11/27 06:29   :30
11/27 14:45   :30   11/27 14:55   :30   11/27 15:11   :30   11/27 15:35   :30
11/28 08:08   :30   11/28 13:36   :30   11/28 14:05   :30   11/28 15:11   :30
11/28 15:36   :30   11/30 06:37   :30   11/30 13:35   :30   11/30 14:15   :30
11/30 15:29   :30   11/30 16:24   :30

=================================================================
                       B I L L I N G   S U M M A R Y
-----------------------------------------------------------------
  32/  :30 Flat Amount     $200.00    Time Charges          $350.00
  30/  :30 sec spots at      $5.00    Agency Commission       $.00
                                      Sales Tax               $.00
                                      Total Amount Due      $350.00
-----------------------------------------------------------------
         The LARRY BERG SHOW Butler's all-time best talk show!!!!
=================================================================
Sworn to and subscribed before me on this
date            as my hand and notary seal.
```

Appendix 5

```
                    Radio Station WISR
                    P.O. Box 151
                    Butler, PA  16001
                    9/01/84
CULLIGAN WATER CONDITIONING                     Sponsor No. 21
                                                Terms: net 30 days
COYNE ADV                                       Logged:
1 PENN CTR W
PITTSBURGH,     PA 15276
```

AFFIDAVIT OF PERFORMANCE

DATE	NO.	EXACT TIMES
84/08/27	6	06:28:00 07:12:00 08:25:00 15:25:00 16:58:00 17:44:00
84/08/28	6	06:25:00 07:26:00 08:05:00 15:39:00 16:55:00 18:25:00
84/08/29	6	06:40:00 07:40:00 08:27:00 15:15:00 16:40:00 17:40:00
84/08/30	6	06:25:00 07:28:00 08:10:00 15:12:00 16:22:00 17:48:00

This announcement was broadcast 24 times, as entered in the station's program log. The times this announcement was broadcast were billed to this station's client on our invoice numbered/dated   at his earned rate of:

        24   0 min 30-sec spots at   10.00 for   240.00

Less agency commission   36.00

Invoice total $204.00

Sworn to and subscribed before me and in my presence

on this   day of

Typed Name and Title   Station

Appendix 5

```
                          STATION WISR-AM
                          BOX 151
                          BUTLER                    PA   16003-0000

                                                    DATE: 02-28-86
                S T A T E M E N T   O F   A C C O U N T S
===============================================================================

        COYNE ADVERTISING              SALESMAN NO:  07
        1 PENN CENTER WEST             TERMS:  AS RENDERED
        PITTSBURGH,         PA  15276  CONTACT: LORRAIN LACONI
        0021-CULLIGAN WATER CONDITIONING      TELEPHONE: 283-1500

DATE       INVOICE     DESCRIPTION     CHARGES    PAYMENTS     BALANCE
--------   --------    -----------     -------    --------     -------
1-31-86    01860012    INVOICE         124.00        .00       124.00
2-28-86    02860011    INVOICE          16.00        .00       140.00
11-30-85   11210200    INVOICE         120.00        .00       260.00
12-31-85   12210300    INVOICE         124.00        .00       384.00

                    A C C O U N T   A N A L Y S I S
===============================================================================
  CURRENT     30 DAYS      60 DAYS      90 DAYS    FIN CHARGE     AMOUNT DUE
-------------------------------------------------------------------------------
   16.00      124.00       124.00       120.00         .00          384.00
===============================================================================
```

Appendix 5

The following is an expiration report for salesman #2 as of Sept 1, 1984 and up to and including 12/31/99 so that all T.F. orders will appear on the report. F indicates that it is ok to bill this order E.O.F. (end of flight):

Expiration Report for 12/31/99

Sls#	Date	Bill	BC#	Sp#	Sponsor Name
2	84 9/15	M	26	477	PEPSI
2	84 9/ 9	M	23	245	MOUNTAIN DEW
2	84 9/ 9	M	27	365	PEPSI THEMATIC
2	84 9/10	M	28	379	PEPSI JACKSON UTC
2	84 9/15	M	172	6	HOOVER
2	84 9/20	F	38	142	WPPCO
2	84 9/22	M	198	379	PEPSI JACKSON UTC
2	84 9/22	F	210	199	SENECA FIRST/AUTO LOAN
2	84 9/22	M	20	262	MCDONALD'S/BREAKFAST
2	84 9/25	M	37	142	WPPCO
2	84 9/26	M	30	132	PIRATES
2	84 9/26	M	31	132	PIRATES
2	84 9/26	M	32	132	PIRATES
2	84 9/28	M	21	262	MCDONALD'S/BREAKFAST
2	84 9/29	M	178	379	PEPSI JACKSON UTC
2	84 10/ 2	F	229	142	WPPCO
2	84 10/ 6	M	220	379	PEPSI JACKSON UTC
2	84 10/ 6	F	221	190	SENECA FIRST
2	84 10/16	F	245	142	WPPCO
2	84 10/18	F	266	316	PITTSBURGH NATL BANK
2	84 10/23	F	289	142	WPPCO
2	84 10/27	F	211	199	SENECA FIRST/AUTO LOAN
2	84 10/27	F	239	190	SENECA IRST
2	84 10/29	M	253	477	PEPSI
2	84 11/ 1	M	254	477	PEPSI
2	84 11/15	F	329	142	WPPCO
2	84 11/20	M	206	459	FIRST FEDERAL SAVINGS
2	84 11/20	F	330	142	WPPCO
2	84 12/29	M	33	239	PITTSBURGH HOME SAVINGS
2	84 12/29	M	34	239	PITTSBURGH HOME SAVINGS
2	85 2/19	M	79	42	DR. J VERNON MAGEE
2	99 5/ 4	M	123	236	N MAIN CHURCH OF GOD
2	99 5/ 6	M	122	236	N MAIN CHURCH OF GOD
2	99 6/23	M	153	399	WILLIAM WILKEN
2	99 10/ 1	M	75	505	CORNERSTONE BAPTIST
2	99 12/31	M	55	265	BELLO'S AUTO BODY
2	99 12/31	M	74	22	CONLEY'S COUNTRY CLUB
2	99 12/31	M	111	226	LLOYD JOHNSON
2	99 12/31	M	137	89	REV. N.K. POWELL

Appendix 5

WISR Sales Journal

Day	Value	Average
84/09/03	1318.12	9.34

BREAKDOWN BY HOUR

Hour	Value	Average
0	0.00	0.00
1	0.00	0.00
2	0.00	0.00
3	0.00	0.00
4	0.00	0.00
5	0.00	0.00
6	67.08	7.30
7	132.52	8.84
8	140.98	10.06
9	68.04	17.00
10	131.50	13.16
11	170.00	24.80
12	135.88	11.32
13	74.60	8.28
14	81.50	9.06
15	39.76	4.96
16	88.06	8.00
17	82.12	7.46
18	70.08	7.00
19	30.00	7.50
20	0.00	0.00
21	0.00	0.00
22	0.00	0.00
23	0.00	0.00
24	0.00	0.00

BY SALESMAN

Salesman	Value
1	0.00
2	290.38
3	100.10
4	0.00
5	340.40
6	0.00
7	130.20
8	589.04
9	0.00

BY SPONSOR TYPE

Sp Type	Amount
LOC	793.90
NAT	359.48
PSA	0.00
REG	164.74

Appendix 5

ACCOUNTS RECEIVABLE AGING
-- by Sponsor Number --

PAGE: 20

Date: 11-30-84

SP#	SPONSOR NAME	SL MN	INVOICE	DATE	CURRENT	31-60	61-90	91 & OVER	FINANCE CHARGE	BALANCE DUE
496	LINDA HUGHES/DEM/POL	8	10840153	10-31-84	.00	-100.00	.00	.00	.00	-100.00
		8	11840164	11-30-84	100.00	.00	.00	.00	.00	-100.00
		** Sponsor Total			100.00	.00	.00	.00	.00	.00
503	EICHENLAUB TROPHY SHOP	1	11840165	11-30-84	80.00	.00	.00	.00	.00	80.00
		** Sponsor Total			80.00	.00	.00	.00	.00	80.00
504	PAPPAN'S	5	07050402	6-30-84	.00	.00	.00	80.00	.00	80.00
		5	08050403	7-31-84	.00	.00	.00	80.00	.00	80.00
		5	09050404	8-31-84	.00	.00	.00	80.00	.00	80.00
		5	10840154	10-31-84	.00	.00	.00	.00	.00	.00
		5	11840166	11-30-84	.00	.00	.00	.00	.00	.00
		** Sponsor Total			.00	.00	.00	240.00	.00	240.00
505	HILL'S/RECORDS	8	11840167	11-30-84	52.05	.00	.00	.00	.00	52.05
		** Sponsor Total			52.05	.00	.00	.00	.00	52.05
506	CORNERSTONE BAPTIST	2	07050602	7-31-84	.00	.00	.00	80.40	.00	80.40
		2	07050603	8-31-84	.00	.00	.00	72.00	.00	72.00
		2	09840167	9-30-84	.00	.00	90.00	.00	.00	90.00
		2	10840155	10-31-84	.00	72.00	.00	.00	.00	72.00
		** Sponsor Total			72.00	72.00	90.00	152.40	.00	386.40
508	HILL'S/INTERBATH	8	11840169	11-30-84	32.03	.00	.00	.00	.00	32.03
		** Sponsor Total			32.03	.00	.00	.00	.00	32.03
513	BLACKBERRY PATCH	8	09840168	9-30-84	.00	.00	60.00	.00	.00	60.00
		8	10840156	10-31-84	.00	65.00	.00	.00	.00	65.00
		8	11840171	11-30-84	65.00	.00	.00	.00	.00	190.00
		** Sponsor Total			65.00	65.00	60.00	.00	.00	190.00
524	HARDY FURNACE	8	10840157	10-31-84	.00	40.00	.00	.00	.00	40.00
		8	11840172	11-30-84	130.00	.00	.00	.00	.00	170.00
		** Sponsor Total			130.00	40.00	.00	.00	.00	170.00
		**** Total			19863.01	13486.75	5907.89	16436.99	388.92	55694.64

Appendix 5

PRELIMINARY BILLING REPORT

Broadcast Dates: 8-27-84 thru 9-30-84
Calendar Dates: 9-01-84 thru 9-30-84
Page: 11
Printed: 9-30-84

LINE	SP#	SPONSOR NAME	SRC	INVOICE	ORDER	SLMN	LGTH	UNITS	RATE	GROSS	AGY-COMM	NET AMT
208	322	ANNA MARIE'S/BONUS	01	09840147	43	8	:30	43	$.00	$.00	$.00	$.00
								Sponsor Total:		$.00	$.00	$.00 **
209	338	BASILON S TUXEDOS/BONUS	01	09840148	51	5	:30	32	$.00	$.00	$.00	$.00
210	338	BASILON S TUXEDOS/BONUS	01	09840148	52	5	:30	6	$.00	$.00	$.00	$.00
								Sponsor Total:		$.00	$.00	$.00 **
211	342	DBA/ETHNIC	01	09840149	167	8	:15	9	$3.80	$34.20	$.00	$34.20
212	342	DBA/ETHNIC	01	09840149	167	8	:15	4	$3.80	$15.20	$.00	$15.20
								Sponsor Total:		$49.40	$.00	$49.40 **
213	345	CLEARVIEW TIRE/BONUS	01	09840150	73	8	:30	37	$.00	$.00	$.00	$.00
								Sponsor Total:		$.00	$.00	$.00 **
214	355	LITE 1L4GTL-CODE 13	01	09840151			SEPT AD			$160.38	$24.06	$136.32
								Sponsor Total:		$160.38	$24.06	$136.32 **
215	366	PEPSI THEMATIC	01	09840152	27	2	:60	14	$5.88	$82.32	$12.35	$69.97
								Sponsor Total:		$82.32	$12.35	$69.97 **
216	379	H P STARR & SONS	01	09840153	97	5	:60	25	$8.50	$212.50	$.00	$212.50
								Sponsor Total:		$212.50	.00	$212.50 **
217	380	PEPSI JACKSON UTC	01	09840154	28	2	:60	6	$5.88	$35.28	$5.29	$29.99
218	380	PEPSI JACKSON UTC	01	09840154	178	2	:60	12	$5.88	$70.56	$10.58	$59.98
219	380	PEPSI JACKSON UTC	01	09840154	198	2	:60	6	$5.88	$35.28	$5.29	$29.99
								Sponsor Total:		$141.12	$21.16	$119.96 **
220	387	BON TON	01	09840155	59	7	:30	5	$4.20	$21.00	$.00	$21.00
221	387	BON TON	01	09840155	170	7	:30	30	$4.20	$126.00	$.00	$126.00
								Sponsor Total:		$147.00	$.00	$147.00 **
223	398	JACK'S RESTAURANT	01	09840156	102	5	:60	4	$10.00	$40.00	$.00	$40.00
								Sponsor Total:		$40.00	$.00	$40.00 **
224	400	WILLIAM WILKEN	01	09840157	153	2	3:00	5	$20.00	$100.00	$.00	$100.00
								Sponsor Total:		$100.00	$.00	$100.00 **
225	416	GALIDA'S SPORTING GOODS	01	09840158	175	7	:60	8	$10.00	$80.00	$.00	$80.00
								Sponsor Total:		$80.00	$.00	$80.00 **
226	417	MOYER'S CUSTOM/BONUS	01	09840159	121	5	:30	10	$.00	$.00	$.00	$.00
								Sponsor Total:		$.00	$.00	$.00 **
227	424	HILL'S/UNION UNDEROOS	01	09840160	162	8	:60	5	$4.71	$23.00	$3.53	$20.02 **
228	431	CALVARY PRESBYTERIAN	01	09840161	71	3	9:00	5	$23.50	$117.50	$.00	$117.50

Appendix 5

BILLING SUMMARY

Broadcast Dates: 8-27-84 thru 9-30-84
Calendar Dates: 9-01-84 thru 9-30-84
Page: 13
Printed: 9-30-84

SOURCE	CASH	TRADE	GROSS	AGY COMM	NET BILLING
01	$17,898.03	$.00	$18,762.21	$864.18	$17,898.03
TOTALS	$17,898.03	$.00	$18,762.21	$864.18	$17,898.03 **

Appendix 5

SALES MAN COMMISSION SUMMARY

Broadcast Dates: 8-27-84 thru 9-30-84
Calendar Dates: 9-01-84 thru 9-30-84

Page: 14
Printed: 9-30-84

SLMN	SOURCE	NET BILLING	COMMISSION
1	01	$120.00	$24.00
		$120.00	$24.00 **
2	01	$2,700.70	$10.20
		$2,700.70	$10.20 **
3	01	$1,723.65	$10.90
		$1,723.65	$10.90 **
4	01	$332.50	$.00
		$332.50	$.00 **
5	01	$3,125.41	$285.96
		$3,125.41	$285.96 **
7	01	$3,103.13	$306.01
		$3,103.13	$306.01 **
8	01	$6,792.64	$679.25
		$6,792.64	$679.25 **

Appendix 5

```
                              PROJECTED REVENUE
Page:   3                      --- by Salesperson ---                              Date: 07-20-85
                              PERIOD: 07-01-86 TO 07-31-86
================================================================================================
SL                  SP   PR
MN   SPONSOR NAME           SP#   TYP  CD   ORD#   UNITS   GROSS       NET      COMMIS'N   SR
--   -------------------    ----  ---  ---  ----   -----   --------   --------  --------   --

08   BARTOLI'S CLEANERS     0009  LOC  007  0049   00009    76.50      76.50      7.65    01
08   BARTOLI'S CLEANERS     0009  LOC  007  0050   00013    71.50      71.50      7.15    01
08   BUTLER AMERICAN SALES  0010  LOC  015  0064   00013    78.00      78.00      7.80    01
08   J. M. BEATTY AUTOMOTIVE 0013 LOC  027  0101   00013   110.50     110.50     11.05    01
08   MILLIE'S NOTARY SERVICE 0036 LOC  017  0117   00022    35.00      35.00      3.50    01
08   FRIEDMAN'S FOODLAND    0039  LOC  098  0089   00050    80.00      80.00      8.00    01
08   FRIEDMAN'S FOODLAND    0039  LOC  098  0265   00126   630.00     630.00     63.00    01
08   MARTIN SALES           0044  LOC  015  0112   00008    80.00      80.00      8.00    01
08   HUNTER'S TRUCK SLS AND SER 0050 LOC 027 0099  00013   110.50     110.50     11.05    01
08   GEORGE KERR TV         0059  LOC  015  0090   00295   330.00     330.00     33.00    01
08   GEORGE KERR TV         0059  LOC  015  0091   00004    20.00      20.00      2.00    01
08   R.W. MCDONALD & SONS   0068  LOC  015  0134   00044   330.00     330.00     33.00    01
08   MILLER'S SHOES         0076  LOC  091  0115   00005    42.50      42.50      4.25    01
08   MILLER'S SHOES         0076  LOC  091  0116   00004   100.00     100.00     10.00    01
08   PANEL & TILE MART      0095  LOC  083  0128   00022   165.00     165.00     16.50    01
08   RALPH'S SHOES          0101  LOC  091  0136   00004    34.00      34.00      3.40    01
08   SEAMAN TIRES           0106  LOC  014  0140   00009    67.50      67.50      6.75    01
08   SAXONBURG DRUG STORE   0108  LOC  070  0139   00009    45.00      45.00      4.50    01
08   TRAVAGLIO WASHER PARTS 0114  LOC  015  0145   00004    40.00      40.00      4.00    01
08   FLOWERS BY TWILA       0127  LOC  150  0088   00009    67.50      67.50      6.75    01
08   WEAVER'S RENTALS       0149  LOC  051  0150   00009    67.50      67.50      6.75    01
08   EASTLAND DINER         0170  LOC  108  0082   00013    97.50      97.50      9.75    01
08   BILL'S BEER BARN       0176  LOC  025  0057   00009    63.00      63.00      6.30    01
08   BATHMASTER OF PA.      0214  LOC  003  0053   00004    40.00      40.00      4.00    01
08   SARVER DALE/MUFFLER    0259  LOC  015  0138   00004    20.00      20.00      2.00    01
08   BUTLER PACKING         0261  LOC  089  0068   00026   260.00     260.00     26.00    01
08   KIRK'S                 0269  LOC  035  0106   00004   100.00     100.00     10.00    01
08   KELLY CHEVROLET        0271  LOC  015  0105   00004    20.00      20.00      2.00    01
08   UNICORN CARD & GIFT    0318  LOC  016  0146   00009    67.50      67.50      6.75    01
08   BLACKBERRY PATCH       0513  LOC  016  0058   00013    65.00      65.00      6.50    01
08   HARDY FURNACE          0524  LOC  105  0283   00013   130.00     130.00     13.00    01


        ** TOTAL **                                00793  $3,443.00  $3,443.00   $344.30

NET SPOT AVERAGE: Salesman 08    $4.34
```

Appendix 5

PROJECTED REVENUE SUMMARY

Page: 4　　　　　　　　　　　　PERIOD: 07-01-86 TO 07-31-86　　　　　　　　　　Date: 07-20-85

SOURCE	SALESMAN	UNITS	GROSS	NET	COMMIS'N	NET SPOT AVG
01	02	00381	1,713.00	1,713.00	256.95	4.50
01	05	00086	635.00	635.00	42.33	7.38
01	08	00793	3,443.00	3,443.00	344.30	4.34
** TOTALS **		01260	$5,791.00	$5,791.00	$643.58	$4.60

BV 656 .D87 1986

DATE DUE